THE SUSTAINABLE GARDENING COLLECTION

A COMPLETE BEGINNERS GUIDE TO PERMACULTURE,
SEED SAVING, AND COMPANION PLANTING FOR
THRIVING, ECO-FRIENDLY GARDENS

P. JOSEPH RICHARDS

TABLE OF CONTENTS

PERMACULTURE GARDENING HANDBOOK

THE COMPLETE BEGINNERS
GUIDE TO SEED SAVING

THE COMPANION PLANTING PLAYBOOK FOR BEGINNERS

PERMACULTURE GARDENING HANDBOOK

THE 9-STEP HANDS-ON BEGINNERS GUIDE
TO DESIGN A SELF-SUSTAINING
ECOSYSTEM

INTRODUCTION

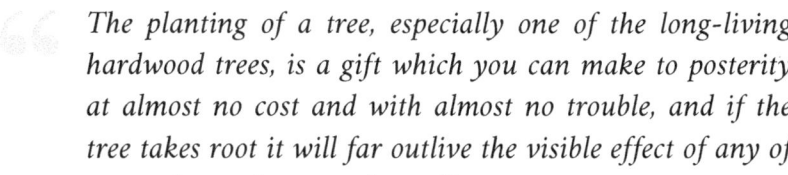

The planting of a tree, especially one of the long-living hardwood trees, is a gift which you can make to posterity at almost no cost and with almost no trouble, and if the tree takes root it will far outlive the visible effect of any of your other actions, good or evil.

— GEORGE ORWELL, *A GOOD WORD FOR THE VICAR OF BRAY*

George Orwell's rather direct quote carries more weight than you'd think. It reflects how much every form of life on earth depends on the blossoming of nature. The very element of green is beneficial–and essential–to sustain the circle of life.

If you look around any park, garden, farm, meadow, pond, or forest, initially, it will seem like little is happening. But when you allow your senses to adjust to the ecosystems held within the palms of nature, you'll find that many creatures—big and small– are co-dependent and co-habitant with the flora around them.

In a way, it's humbling to realize that trees, shrubs, and even the grass under your shoes contribute to the survival of animals and other plants around them without you being aware.

Raising and building a garden that mimics the workings of the surrounding ecosystem can have a majorly positive impact, not only for the balance of nature but also for you and your family.

"Sustainability" has become a buzzword in the modern era, commonly used in media as a sidekick to the word "green." And while these words are powerful concerning marketing tactics and allude to the fact that it's good for the environment, what does it mean?

Living and gardening sustainably mean using the resources available to us to meet our needs while keeping future generations' needs in mind.

The term, while relatively new, is rooted in social justice, conservationism, internationalism, and sustainable development. That came into the spotlight in 1983 when former Norwegian prime minister, Gro Harlem Brundtland, started running the *World Commission on Environment and Development.* In addition, many countries struggled with food security and poverty, even after the industrial revolution; this made it clear that economic development that led to the destruction of environmental health was not a long-term solution.

Sustainability isn't just about finding renewable energy sources and reducing plastic waste; it's a way of life that protects the environment without affecting our quality of life. It's about innovation and using technology to advance further while maintaining the balance of the ecosystems around us.

Every day we make decisions that affect us and the world around us. These decisions may seem minuscule in the grand scheme of things but added up over the entire course of your life (multiplied by millions of other people who make the same decisions) will affect the sustainability of the resources available to future generations.

By setting the example to implement change and be mindful of these choices to our children, we can ensure that, over time, the impact we can collectively have on the environment has the potential to be tremendous.

Permaculture or sustainable gardening differs from regular gardening to make your backyard look green and lush. You could have researched sustainable gardening, heard about it, or even seen it firsthand, and that piqued your interest.

You don't just want a beautiful garden; you want a natural, thriving, self-sustaining ecosystem—but you don't know how to achieve that or even where to start.

In the vein of permaculture, a sustainable garden can provide you with fresh produce sans harmful chemicals and processing and offer you other resources you can use to further sustainability.

The scattered bits of information you find online get overwhelming and complicated. You want an easier, more approachable way to gain all the necessary knowledge about sustainable gardening practices and permaculture to do it right from the get-go, even as a beginner.

This book will summarize all the relevant information regarding permaculture ethics and practices for a lifelong sustainable garden. An easy-to-follow nine-step process will teach you how to; design a garden by observing nature, making the necessary preparations, choosing the right plants, propagating the right way, creating a biodiverse ecosystem, and using nature-inspired integrated pest management, maintenance, and zero-waste practices.

Your road to a beautiful, sustainable, self-sufficient ecosystem starts right here. A flourishing garden will reciprocate tenfold in the form of fresh produce, herbs, and other interconnected resources in a serene environment where all forms of life (including yourself) work together to provide for all.

Growing up on a farm and experiencing a sustainable way of living that didn't take anything away and instead made me feel more fulfilled than anyone I've ever met.

This way of living made me aware of how every action has a consequence on nature. And with nature being the giver of life to us all, I knew this was what I wanted—no, I needed to continue learning about and practicing myself.

Even though my family and I were already living pretty sustainably on the farm, within months of me doing extensive research on the topic, we had converted a small piece of land next to one of the farmhouses into a permaculture garden. The local community also got involved, providing additional resources and produce for everyone.

I also saw how this impacted the surrounding landscape and soil quality. Our little ecosystem oasis attracted birds, tiny animals, and insects that all contributed to the well-being and fertilization of the plants and trees.

Knowing that it took me a long time to gather and siphon through all the knowledge and information to get where I am today, the idea of a less intimidating, all-inclusive permaculture handbook for beginners was born.

I want to help other people experience the lifestyle that only this way of living can provide.

1

THE PERMANENCE OF PERMACULTURE

The search for something permanent is one of the deepest of the instincts leading men to philosophy.

— BERTRAND RUSSEL, *A HISTORY OF WESTERN PHILOSOPHY*

Although permaculture and sustainable gardening are not the same, they do go hand-in-hand when designing a self-sufficient, self-sustaining ecosystem of your own.

To start the garden of your dreams, you need to know a few things before you can dive into the practical steps to achieve it. This chapter will expand on permaculture, what it is, the history and philosophy behind it, as well as the ethical codes that drive it.

WHAT IS PERMACULTURE?

It takes conventional farmers, or even gardeners, much work to cultivate crops or keep the plants alive. However, plants and biodiversity need much more than good soil, water, and sunlight to reach their true potential. They require productive ecosystems that promote diversity, stability, and resilience.

Permaculture is a fusion of "permanent" and "culture." The principle of designing the layout of certain plants and trees in landscapes (including agricultural landscapes) is that it improves and supports the diverse ecosystem around them.

Meaning that a garden that implements permaculture ethics and practices can sustain itself for many generations, just as naturally occurring forests and other ecosystems are if not interrupted.

The Philosophy Behind It

Instead of working against nature and forcing something to grow where it's not favorable, safe, or lacking the resources it needs, permaculture focuses on creating an environment where every plant gets everything it needs because of co-habitant plants, flowers, animals, and insects.

Permaculture focuses on the future outcome of our actions to grant an abundance of produce for multiple lifetimes reinvested into the community and the ecosystem.

Bill Wilson, the founder of Midwest permaculture, has devoted most of his adulthood to teaching its fundamental principles. Wilson often uses a metaphor that permaculture is a four-legged stool that depends on all four factors to be stable.

1. The first leg represents the environment and the cultivation of produce. Even though this is a significant factor, especially regarding sustainability and food security, it remains a small portion of what permaculture stands for.

2. The second leg is about water and energy usage, which are both very important for all life forms; thus, this factor is the same in permaculture development. It's essential to discern whether we're using water and energy resources responsibly to create an abundance instead of draining them—permaculture advocates for using these resources mindfully and finding renewable, sustainable sources that store effectively.

3. Permaculture's third leg rests on the artificial environment and waste reduction. With proper design and a bit of forward-thinking, we can reduce waste produced by construction practices and consumables that generate massive pollution.

4. The last leg of the permaculture philosophy is our relationship and how we receive all we need to maintain our livelihoods. How we manage funds, healthcare facilitation, and govern the people could determine the ultimate success and indefinite implementation of this principle that leads to an autonomous world.

THE PRIME DIRECTIVE OF PERMACULTURE

A quote by Bill Mollison sums up the prime directive of permaculture in a nutshell: "The only ethical decision is to take responsibility for our own existence and that of our children."

These wise words serve as a guideline for all that permaculture ethics represents. Taking responsibility for using our limited resources to ensure future generations' longevity while still providing for our own needs is all that permaculture is.

It doesn't mean we should revert to pre-industrialization times or resort to our own devices regarding what or how we feed our families and live in total isolation. Instead, it means we are responsible for eliminating our superiority complexes and considering our impact on the world.

Permaculture Ethics and Principles

In its purest form, a permaculture is a holistic approach to agriculture by leveraging the natural design in which nature occurs. Naturally occurring, serene landscapes should serve as the ultimate guidance instead of being flattened to make way for manufactured crops drowned in pesticides and drain the soil of nutrients that need replenish

ing.

No matter how much power we hold as–debatably–the most intelligent species, the world does not belong to us. Though when it comes to ensuring the survival of the future of humanity, the death of the planet doesn't seem to come up as a massive concern regarding modern agricultural and industrial practices.

The lack of ethics around our modern way of living and providing for ourselves has already proven to hold nothing but destruction, which is why permaculture practices are the only way forward.

The self-explanatory ethics of permaculture are summarized as follows:

1. Care for the earth.
2. Care for the people.
3. Reinvest the surplus.

Care for the Earth

Without the earth and its invaluable resources, we are nothing. When we look after the planet, it will look after us; we can't thrive if the world isn't.

All the resources available to us are because of the delicate ecosystems that have existed even before our time. Nurturing the well-being of forests, rivers, and the incredible microbiomes everywhere will ensure the replenishment of these resources.

But besides simply nurturing the balance of nature, we need to encourage fertility and biodiversity so they can expand and grow instead of just sustaining our current needs-this process generates abundance.

With every action we take, we need to consider if they hurt or further the ecosystem's health and if there's a more efficient way to go about it. Taking a leaf (pun intended) from mother nature to determine how she would fix the problem is often the smartest thing to do.

Care for the People

Caring for yourself and your family or dependents should come with the mindset of taking and using what you need and no more. This mindset includes taking a step back from consumerism and avoiding people and businesses that exploit or convince people to buy or use products or services that aren't necessary.

While helping care for other people can be very fulfilling, we still need to leave some room to take care of ourselves. Charity starts at home, and once you've achieved your desired level of self-sufficiency and reduced the behavior that negatively impacts the environment, you can begin to focus your energy outwards.

Inspiring others through our initiatives is the best way to show them that things don't have to be how they are. Having or buying more things doesn't bring about happiness and certainly doesn't benefit the planet.

Reinvest the Surplus

As mentioned before, the goal of becoming self-sufficient isn't to maintain the community's current needs but rather to grow. Not only will this lead to an abundance of food, but it will also increase other resources and lead to more biodiversity, a healthy planet, cleaner air, cleaner water, and a thriving environment.

And any abundance or surplus in these resources should be used to improve further and grow permaculture. For example, rainwater can be collected and stored in systems that redirect it back into the ground as needed; compost piles can replenish the soil; a public garden can provide products for the community, and so on.

Becoming self-sufficient can take many forms; growing fresh herbs on the kitchen windowsill, making your cleaning products, using gray water to water the lawn, shopping local, supporting businesses that implement permaculture ethics, etc. As long as you try to do what's best and consider your actions' effect on the environment, you're already halfway there!

Caring for ourselves and being responsible for our consumption will lead to a life of abundance and resilience (financially and otherwise).

The Importance of Ethics

Ethics are like a set of objectively correct rules. In permaculture, these ethics emphasize protecting the balance of nature. Ethics are important because they keep people from doing something poten-tially harmful.

However, how do we distinguish right from wrong without bias? How do we measure the validity of ethics regarding anything?

Deciphering this concept is where things get tricky. It's harder to do the right thing when doing the wrong thing benefits us in the short term. So while morality and ethics can change over time according to social and economic development concerning every-thing else, when it comes to permaculture and what's best for the planet, we need to look at the scientific and evidence-based trajec-tories. If we continue on this path, the likely outcomes indicate that we are doing something wrong.

While things like politics, laws, ideologies, culture, religion and individual morality are subject to change over time, some practices are indisputably wrong.

Having strict ethics and principles that serve nature and every-thing in it to guide our actions is necessary to stay on track with permaculture's outlook and end goal instead of spinning into something only for personal gain.

WHAT'S IN A PERMACULTURE?

Is permaculture another term for living off the land and the grid; is it just a gardening technique? Is it science, biodynamics, horti-culture, sustainability, or lifestyle?

Well, that's where most people need help to grasp how complex permaculture is. It's all of the above and more!

Permaculture is a best-case scenario where everyone lives in harmony with nature by integrating our needs instead of trying to bend nature to fit our needs.

For many years, it has been an underground social movement labeled as "hippie" culture, though this hasn't stopped the message that their practices have been sending and even managed to reach mainstream news in recent years for a good reason.

Ethics of permaculture are embedded in every message about sustainable living and "going green." Here are five concepts that are directly derivative of the principles and ethics of permaculture:

Closed Loop Systems

A closed-loop system is when an ecosystem provides the energy it needs. With plants, this usually refers to "inputs" such as fertilizer but extends to other concepts such as biofuel and solar power.

An example of a closed-loop agricultural system is when it supplies its fertilizer, or the fertilizer is collected locally instead of imported using manure from livestock or composting piles.

The idea of a closed-loop system is turning waste into resources and problems into solutions. "You don't have a snail problem; you have a duck deficiency" is another quote by Bill Mollison.

Perennial Crops

Perennial crops need planting once and continually produce fruit or vegetables yearly–when in season–without having to turn the soil and replant crops (which isn't very great for retaining the soil quality).

An alternative to monoculture (wheat, soy, and corn fields) is agroforestry, edible tree crops with other vegetation underneath that thrive in the shade. Agroforestry creates an excellent sustainable solution and will also require less work than turning soil and growing food from scratch every year to feed the entire population of the earth.

The problem is most of the food in our pantry right now is non-perennial crops, which are unfortunately not sustainable and hard to maintain, and therefore harmful to the local ecosystem. However, there's still room for annual crops (crops that need planting every year) in permaculture, but your garden should mainly consist of perennials.

Stacking Functions

Stacking functions is the original idea of permaculture and for what it's more famously known. "Stacking" functions refer to creating a space where the landscape and all the elements that make it up are multifunctional, strategically designed, and placed.

For example, if you need to construct a fence, you can design it, so it also functions as a barrier against wind, a trellis for tomato plants, or a reflective surface to provide extra heat to some plants or crops. Likewise, rain barrels can house aquatic plants and edible fish, and the overflow from rain can be directed back to the ground for irrigation.

Eco-Earthworks

Another significant component of permaculture is carefully managing water consumption and putting measures to conserve this precious yet very finite resource that gives life to everything.

By using water collection methods such as sculpted land, swales, and canals, we can ensure that the garden will consume every drop of water efficiently.

For example, rainwater needs more time to soak wherever sloped landscapes exist. Instead, it simply rolls down into places that might not need it or even polluted areas that ruin the water quality (this doesn't pertain to naturally occurring rivers or pre-existing reservoirs). Therefore, we circumvent this issue by digging swales (broad but shallow ditches on moderately sloped areas). The rainwater can penetrate the earth and allow for cultivation in these areas.

Furthermore, these ditches (or swales) can also collect water that flows down channels for preservation or redistribution to where it is needed.

Letting Nature Do the Heavy Lifting

This principle encapsulates letting nature be nature and using it to your advantage rather than implementing thoughtless labor.

The ecosystem has evolved over many millennia to be what it is today. Without humans, nature would flourish; it doesn't need us nearly as much as we need it. The circle of life is beautiful by observing everyday life.

Permaculture lays heavy emphasis on this fact. By letting nature do the heavy lifting, you minimize the amount of effort and maintenance that has to go into a self-sustaining garden; hence the term "self" sustaining.

A prime example is using "chicken tractors" to rid crops of pests and bugs that destroy the product or prepare land for planting food. The chickens will naturally scratch through the top layer of soil in their search for bugs. In this process, the earth turns over, and the weeds are cleared—along with the pests. In addition, the chicken's nature to go wherever will add to the fertilization of the area. And all you have to do is put the chickens where you need them.

Another example is planting mashua (a vine that is very tolerant of shade but needs a support structure) under a locust tree (known to release nitrogen into the ground, thus eliminating the need for fertilization in that area) near crops or gardens. The tree provides shade to the vine and fertilizes the soil, and the vines deliver a nectar source for bees that encourages pollination of fruit trees and other plants. And as a bonus, you have a majestic-looking garden.

PERMACULTURE VS. ORGANIC

There are similarities between permaculture and organic farming. However, permaculture takes this to the next level.

In permaculture, the natural underground microorganisms remain fertile, ensuring the soil is full of vitamins and minerals. Another way permaculture differs from being labeled organic is that crops and plants are often grown in a mixed culture and variety. In contrast, organic produce might still use non-perennial crops and other harmful agricultural practices.

Food that comes from permaculture gardening might also differ in size from those that come from organic farming since they're grown in even more natural circumstances. Also, permaculture produce will always contain seed-safe seeds and not be available outside of their harvest times. Unlike organic products, there are also no international trading or long transportation routes with permaculture farming.

If these differences still seem too subtle, here are some more substantial differences that will paint the picture of why permaculture isn't just organic farming:

1. Type of crops.

Primarily, organic farming focuses on annual crops (crops that need planting yearly). In contrast, permaculture farming avoids this and only farms crops that yield produce for many years, if not indefinitely.

Permaculture also farms many different types of crops, whereas organic farms might only limit themselves to one.

2. The techniques.

While organic farming promotes "green" or "eco-friendly" outputs, some farms that pass the bar as organic may still use problematic or harmful practices that damage the environment, such as monocropping and wasteful irrigation systems. Therefore, as long as organic farms don't use chemical fertilizers or pesticides, they can still be certified as organic no matter the other practices that go into cultivating these foods.

Permaculture farming is firmly against this and follows solid principles and ethics that benefit the crops, the ecosystem, and the environment. Every single system promotes minimizing the waste of resources and maximizing efficiency.

3. The control.

Even though the entire catchphrase of organic produce is "no harmful chemicals or pesticides," organic farms still use organic compounds to eradicate pests, weeds, and anything else that might challenge the crop the farm is growing.

Of course, this is still a considerable step up from using chemicals that damage the soil and pollute nearby water sources; however, in a permaculture setting, even these organic pesticides and fertilizers are often optional or permitted. Permaculture ethics strive to create an environment where plants, animals, and even pests live together in balance and harmony.

4. The soil.

An industrial farmer will treat or prepare the soil by tilling and adding pesticides and fertilizers when they want to plant crops. Organic farming also follows a very similar approach (except they use organic pesticides and fertilizers). However, this method still damages the soil and the delicate ecosystem.

On the other hand, in permaculture practices, they might turn the soil once and then keep adding enriching components to the top layer, such as compost and mulch, which protects the sanctity of the ground. This no-tilling policy ensures that the integrity and fertility of the soil stay intact and instead is built upon rather than broken up, which makes it difficult for the underground ecosystem to regenerate and serve its purpose.

Regardless of the differences, both are still trying to do better than the past has taught us. With the environment and well-being of all the earth's inhabitants in mind, organic and permaculture practices should continue to find the best way to feed us all that is least harmful to the environment.

LAYERS OF PERMACULTURE

A food forest (also known as a food garden) is a standard permaculture farming regime where huge gardens mimic the structure of a regular forest in the sense that it's self-sustaining, just with produce-yielding plants and trees.

Food forests rely heavily on "polyculture," extensive knowledge of how different plants can co-exist and serve each other and the environment.

The benefits of food forests are plentiful. Besides providing food, it only requires a little maintenance if designed properly; it creates a habitat for many small animals and creatures and integrates pest control and pollination. In addition, it is self-fertilizing and provides other resources such as fibers, fuels, green manure, and building materials.

A food forest has functions at as many as seven layers:

1. At the very top, we have trees that act as canopies and shelter for some plants.
2. Next, we have smaller trees or larger shrubs.
3. A small shrub layer below larger shrubs.
4. An herbaceous layer.
5. A layer of low-growing plants covers the ground
6. Vining plants or plants that grow vertically.
7. Underneath the soil, these plants have unique rooting systems that benefit each other in different ways and minimize competition.

BENEFITS OF PERMACULTURE

The ethics and ultimate goal of permaculture are to benefit and sustain all life on earth while ensuring the re-establishment of resources. This goal, of course, is not only in the best interest of the longevity of the human race but the environment as well.

Here's a breakdown of all the benefits that permaculture practices and ethics could hold in store:

- Reduced cost.

Because we use natural resources to service or maintain permaculture and our sustainability, there's less cost involved than conventional farming.

- Reduced waste.

In permaculture, all waste products or output is optimally recycled by either composting and returning it to the earth or using it in other ways to benefit the ecosystem. Since there's a responsibility policy concerning permaculture practices, the ecosystem consumes waste as efficiently as possible.

- Chemical resistance.

In a permaculture garden or agricultural setting, there is no use for chemical fertilizers or pesticides since nature is the primary way to uphold the balance between pests, weeds, and soil fertility.

- Less pollution.

The no-waste, no-chemical ethics, and ideologies of permaculture result in the most natural way of providing food and other resources, contrasting a large amount of waste and pollution in industrial agriculture practices. A proper permaculture zone will be completely free of pollution.

- Community values.

Many permaculture values center around the community working together to reduce pollution, helping each other, and using what you need from all available resources.

- Self-reliance and diversity.

With only a tiny area of land, you can grow a diverse range of produce for consumption or preservation. As a result, you are creating a sense of self-reliance and fulfillment, knowing that you and your family are taken care of even when tough times arise.

- Promotes green living.

Because your product is not subject to harmful chemicals, it's healthier and better for you and the environment. In addition, green living improves environmental conditions that might harm wildlife or ecosystems.

- Improved mental health.

Besides a sense of purpose and belonging, having your permaculture garden can significantly impact your mental health.

If all this sounds complicated, it's because it is. You have many questions that this book will answer in time. It's a lot to take in, but it's essential to have the basic knowledge and understanding of permaculture to get started on your self-sustaining garden and succeed at it for all the right reasons.

2

DESIGN PRINCIPLES OF PERMACULTURE

 Perfection is achieved, not when there is nothing more to add, but when there is nothing left to take away.

— ANTOINE DE SAINT-EXUPÉRY, *AIRMAN'S ODYSSEY*

Whether you want to transform acres of land into a food forest or a small back garden into a self-sufficient oasis, the design principles of a permaculture environment remain the same.

The design principles of permaculture are an extension of the ethics of permaculture. The regulations consider ecology, landscape design, environmental science, and the local ecosystem.

PRINCIPLE 1: OBSERVE AND INTERACT

When it comes to recreating the efficiency and sustainability of nature, what better source is there to learn from than nature itself? Ancient Greek philosophers considered nature an eternal divine for a good reason. Nature is one of the only things on earth that has always been self-sufficient and efficient when left alone.

Therefore, the first and most important principle of permaculture design is to observe and interact with nature.

Plan as Efficiently as Nature

The goal of permaculture is to set up a system that still produces resources and food for consumption while maintaining itself with little to no help. Industrialization could be more sustainable concerning energy consumption and usage. This lack of sustainability is why permaculture observes how nature interacts with elements and seasons to find new ways of conserving and using energy.

Know Your Environment

Before you even start setting up a permaculture garden, you want to know the surrounding environment and how it reacts to every season. Therefore, novices should collect essential data on the area and surrounding ecosystem.

Note the natural positioning of plants around the area and any bugs, insects, and animals that appear. It could also help to research the plants, bugs, insects, or animals you see and their needs and natural predators. Observe where the sunlight and shaded areas are and if anything could obstruct rainfall or air circulation.

Anything that could benefit, interfere with, or disrupt your permaculture balance is worth considering. Furthermore, consider the surrounding environment since neighbors using chemical fertilizers or pesticides, nearby water sources, construction sites, and parks can affect your garden.

PRINCIPLE 2: COLLECT AND STORE ENERGY

In a capitalist world where maximizing capital—even to the detriment of nature—is the main focus, a permaculture garden should always use renewable resources that don't affect the environment and instead make the most out of them.

Investing in the Long Term

Renewable energy sources will require an initial investment that results in non-financial returns, which is why it could be a better go-to for capitalism and industrialization. But on the other hand, permaculture principles are less interested in financial gain and more focused on providing us with everything we and our future generations will need to live a good life.

Renewable resources such as solar, wind, and hydropower energy, fertile soil, perennial plants, water tanks, and passive houses provide everything any living human needs to survive with minimal need for financial income.

What need is there for financial "freedom" in retirement if you own a home that's off-the-grid with a garden that supplies you with resources such as products to consume, sell, or trade? Not only will this benefit you, but it will also benefit your children, their children, and so on.

You may still need money for things you cannot provide through your garden, like taxes, a mortgage (if your home still needs to be paid off), and other services or items. But this is pale compared to the amount of money you'll need to save for retirement without a permaculture garden and sustainable living practices.

I'm not saying you shouldn't save for retirement but investing at least a portion of your savings in something that you can benefit from for years or indefinitely is—according to my limited knowledge of investing—a good move.

PRINCIPLE 3: OBTAIN A YIELD

The process of moving from consumerism to self-sustainability is, for lack of a better metaphor, a race and not a sprint. Investing all our money and resources into something that will only generate a yield many years from now is not realistic or beneficial to us in the present.

Immediate Yield Prevails

While thinking of the future is a big part of permaculture principles, we must also consider our current needs. Therefore, we need to do both. A system that provides an immediate, usable return on investment is preferable over one that will only serve you in the long run, at least for the foreseeable future.

You must invest in permaculture practices that benefit you immediately or as soon as possible, promoting development and growth.

For example, you might be waiting months for your fruit or vegetable garden to mature and yield fresh produce for you and your family. In the meantime, switching to solar power will have an immediate positive effect since you'll save on your electric bill, which means you have more money to invest in other areas that promote sustainability, such as rainwater collection, filtration, and storage.

PRINCIPLE 4: APPLY SELF-REGULATION AND LEARN FROM FEEDBACK

You won't have a thriving, self-sustaining garden on the first try. No matter your knowledge, there will always be an unaccounted element. The goal of this principle is better to understand the feedback—positive and negative—and respond appropriately.

Your garden will tell you exactly what's wrong if you pay close attention. Once you know what's wrong, you can implement self-regulatory, corrective systems that, once implemented, need minimal action to maintain.

Autonomous and Self-regulating Systems

As is the theme of permaculture, autonomous and automated systems are the ideal option since they will inadvertently promote self-sufficiency and balance.

The process of bringing this into action is observing negative feedback and making subtle changes until there is positive feedback. But be aware that it might take some time for the negative feedback to turn to positive feedback as nature is not in a hurry.

PRINCIPLE 5: USE RENEWABLE SOURCES AND SERVICES

Continuously withdrawing money from an account with a limited amount of funds could be better in terms of longevity since the money will eventually run out. But unfortunately, this is what will happen concerning non-renewable energy sources.

Permaculture principles advocate for the implementation of renewable resources. When a resource can naturally replenish, we can sustainably benefit from it, given we don't pollute or poison the source.

Resources Without Destroying the Host

There are many alternative ways to generate energy and other services from nature other than burning fossil fuels. Not only are the alternatives better for the environment, but there's also less need for manual labor once these measures are in place.

Using renewable resources responsibly means they can replenish quicker than we consume. As long as the source thrives, it will continue producing energy or other resources.

PRINCIPLE 6: DON'T PRODUCE WASTE

Permaculture ethics aims to minimize or, better yet, eliminate waste by utilizing most, if not all, of the output generated by simply going about your daily business. By actively looking for ways to reduce waste by reusing it in a way that is both productive and beneficial to the environment, we can avoid polluting our beautiful planet and preserve valuable resources.

Waste to Resources

In nature, all waste outputs always serve as a resource in some other way. For example, the worms mentioned above still serve a purpose by feeding on the remains of plant matter which provides nutrients to the soil when the worms defecate underground; their tunneling systems also ensure that the ground has air pockets and effective draining methods. So, all in all, you don't want to get rid of them completely.

Permaculture tries to follow this exact rule when it comes to the consumption of resources and the production of waste.

PRINCIPLE 7: DESIGN FROM PATTERNS AND DETAILS

From here on out, the principles of designing permaculture take a step back to look at the bigger picture instead of focusing on the elements at eye level.

Patterns and Holistic Understanding

Designing an impressive permaculture garden means nothing if it doesn't work. Patterns can be a great precursor and guide when you're stuck on all the complex options available.

Let's use a spiderweb as an example. Much like snowflakes, every spider web is unique; however, there's a clear pattern visible to every single web. Recognizing a pattern's simplicity instead of getting caught up in all the details will help you combine simplistic systems that function.

Therefore, finding the correct pattern for a layout or design is much more important than knowing all the complexities that go into it.

PRINCIPLE 8: INTEGRATE, DON'T SEGREGATE

A system is not just about the individuality of all the parts involved but the connections, interactions, and relationships amongst every independent subsystem that make it function the way it does.

The Importance of Connection

Regarding permaculture, the connections between the elements in any given ecosystem are just as meaningful as the element itself. That's why it's vital to arrange or design a permaculture garden so that each one serves the other plants and features and benefits from the surrounding elements. This phenomenon is commonly referred to in nature as symbiosis or mutualism.

If we look at industrial agriculture, we can see that the elements are split into acres of monoculture crops, leaving the entire system vulnerable and unstable to many potential pitfalls. Therefore, the maintenance that needs to go into this kind of farming is often expensive and extensive.

Meaningful Placement

Designing a permaculture garden to strengthen the interconnected relationships and connections between elements is necessary for self-sustainability and sufficiency.

Remember, the elements—even those that seem to be to the garden's detriment—play a vital role that fulfills many functions. Keeping things balanced is the ultimate goal in permaculture practices.

PRINCIPLE 9: IMPLEMENT SMALL AND SLOW SOLUTIONS

Our economy focuses on the idea that *bigger is better.* However, the ideology of permaculture is always to try to help nature by implementing the least amount of change that has the most significant positive impact on the ecosystem and environment as a whole.

Slow and steady wins the race when it comes to sustainability and the health of the planet. But unfortunately, not only are fast-paced economic processes inefficient, but we also see the same thing when it comes to nature.

Various examples concur with this; fast-growing trees don't live as long, and fast-growing livestock that consumes concentrated nutrients are more likely to develop fatal diseases or illnesses and have a shorter life expectancy. In contrast, slower-growing plants, trees, and animals contribute to the ecosystem more extendedly and tend to become more valuable as they age.

PRINCIPLE 10: USE AND VALUE DIVERSITY

The vast diversity of nature is not only something to be amazed by, but it's something we should value. As stated before, the connections between different ecosystem elements make it self-sustainable and efficient. Since diversity brings about even more opportunities to foster beneficial relationships among the details, we should encourage and embrace diversity. After all, it's a sign that the ecosystem is healthy and that you're doing something right.

PRINCIPLE 11: USE EDGE ZONES AND VALUE THE MARGINALS

Edge zones or boundary zones serve as a complex merge between two biological communities, such as where forest turns into grass-lands or land and water meet.

For example, areas where land meets water, such as beaches, lakes, rivers, ponds, etc., offer a distinct benefit to the ecosystem. Shallow water is penetrated by sunlight, allowing algae and aquatic plant growth and microorganisms to form an entire ecosystem in this marginal zone. Additionally, it's also a feeding place for birds and other animals.

Edge Zones Are Opportunities

Edge zones are arguably the most neglected regarding industrial and agricultural practices. They see it as a problem since you obviously can't grow crops there, which leads to the destruction of these marginal zones where there are plenty of growth opportunities.

These overlapping edge zones can foster biodiversity from ecosystems (aquatic and land, forests, grasslands, mountains, and forests, etc.) and species that exclusively live in the edge zone. By expanding and encouraging the development of permaculture in this area, we further biodiversity and productivity.

PRINCIPLE 12: CREATIVELY RESPOND TO CHANGE

Change is much a part of nature as it is within ourselves, and it can be another excellent opportunity for betterment if done consciously and cooperatively. It especially applies to significant natural changes that aren't in our control.

Permaculture ethics urges us to work with natural changes to avoid wasting large amounts of energy or resources to fight them. Instead, you can turn a potential problem into value that either furthers the ecosystem or generates resources if you use your imagination.

For example, weeds can be great for soil fertilization, serve as pest control, and attract specific bugs that benefit the surrounding plants. The abundance can be removed and turned into mulch or composted.

Flexibility and creativity are the best ways to respond to changes in a natural environment. Permaculture is rooted in its ability to adapt, which also applies to the biodiversity that resides within it.

This adaptiveness is all great in theory, but how does all this play out practically? At its core, permaculture is all about creating and fostering an ecosystem. And to get started on that, it's essential to familiarize yourself with the concept of zoning.

3

CREATING A NATURAL ECOSYSTEM—ZONE PLANNING

 Land is the only thing in the world that amounts to anything.

— MARGARET MITCHELL, *GONE WITH THE WIND*

Permaculture zones are all about planning the placement of design elements—including trees, plants, animals, structures, and buildings—to make the most of all the available resources and energy.

Natural elements like sunshine, wind, water, and heat should always remain at the forefront when designing your permaculture garden or forest.

Planning for efficient energy usage can be divided into three categories: zone planning, sector planning, and slopes.

ZONE PLANNING

This plan considers how often we need to use the element and how often we need to maintain or service the aspect. Logically, the parts we use most and need the most attention should be the closest to you.

Consequently, the elements you use the least or need the least attention can be further away. Therefore, every zone in between should be arranged accordingly from most used and attention required (closer) to least used and attention required (further away).

This planning enables you maximal accessibility and efficiency, so you expend the least energy getting to them. An excellent example is a kitchen garden with the most used ingredients, like vegetables and herbs. It would make sense to place it as close to the kitchen as possible, so obtaining produce is as easy as stepping through the back door instead of having it to the side of the house or the back corner of your yard.

Zones will include a numerical priority from 0-5 based on their accessibility and frequency of use. Zone 0 is the house and will elements of your permaculture garden that you use daily and need the most attention. Zone 5 is far from zone 0 and will include features or plants you use the least, requiring little to no attention or maintenance.

Before we go into more detail about what we put into the individual zones, it's worth mentioning that zones aren't rigid boundaries separated by fences or other structures and can blend in seamlessly together, just like they do in nature. Additionally, they can be in any shape or form defined by how accessible the area is.

Zone 0

Unless you're designing a permaculture for an empty piece of land, zone 0 is the building or housing structure. Your house should be as energy and resource efficient as possible so everyone living in the home can function correctly.

Zone 1

This zone will be used most frequently and should be as accessible as possible. Zone 1 is the area directly around the house and includes pathways and outside living areas that are easily accessible. So even if a particular site is against the house but is not easily accessible, it wouldn't fall under zone 1.

Elements that are usually enhabiting in zone 1 are:

- A kitchen garden that provides often-used ingredients that replenish quickly, such as vegetables, salad greens, and herbs
- Small trees providing fruit, such as lemon trees, and other fruit bushes like strawberries, blueberries, tomatoes, etc
- Worm farms to turn kitchen waste into fertilizer
- Greenhouse, cold frames, and propagation areas
- Workshops or sheds
- Rainwater tanks, boreholes, and wells
- Wood or gas for heating or cooking
- Animal pens for rabbits, guinea pigs, or other small animals

Zone 1 is an intense activity zone, meaning it needs frequent human interaction and maintenance to thrive since these systems usually don't occur naturally. In addition, this zone needs irrigation or drip systems and complete mulching to continue to thrive.

If you have a small yard, you'll only have these two zones. For bigger yards, you can fit in one more zone.

Zone 2

This zone requires less human interaction than zone 1 but often requires frequent attention or maintenance. More sizable elements or plants flourish in this zone, such as:

- Perennial vegetables that have a longer growing season
- Fruit trees and small-scale orchids
- Composting bins or heaps
- Beehives
- Ponds
- Chicken or other poultry enclosures
- Larger animals that require monitoring and frequent maintenance

The plants and elements in this zone may still need manual intervention, such as irrigation and mulching, to ensure they stay productive. Trees and large shrubs may need extra support until they are more established; the larger animals might need rotating to avoid overgrazing or damage to the plants, etc.

You'll need to maintain this area often, so keep it close to zones 0 and 1.

Zone 3

If you're converting a larger area of land, such as a farm, into a self-sustaining permaculture, from here, the zones will likely only apply to you since urban homes need more space to implement these.

This zone will house all the larger scale elements that need way less attention and upkeep if the permaculture practices are implemented correctly, such as:

- Large-scale trees, orchids, and main crops
- Pastures for livestock to graze on
- Livestock enclosures or structures
- Semi-managed bird flocks
- Foraging landscape for small animals
- Dams for water storage that also supply water sources for animals

Zone 3 also uses living mulch in the form of ground-covering plants that are kept unpruned and unmanaged. Of course, some trees might still need regular irrigation, but they're often the exception to the rule.

Zone 4

This zone serves as an in-between for managed versus unmanaged land. The primary use of zone 4 is for collecting wild-growing foods and wood, but it is also used as a source for larger free-roaming animals—like deer—to forage and graze on.

Human interference is unnecessary for this zone to thrive, assuming the natural resources (such as wood and wildlife) are not being used up or hunted at a higher rate than they can naturally replenish. Therefore, this zone is left alone for nature and the animals that inhabit it to do their thing.

Zone 5

This zone is completely unmanaged and wild without any human interference or maintenance. Instead, zone 5 is to be conserved and used only for observation purposes to step back and experience the balance of nature without having any control exhibited over it.

It provides a space to connect fully, witness nature, and learn from it.

Natural, self-sufficient ecosystems under zone 5 include bushlands, forests, and other similar landscapes. But, again, this zone doesn't have to be restricted to far outer parameters of your owned land; it can extend close to zone 0 via a "corridor" that brings a natural ecosystem closer to your home as part of your design.

In urban or suburban areas, zone 5 could be a nearby area of vacant land or a creek.

PRACTICALITY

If you look up zone diagrams online, it's usually depicted as circles increasing in size as they get farther away from the middle (with the smallest one as zone 0—or your house). However, this is not practical since land is uneven and irregularly shaped; some of it can be hard or impossible to access.

These perfectly even-spaced, circular diagrams exist only to explain the zones in an easily understandable way, but in practice, the zones can be flexible, overlap, be odd-shaped, etc.

The only thing you should consider is the sizes of the zones. There are no strict specifications for how big each zone should be; however, keep in mind that the zones should be small enough to cover on a human scale. The amount of product you're planning on growing will give you an idea.

SECTOR PLANNING

Planning out sectors will have an impact on where and how you lay out your zones and heavily depend on the external energies and elements that are entirely out of our control, including:

- Wind strength and temperature from hot summers or cold winters
- The position and angle of the sun throughout all seasons
- Water flow and flooding
- Unwanted views
- Fire prone areas

Considering these natural elements, we can strategically design our permaculture and supporting components to block, channel, or even take advantage of external energies.

Blocking External Energy

Suppose the external energy source (such as strong winds that are too hot or cold, or wind that carries salt from the seaside or dust) is damaging to our permaculture. We can block this with a wind-break, usually by densely planting resilient trees or other artificial structures.

With regards to heat, planting trees next to a house will keep it cool in the summer, and with the leaves falling off just before winter, the sun will again be able to warm the home until summer rears again.

In dry, hot summers where fire warnings are issued, we can build firebreaks to minimize the damage in the event of a fire. Firebreaks take the form of roads, rocks, stone walls, clearings, and even rivers, marshes, or ponds. Fire-resistant trees are also planted along these firebreaks to create a kind of shelter belt: oak, elms, willows, poplars, aspen, cottonwood, figs, carob, mulberries, and mirror bushes, to name a few.

Additionally, robust trees and shrubs can provide further privacy to your home or garden, adding a more aesthetic look and feel to your backyard area.

Channeling External Energy

The principles and ethics of permaculture advocate for reinvesting the surplus, but this doesn't just apply to products or other resources from your garden. Using natural external elements such as strong winds and heavy rainfall to our advantage is reinvesting the abundance.

Water flooding your site, either from rainfall or otherwise, can be collected and stored on-site or redirected to a nearby lake, pond, dam, river, or other storage solution for preservation.

Furthermore, suppose you can collect water at an elevated point such as a hill. In that case, you can use that potential energy that gravity provides for things like hydroelectric power generators, irrigation, or water supply to your garden.

Windmills or turbines are a great way to use high winds and provide a free source of electricity; the same with solar panels that convert and store the sun's energy into electricity for personal or commercial use.

Opening Areas to External Energy

The goal is to keep your garden open to only some external elements since they still need some to survive and be productive. Try to cater to your garden's needs; every plant will need wind, sunlight, and water.

A large tree obstructing the sun from shining on your kitchen garden will prevent it from thriving. Instead of relocating the planting area, prune the tree by removing some branches and utilize the removed branches and leaves for mulching in other garden areas.

You can also keep a particular area with a pleasant view (such as mountain landscapes or lakes) unobstructed to allow for some airflow through your garden while still keeping the advantage of having a serene or inspiring view of nature.

Mapping Sectors

With some strategic designing, we can block, channel, or open up our permaculture garden to the various external and unpredictable elements that optimize energy usage in every zone.

Zone and sector planning is about managing energy income and expenditure and ensuring we sustainably utilize everything nature offers.

There is one more thing that is highly important when designing permaculture, and that is the *slope*. As we all know, the land is rarely even, and this should work with your area when creating a permaculture garden or food forest since it can impact plants and their ability to thrive, as well as how external elements react to the slope.

SLOPE

Mountains, hills, valleys, and other uneven landscapes will also have to factor into permaculture design. This unevenness is worth evaluating because energy flow in these areas can vastly differ from a more even landscape area.

Gravity naturally wants to move things with mass from top to bottom. In this case, it is generally water.

Water

Water from rainfall will always flow from the highest point to the lowest. This flow is great if that's what you're looking to achieve, but it can result in flooding or damage to your garden or a particular zone if left alone.

We can use gravity to our advantage by building collection structures that channel the excess water to a nearby body of water like a river, lake, or pond. Alternatively, gravity can direct excess rainwater from uphill to orchids or crops further downhill.

Water from the roofs of structures, like homes and greenhouses, can also be collected and channeled elsewhere.

Using gravity to direct water flow uses little to no energy besides building the structures. Gravity can supply water directly to your home, and wastewater can flow to marshes or reed beds that clean the water before it flows to where it has reached a natural collection point.

Heat

Bodies of water situated downhill reflect heat and light and retain it to be released when temperatures drop. Since hot air rises, downhill water sources will act as a thermal mass and direct heat upwards, warming homes in the winter.

Furthermore, we can plant trees on a slope that will further preserve the heat generated and release it, supplying more heat when the wind blows the hot air over the home.

Erosion Control

Planting trees on slopes can also help avoid soil erosion. As water runs downhill, it can take some of the top layers of soil with it, exposing the underground ecosystem to harsh elements of nature above the ground.

Trees, living mulch, and other ground-covering plants keep the soil from being washed away and help the ground retain more water.

Trenches and swales also help as they slow down the speed at which the water travels. Constructing pathways and roads on the contours of slopes further slows down the water flow, forces it to stick around for a bit longer, and, therefore, absorbs better into the soil.

Fire Control

The biggest concern for a fire breaking out near a slope is what's known as *upslope fires*. This phenomenon occurs when fires climb the slope uphill, and the steeper the hill, the quicker it happens.

This direction is concerning because the heat from the downhill fire will dry out the material uphill, making it easier to catch fire and spread. Furthermore, the hot air draws in more oxygen-rich air from downhill, further feeding the fire.

For this reason, building a house on a hilltop is not recommended. Not only are you exposed to fire from all angles without any potential escape route, but the fire also will move exceptionally quickly.

You should also not build your house on the side of a mountain sheltered from the wind. The wind that blows around the sides and crests of the hill creates a lot of air circulation and could essentially form a cyclone of fire directly on top of the house.

Houses on plateaus or level land with firebreaks are the best option to reduce the risk of being caught in a fire.

Aspect

The aspect of slopes or hills is merely the direction it faces. Therefore, you want to situate your permaculture garden in a sun-facing part of the slope.

This layout allows the area to receive enough sun energy and minimizes the amount of potentially harmful frost in the winter.

A MULTIFUNCTIONAL APPROACH

How we, as humans, need many things to be happy, and so do plants. Unfortunately, in a conventional gardening or agricultural setting, every plant's needs must be manually supplied, which takes a lot of work.

Permaculture aims to eliminate as many manual functions as possible by layering and outsourcing as many labor-intensive functions to nature.

The easiest way to ensure you maximize the efficiency in your permaculture garden (if you're a beginner) is to ensure that every element has at least three different functions. Here are a few examples:

- A tree provides shade, produces, and acts as a windbreak.
- Dill is helpful in food preparations, attracts valuable insects, and adds to the garden's look.
- Mulch suppresses weeds, feeds plants, and stores moisture and humidity.
- A wall provides privacy, supports climbing plants and vines, and stores heat.
- Comfrey attracts bees for pollination, the leaves make for an excellent source of mulch, and the roots break up compressed soil and draw deep underground nutrients to the surface for surrounding plants to use.

It's of utmost importance that you know what every element can provide, and its needs. Furthermore, you want to ensure that these critical needs are met or supported in at least two ways.

First, let's look at the essential functions of every single element that need evaluating when designing permaculture:

- Water.

This element is the most important one and should be at the forefront when designing for sustainability. Unless you're entirely off-the-grid, you likely have access to clean water already. Rain will also help in this regard, and it doesn't hurt to try and store as much rainwater as you can to reduce the amount of water you're using on your permaculture from your local municipality.

When something happens to the main water supply, you, your animals, and your garden will be affected drastically. Therefore, storing rainwater and investing in a filtration system (even small scale specifically for irrigation) will ensure you have at least two water sources.

Other potential water sources include bores, dams, rivers, creeks, etc.

- Food.

It might be a good idea to plant trees and vegetation that supply a steady food source all year round, growing a variety of foods that produce different fruits, berries, vegetables, nuts, and grains. Moreover, having at least two plants of each will ensure you have at least one source of a specific food group if something happens to the second plant.

Extending the harvest season means you have a more significant yield. You can do this by planting vegetable seeds or herbs a few weeks earlier, indoors or in a greenhouse, giving them a head start. They'll start to mature and produce much earlier during the season.

Also, a mixture of annual and perennials will further expand the food supply. Keep in mind that yearly crops grow much quicker and need many nutrients and resources in a short time.

- Energy.

Any system requires an input of energy to foster growth, change, and productivity. So, having more than one energy supply is helpful to avoid any potential points of failure if we lose the main supply.

Permaculture advocates for using and producing renewable energy sources since this method of energy production is sustainable. However, supplementing renewable and non-renewable energy sources is still better than relying strictly on the former.

But ideally, you'd want to use only renewable energy and additional renewable energy production as a backup. For example, by combining solar panels and wind turbines, solar panels provide the majority of electricity in the summer. In the winter, the wind turbines pick up the slack from having less sunny days.

An example of this setup could be grapevines and strawberry bushes planted under an apple tree sitting next to a fence or trellis.

The apple tree provides the strawberries and grapevines with shade, and the leaves that fall from the tree create mulch for the strawberries. The strawberry bushes act as living mulch for the tree and keep the ground moist for the tree and the grapevines, creating a microclimate for the strawberries. Lastly, the trellis or fence supports the climbing of the grapevines and provides extra privacy.

This setup also allows you to add another garden bed close by where the trees and grapevines shade the small vegetable or herb garden from receiving too much sunlight.

Besides this system's cross-functionality, you have a small amount of fruit, vegetables, or herbs. This limited number of apples, strawberries, grapes, and vegetables is not enough to support an entire family for a whole year, but it will still make a difference to your food bill.

NATURAL VS. UNNATURAL ORDER

A big part of permaculture principles is about the order. However, when people hear the word "order," they immediately think or assume it means neat, well-manicured shrubs and straight lines, but is that truly natural?

The answer is no. The order does not equal tidiness—at least in permaculture and nature, it doesn't. Grouping the same crops, orchids, or plants in unnatural shapes and patterns is great for aesthetics and convenience but is wasteful and unsustainable.

The natural order is just a random collection of plants growing together uncaringly, except it isn't. In nature, if certain plants group together, they've managed to attain stability and self-sufficiency.

Ultimately, the most crucial aspect of a permaculture garden is the number of connections and functional relationships, not the number of plants you have planted together. There are always reasons behind the apparent chaos in an autonomous system.

Just as some plants work together in harmony, some plants and crops compete or even harm particular species. Therefore, thorough research needs gathering on every element or plant you wish to add to your garden to ensure they are compatible with the components already established in your permaculture. If they aren't, you'll have to separate them or grow them in a different guild or zone with elements that benefit them and vice versa.

Guilds

Plants that support the overall growth of the local ecosystem and the supporting network are called a guild. It's generally a collection of plants grown around a central focus point, another plant, tree, or even an area where certain animals roam to assist with joint health, growth, pest control, competition management, fertilization, and protection from natural elements.

Plant Stacking

In the introduction, I mentioned the several—seven, to be precise —layers on which permaculture works to efficiently utilize vertical space to grow various crops in a relatively small area.

The seven layers in more detail are as follows:

1. Tall trees: Large fruit and nut trees provide a wide canopy at the top.
2. Smaller trees: Right underneath the high ceiling of the first layer, smaller, lower-growing dwarf fruit trees.
3. Shrubs: Below the smaller trees, current and berry trees of different varieties.
4. Herbaceous plants: Herbs for culinary, medicinal, companion plants, or for bee and poultry foraging.
5. Ground-cover plants: Takes up any remaining space on the ground and protects the soil from erosion, reduces water evaporation, prevents weeds, and acts as living mulch.
6. Rhizosphere or root plants: Below ground level, root crops like carrots, onions, and potatoes take up very little space above the ground.
7. Vines and climbing plants: Supported by trellis, fences, and other structures, they occupy any remaining vertical space while producing berries, grapes, other fruits, and legumes.

Succession Planting

To ensure you have access to produce all year round, you want to implement fruits and veggies of different seasons, so the soil is always fresh and productive.

This rotation is called succession planting, which means that when one plant comes to the end of its harvesting period, another is already sprouting and taking the place of the dormant plant.

For example, as soon as your tomato plants start to decline at the end of summer, you can plant a cold-season crop such as broad beans in the same garden bed. Then, when the tomato plants stop producing, the beans will have already sprouted.

THE NINE STEPS TO PERMACULTURE

In the following chapters, we will go over nine beginner-friendly steps based on all the information provided to help you get started on your permaculture garden.

The nine steps—which we will be covering in great detail under a chapter of their own—are as follows:

1. Site survey and zone mapping.
2. Waterworks and water management.
3. Improving soil quality.
4. Guilds and companions.
5. Permaculture-based garden space design.
6. Planting and propagation.
7. Creating a biodiverse ecosystem.
8. Pest management.
9. Maintenance and zero-waste practices.

Tools

Before we jump into the steps of starting your permaculture, let's discuss all the possible tools you'll need to create and maintain your self-sustaining garden.

Don't panic! The rhetoric behind permaculture is that minimal maintenance goes into it, and heavy or expensive machinery or tools are unnecessary. But there are still a few things that can help you get the job done as quickly and efficiently as possible, and they are:

- A wheelbarrow to move materials such as mulch, compost, or other resources around the permaculture site. Make sure to invest in a wheelbarrow that's of decent quality that suits your height and strength.
- A hoe for weeding, dragging or tilling the soil, and preparing plant beddings. Again, invest in a quality hoe that won't break easily under pressure and is suitable for your height to avoid back injuries.
- A trowel will be handy for digging sizable holes without damaging nearby plants and moving back the mulch. Trowels with wooden handles are preferred since they last longer and are better for the environment than plastic.
- Garden gloves will protect your hands from calluses, thorns, sharp rocks, and critters that bite. Be sure to get the right size since gloves that are too big will make specific tasks a lot harder than they should be.
- Hose or irrigation systems. Hoses should be long enough to reach every inch of your garden without dragging over other plant beds or crops, as this can damage the plant. Drip-line irrigation or sprinkler systems are usually the preferred methods of providing water to the plants as this

is more convenient and time-efficient. Channeling water flow, so only certain zones receive water is also helpful.

- A pickaxe is especially useful when building raised garden beds and breaking up hardened or compacted soil. However, be sure to learn the correct use of a pickaxe since they are heavy and can easily cause back injuries.

Without further adieu, grab your notebook and a beverage and take a seat in your back garden because the first step in creating permaculture is simply watching and learning.

4

STEP 1—SITE SURVEY AND ZONE MAPPING

Adopt the pace of nature: her secret is patience.

— RALPH WALDO EMERSON, *THE COMPLETE WORKS*

Permaculture focuses on and relies on biomimicry to create a garden that is the most self-sufficient and productive it can be.

You can find examples of biomimicry all around you because nature has found the best ways of preserving and healing itself over billions of years of evolution. The methods that work stick around because, well, they work.

NATURAL PATTERNS

With biomimicry at the forefront of your intentions, spend a week going out into nature—or just your garden—and pay attention to the patterns you see. Some designs that are a common occurrence in nature are:

- starbursts
- spherical (or bubbles)
- spirals
- lobe (or clusters of spheres)
- stacked
- waves
- branched
- honeycombs
- scaled

While you're taking notes on the patterns that naturally occur around you, also take note of your daily habits or emotional patterns and ask yourself the following questions:

- What do I eat?
- Where do I go?
- What do I see?
- What do I buy?
- What do I waste?
- What do I create?
- Am I taking more than I give (from an ecological point of view)?
- How can I create a better balance?

Since permaculture is all about doing what's best for the environment and the planet, we should also consider our habits and do what we can to reduce our negative impact on the ecosystem.

There are nine basic principles of biomimicry that we can also apply to our rules or ethics:

- Nature runs on sunlight.
- Nature uses only the energy and resources it needs.

- Nature focuses on functionality.
- Nature recycles everything.
- Nature rewards cooperation.
- Nature thrives on diversity.
- Nature demands local expertise.
- Nature curbs excesses from within.
- Nature taps the power of limits.

SITE SURVEY 101

Many factors come into play concerning what to plant where. Unfortunately, some of these factors require implementation and, if done incorrectly, could foil your plans and visions for a lush, self-sufficient garden.

Practicing critical thinking and sustainable solutions would be best when observing the site where you want to start your permaculture.

To make it easy to remember and pay attention to, here are the most important things that need observing and noting when performing a site survey:

- Soil. What is the soil type on the site (sandy, silt, clay, or loamy)? What pH is the ground? How efficiently would it drain?

Loamy soil is preferred for growing vegetation since it contains the right balance of minerals, drains well, and contains humus. If you have very sandy, silty, or clay soil, consider creating a raised garden bed with the right soil type.

To test the pH of your soil, you can place two tablespoons of the earth in two separate containers. To one container, add half a cup of vinegar; if it fizzes, you have alkaline soil. To the other cup, you pour just enough distilled water to moisten the soil before adding half a cup of baking soda; if it fizzes, you have acidic soil.

- What is currently growing?

Unless nothing is growing in your backyard, you have decent soil. Although, you might have to do some preparations before planting, such as removing the weeds, mulching the area, and adding compost to the top layer to encourage the underground ecosystem to do its thing.

You should also consider what type of weeds are growing in the area and how they benefit or damage the soil.

- What animals, critters, or wildlife visit the area?

Birds, frogs, lizards, insects, squirrels, and other creatures indicate that your garden will have frequent visitors that benefit from it. Once you have a good idea and record of what wildlife frequents your garden, you can do additional research on them with regards to how they can benefit permaculture and how to keep them at bay.

- How much sun, wind, shade, and water does the area get?

Please spend some time in your backyard (or wherever you plan on setting up your permaculture garden) during different times of the day and note how much direct sun it gets and where the shaded areas are. Also, surrounding trees and solid fences will reduce the wind the site gets, so be sure to keep that in mind.

Furthermore, a quick google search will provide you with the amount of rainfall your area typically gets in a year. Jot down if and how you want to collect rainwater and devise a few practical ideas.

All this information will be vital once you plan out the different zones and what type of plants you could really grow based on their needs and what the area can provide naturally.

- How is the area affected by storms and droughts?

Again, you can search online for this information to become more familiar with the area. Also, consider the climate every season and devise creative ways to solve potential obstacles such as hot and dry summers, cold and icy winters, floods during spring, etc.

Planting warm-seasoned vining plants can help provide shelter in the summers, while a greenhouse is an excellent idea to protect your plants during snow in winter, and building water channels or raised garden beds can prevent your plants from drowning in spring.

- What are the best plants to grow here?

Considering all the information from the above points, what you *want* to grow is different from what you *should* grow. However, you can use what you know and research vegetation that thrives in the elements and with the resources you and your backyard can provide.

Planting tomatoes that require full sun in your yard where sunlight isn't readily available isn't practical. The plant won't thrive or bear fruit.

The Sit Spot

Observing nature is crucial for growing a thriving permaculture garden. However, to monitor the ecosystem of the area where you want to start your garden, you'll have to spend ample time there to get to know it.

For this reason, it's best to set up a spot near or even in the middle of the area you want to observe. This location needs to be where you can comfortably spend at least an hour connecting with the site as if it's your best friend.

"The sit spot" will become the heart of your observation routine, where you will build an intimate connection with that piece of nature. Return to it daily, sit quietly before exploring curiously, almost looking at the area through the eyes of a child.

This spot is where you will uncover the lessons of nature, a place that will become private and intimate to you, where you will get to know yourself and the surrounding ecosystem fully. Connect with this spot using all your senses and become an accepted and unobtrusive guest of the wild.

Vision

Something productive you can do while spending so much time in your "sit spot" is daydreaming. Try envisioning what you want for your permaculture and why you're doing it. Again, what you wish might only sometimes be what you get, but it will guide you for future reference.

You may want to grow at least 50% of your products or ingredients; you may have a certain way you want your garden to feel when walking through it. Whether you want to fully commit to the no-waste movement or reduce your waste as much as possible, make sure to avoid setting yourself up for failure by having unattainable short or long-term goals.

Creating a wish list for all your zones on your site could be a great way to keep you on track with your progress and vision.

For example, a wishlist for zone 0 could be to switch to solar energy production, reduce waste, and build a rainwater collection system. For zone 1, it could be to plant a kitchen garden with herbs and teas, start a composting pile, and construct a structure for a couple of chickens. Finally, if you have zone 2, its goals could be to build a greenhouse for more vegetation and extended harvest periods and start a water garden.

Maps

To help with your vision and design, you can also draw a map of the yard or area where you want to grow your permaculture and define the zones. You can do this even if the site is small, but this would likely only fall under one or two zones.

Several different maps are critical for knowing the ecosystem and what elements it's exposed to daily:

- Base map: A base map is essential in designing your permaculture garden because it's the starting point for laying out different elements while referencing existing structures.

A base map also records our observations and provides a canvas when designing. Therefore, the base map should be as accurate as possible concerning the layout and scale. You can make copies of this base map to test out a few different designs without having to redraw it every time.

- Sun map: A sun map represents where the sun falls on the site from sunrise to sunset. This pattern is helpful information since some plants have different solar needs than others. Also, bees and other animals (chickens, fish in ponds, pets, etc.) prefer the sun in winter and at least some shade in summer.

Furthermore, if you have solar panels, you want to ensure they get as much sun exposure as possible.

To map out where the sun shines on your yard, you can use a few tools and techniques, but the easiest one is to take a picture of the site mid-morning and mid-afternoon in midsummer and midwinter. Then, use a copy of your base map and illustrate where the sun and shaded areas are in the morning and afternoon in both winter and summer.

- Sector map: This map includes uncontrollable influences that might affect your garden, such as wind, water, weather, people (in community gardens), and so on.

Essential zones you should consider when designing your garden are work zones (where maintenance or harvesting needs completing). Examples include; children's play areas, shaded areas, sunny areas, areas that don't drain rainwater very well, and areas that tend to be dry. All these areas can be considered different sectors with variations of uses, needs, yields, microclimates, inputs (maintenance and use of resources), and outputs (waste and providence of resources).

All these sectors will influence your design and create potential opportunities or obstacles depending on your choices and how you utilize them.

- Zone map: As previously discussed, zone maps are labeled from zone 0 (inside the house) to zone 5 (wilderness). If you have a small back garden as your site, you might only have zones 0 and 1, a more extensive rear garden could stretch from zone 0 to 3, and farms typically have all five zones.

- Water map: The best way to know how the area drains water is to wait for semi-heavy rainfall and record where the soil gets waterlogged or tends to flood. Depending on the outcome, you might have to think of ways to mitigate or remedy this since you want your garden to flourish during storms.

This solution could be done by having raised waterbeds that allow excess water to flow past, living mulch to protect the soil from erosion, and swales around or through the garden.

Inputs and Outputs

Every element, zone, and sector in your permaculture will have different inputs and outputs.

Inputs are what you put into caring for and ensuring the animal or plant has everything it needs to thrive and produce; this includes sunlight, water, fertile soil, mulching, pruning, and other maintenance work.

Outputs come from inputs and the general livelihood of the plant or animal. The output can be beneficial, such as manure from animals that can feed the soil or fallen leaves from trees that can provide mulch. On the other hand, the output can come from waste, especially in zone 0, where humans rely heavily on consumables packaged with plastic and other non-biodegradable materials.

The idea of permaculture is to be aware of the inputs required of the ecosystem you're creating and to find a function for every output so it doesn't go to waste. Most output can double as input for a different element.

A sustainable garden will have no gaps where output doesn't double as a resource or input elsewhere. Composting piles are another great way to use the output from Zone 0 as future input.

Expectation vs. Reality

Whatever your grand vision for your space is, being realistic about the process and the time it will take to get there is a smart move.

Consider how much time, money, and energy you can invest in your design, implementation, and maintenance of the permaculture. Would you be getting help from family members or friends? What resources are available regarding tools, money, or otherwise?

Also, consider your limitations, such as health, age, physical strength, or energy levels, that might restrict you from performing specific tasks.

An example is if you work a typical 9-5 job, you'll have to budget your time, energy, and funds wisely to maintain your permaculture properly. In this case, a miniature garden may better fit you.

Assess All Information

Knowing as much as possible from your observations and further research will give you a solid idea of what you can realistically achieve. Observation and site survey goes beyond just looking at nature, and there are some things that you can't know by observation alone.

Once you have a good knowledge about the particular climate or biome you're in, you can think about providing the best circumstances for the plants that thrive in a specific environment.

The Master Plan

You have observed the site, connected with it on a deeper level, and know what you want to achieve can be done realistically. Now what?

Create an implementation timeline and follow through with it. If you want to bring your vision to life, you have to lay out a personalized step-by-step action plan to make it happen.

This plan of action will vary based on your particular circumstances. For example, you may have all the resources and knowledge about the area to start immediately; however, most people will have to wait until they have enough money or have purchased all the tools.

Whatever the case may be, a good plan of action contains multiple, easily executable steps.

Your first step after completing the site survey could be to research specific vegetation you want to grow to see if it's compatible with the area, which season to plant in, their needs and benefits to the ecosystem, what plants to combine them with, etc.

After that, you want to make sure that the types of fruits and vegetables you pick out for every season have everything they need before you even purchase them. So, this step will include you getting the soil ready, water management, mulching, and other means to prepare the ground.

Consider all the steps on your to-do list, and give yourself a reasonable timeline.

5

STEP 2—WATER MANAGEMENT

 If there is magic on this planet, it is contained in water.

— LOREN EISELEY, *THE IMMENSE JOURNEY*

It's common knowledge that water is vital for keeping all life on earth alive, so essential; life started in the water!

Poor water management is often the most significant reason a permaculture garden doesn't grow and develop as designed or intended. This chapter will discuss the most common issues regarding water management that often result in undesirable outcomes.

WATER IN SOIL AND PLANTS

The type of plants or vegetation you choose and how you treat the soil will determine how much water is absorbed and stored. Depending on your goals, you might want more or less water to be stored. For example, more trees and plants will result in more water consumption from the soil; therefore, you'll need to keep more.

Soil is the best, most cost-effective way to store water. The key to keeping a lot of water in the ground is healthy soil containing lots of organic matter, which helps the soil absorb and hold on to moisture and water.

Excess Water and Flooding

In a climate where it rains often and hard, runoff water or flooding can cause irreparable damage to the plants, vegetation, and soil.

You can prevent this by digging trenches where the water can flow into and away from the garden, though this only works if there is at least a gentle slope. A greenhouse could also be a valid option, as well as drainage systems underground and terracing the area; however, this can run at a higher cost.

Drought

Climates that receive too little rainfall will also need measures implemented to make the most of the rain that does come.

Growing vegetation that is drought tolerant or water-wise can circumvent this problem to some degree, though implementing other ways to preserve and store water is worth considering.

Greenhouses may also aid here because of the humid environment they create, mulching heavily, and collecting rainwater.

WATER HARVESTING AND DISTRIBUTION

When rain first starts to fall, we want as much of it as possible to be distributed evenly and absorbed by the ground. After this, we want to harvest the abundance by either collecting it manually or directing it elsewhere (to a pond, river, or dam) to use at a later stage when and if necessary.

Once the soil has reached its capacity for holding water, it will start to pool on the surface, and you end up with runoff.

Why You Should Harvest Rainwater

One of the most significant issues the world is facing right now is the pollution of water. The current process of supplying clean enough usable water for human and animal consumption is labor-intensive and unsustainable.

Reservoirs and artificial dams that aren't thought out properly—with sustainability in mind—disrupt the ecosystem. And while the world is currently busy working on ways to make seawater drinkable, it doesn't seem necessary, given that we're not using the water resource we now have very efficiently.

Since rainwater is typically drinkable with an easy cleansing process and perfect for irrigation, it doesn't make sense to use the limited amount of clean water from your kitchen sink to water plants—which have built-in filters.

In conclusion, harvesting rainwater is great for the environment, sustainable, and will help you save on your water bill.

Your Garden's Water Needs

The need for water will differ depending on how large the area is and how much vegetation you're planning to grow.

Think about how much water your garden will need and what you plan to do with the water you collect—household use, animals, irrigation, fish ponds, etc.

The math doesn't have to be solid; an estimated amount is acceptable. This calculation is essential when determining the size of storage you'll need, which will also determine what you can realistically afford or build and how much space you have.

If you only plan on harvesting a small amount of rainwater for irrigation purposes, a small tank might be your best and most cost-efficient option.

The Source

How much rainfall your area gets throughout the year and how it's delivered is also important. For example, do you get drizzles frequently during the year or heavy downpours in a specific season only?

From a planning perspective, this information will determine your setup for harvesting water.

Furthermore, you want to be aware of any other sources of water that might come in from the environment around you. For example, some water might travel underground into your garden when a neighbor is watering their lawn. If your yard is sloped, runoff water could also make its way through your garden; this is where swales could be helpful (bearing in mind that you should only build swales on slopes between 3-5% elevation).

PRINCIPLES OF HARVESTING RAINWATER

There are many different techniques for harvesting and collecting rainwater, but permaculture is all about working smarter and not harder. Hence there are a few convenient and helpful tips to go about it smartly.

Observe

For a good reason, we have returned to observation, a running theme in permaculture gardening.

Put on a raincoat, grab an umbrella, and go outside the next time it rains enough for the water to pool. Walk around the site of your present or future permaculture and note the flow of the water.

What paths does it take? Where does it collect? Are there areas where the water flows too fast to absorb into the ground? Where does it erode the soil? The answers to these questions will give you a good idea of what to do or where to start.

From the Top

Instead of dealing with runoff and flooding in some regions of your garden—which is significantly harder to manage and collect —try to minimize it by putting measures in place at the highest point on site.

You could use a contour map of the area or your observations from the previous point.

Easy Does It

Think of designs or implementations you can realistically do yourself with two hands. A lot of small strategies are better than a grand one. It's better to implement small changes at a time based on trial and error.

Not only are smaller strategies easier to maintain and less labor intensive, but it creates a diverse, interconnected system that is more likely to be effective than one extensive system that doesn't work.

Plan Ahead

Always plan for overflow. You never know when a storm might hit or if it will rain more than predicted, so always make sure you have a backup plan for where the water should go if there is too much for your system to handle.

Living Mulch

Shallow-rooted, ground-covering plants will slow down runoff water from rain by acting like a sponge, so the water is better able to spread out and absorb into the soil. It will also protect the soil from erosion.

Planting grass is a good option, though many permaculture gardeners prefer clovers since they release nitrogen into the soil, improving the topsoil's fertility and quality.

Stacking Functions

Another core principle of permaculture is stacking functions; it's the same when harvesting rainwater

—utilizing many ways to collect the rainwater, store it in the soil and manage runoff. This principle can include keeping water at the highest point in tanks, covering the ground with living mulch, and using berms and basins (explained in the following subheading) to direct or contain the runoff around the perimeter of your garden.

Feedback

To ensure that whatever techniques you use to collect and manage watersheds are effective, you must monitor their effectiveness and impact on the environment. Collecting feedback will allow you to change or alter the implementations until they are as effective and sustainable as possible.

RAINWATER HARVESTING TECHNIQUES

Like everything else to do with permaculture, harvesting rainwater should contribute to the success and health of your garden and its ecosystem. Using various techniques to collect and store rainwater and manage abundance, you can have a complex system that efficiently spreads and utilizes all the watersheds.

Sheet Mulching and Plant Choices

Not only is sheet mulching imperative for improving soil quality and eliminating weeds, but it's also a highly effective storage solution for rainwater.

This technique involves tilling the soil and then layering organic matter over the entire surface, creating a humid environment that attracts worms and other microbes, turning the organic matter into humus that later feeds the plants. It also protects the soil from direct sun or strong winds that can dry out the dirt.

Opt for plants that don't need as much water. These plants break up the soil creating air pockets, meaning the ground can hold more water.

Berm and Basin

Berms are similar to swales in that both techniques involve digging into the land to create a guttering system that contains or redirects water flow. Berms and basins are adequate on slopes up to 33% (but never on flat terrain). To implement, start by digging a basin (or hole) into the land, placing the excess soil on the side of the hole that goes downhill (creating the berm).

Thus, water that travels downhill will collect in this hole and have enough time to sink into the soil.

Depending on climate and annual rainfall, berms and basins are usually dug directly in front of plants or behind them. In a dry environment, the vegetation is on the ledge, allowing excess water to flow into the basin and drain into the soil directly underneath. In wet climates, the crops are planted in front of the berm and basins to avoid flooding.

Furthermore, using swales to redirect water flow in the event of flooding, you can direct the overflow elsewhere. It is also essential that the bottom of the basin is level; otherwise, the water will continue to drain in the direction of gravity.

Importing a contour map of your site from *Google* can give you a better idea of where the best areas to build berms and basins are.

Infiltration Basin

Also known as a rain garden, this method of managing or harvesting rainwater occurs on flat land or gentle slopes to store water underground for a group or particular area of vegetation or trees.

For example, digging a shallow "basin" around an anchoring plant (typically a matured tree) that doesn't extend more than 1,5 times the radius of the tree canopy, which means that you don't want to make the basin much more extensive (in radius) than to where the outer perimeter of leaves on the tree extend. You can also build an infiltration basin where rainwater would otherwise go to waste, such as near a rooftop, a driveway, or an overflowing rain-collecting barrel.

The basin should be approximately 2 feet deep to allow the water to absorb into the soil within 12-24 hours, and use a variety of vegetation as filling. You can also set up greywater systems to flow into the infiltration basins.

Sunken Beds

Sunken beds can be beneficial in climates that experience seasonal wet and dry periods. Implementing the garden bed starts by digging approximately 3 feet deep, using most of the soil from the bed to create a lip around the perimeter. Then filling with the remainder of the topsoil along with many layers of mulch which, as we know, will help absorb and store the water and build the soil.

Planting vegetation on the raised part around the sunken bed; the excess water will drain into the open bed, preventing the plants from flooding in the wet season. Then, come the dry seasons, the area around the sunken bed and accompanying mulch layers will have retained a lot of the rainwater from the wet season, so the surrounding vegetation has a solid supply to utilize.

Waffle Gardens

Imagine a waffle and how there are square depressions to distribute and contain the syrup equally; this is how sunken garden beds work and why we refer to them as waffle gardens.

This method is used primarily in dry climates and involves digging squares (2 by 3 feet in size and up to a foot in depth) into the ground. The distance between the walls of the waffle garden will vary depending on how you utilize them.

If you want to create walkways between the squares, the distance between each square should be at least one and a half feet apart; otherwise, they can be closer together. You can create extra support and structure for the walls by using clay which will also act as insulation.

Before planting anything, you should fill each square about a third of the way with mulch and wait for it to break down to ensure the moisture level and quality of topsoil are sufficient.

Permaculture Pond

If there are no existing bodies of water near your area where you can direct the runoff rainwater, you can opt for creating your own —if you have the space for it. A permaculture pond is another way of serving the surrounding ecosystem and dealing with abundant rainwater.

First, you'll have to choose a site for the pond. The pond should be in an area that receives enough sunlight but with a touch of shade, especially in the summer. However, you want to avoid having it directly underneath a tree to avoid having the water covered in leaves.

An area already prone to waterlogging in the rainy months could be ideal since the water will naturally drain into it.

Next, you'll need to build the pond. Regardless of the size of your pond, it should have a gentle slope in at least one area so stranded animals, bugs, or insects can easily crawl out if they fall into it by accident. It should be deeper in the center with a series of contours or steps to allow a variety of aquatic plants and creatures to live there.

You'll also have to decide how to retain the water, so it doesn't drain into the soil. Clay is the most obvious choice here since that's what nature uses.

Lastly, you want to introduce plants that will build the aquatic and surrounding ecosystem so biological creatures favor it, such as floating plants, rooted floating plants, marginal plants, and submerged plants that are oxygenating to the water.

HOW OFTEN SHOULD A PERMACULTURE BE WATERED?

A conventional garden needs watering frequently and manually since it's not built or designed to be self-sustaining. Unfortunately, this is the norm; it's ingrained into our general knowledge. However, in permaculture, the goal is to have a self-sufficient garden—that includes the water needs of the plants in question.

Ideally, you want to set up a foundation for your permaculture garden using all the rainwater harvesting techniques explained above, so you never have to water your garden manually.

It makes sense; when was the last time you saw someone water a forest? Yet it survives without fail, year after year.

Watering from the bottom up rather than the other way around is the best approach, which is why it's the natural ecosystem's route. In contrast, watering from the top down can compact the top layer of soil, meaning the root system of your plants get less oxygen and are more prone to rot and disease.

In a permaculture garden, manual watering and irrigation are often necessary if you're transplanting or planting in a greenhouse setting, your garden is still new and settling, or there has been no rainfall for more than a month.

Mulch is critical for retaining moisture since bare topsoil dries out extremely quickly. Therefore, you should always have 3-4 inches of mulch covering your entire garden bed and beyond.

Irrigation Methods

Watering your garden from the top is not the best way to provide your permaculture with water; a couple more ways to irrigate your garden in a more self-sufficient way (excluding swales, basins, and other natural rain redistribution techniques).

- Clay pot irrigation.

This method uses baked but unglazed clay pots to provide a steady water source to small gardens directly to the roots. The pots have a broad base that's either flat or rounded with a narrow neck—then buried underground, in the middle of an area containing vegetation, .with the neck sticking out just enough so rainwater can collect inside.

The water seeps out of the micro-porous clay pots and into the surrounding soil through the natural osmosis process. This process provides a steady, controlled flow of water. After some time, the roots of the plants surrounding the buried pot will grow around it and automatically extract moisture as needed.

When the soil contains enough water, osmosis stops until the ground becomes dry again, at which point it resumes.

- Dripline irrigation.

This type of irrigation is self-explanatory. A line of tubing extends over the area you want to wet, and water drips (or even mists) down into the soil slowly for however long it takes to wet the soil thoroughly. This method is gentle on the earth, so it won't cause impaction like hosing it down.

After you've decided on your various—preferably combined—water management systems and you're able to keep your garden healthy, it's time to move on to the next step, which is all about the medium in which your garden will grow: soil.

6

STEP 3—IMPROVING SOIL QUALITY

 The soil, it appears, is suited to the seed, for it has sent its radicle downward, and it may now send its shoots upward also with confidence.

— HENRY DAVID THOREAU, *WALDEN*

Soil is the top, loose layer of earth formed from rocks that have broken down over thousands of years. For any plant to survive, the soil has to contain air, water, various mineral particles, biodegradable organic matter, and living organisms that maintain the underground ecosystem.

SOIL SCIENCE 101

The best soil is a balanced mix of three soil types (clay, silt, and sand) called loam. It allows living microorganisms to break down organic material into what is known as humus, which acts as a plant super-food.

The structure of loam—along with humus and other organic material—allows the soil to absorb and retain moisture and oxygen and provide a stable supply of nutrients to the vegetation.

All plants need both macro and micro-nutrients to survive.

Macronutrients have either positive or negative charges. The charge is vital since soil particles carry a negative charge that grabs onto positively charged macronutrients (calcium, potassium, sodium, magnesium, iron, ammonium, and hydrogen). In contrast, the soil repels negatively charged macronutrients (chloride, nitrate, sulfate, and phosphate) and washes away unless the ground contains living microbes.

Healthy soil is just a circle of life taking place on microscopic levels between single-celled organisms. The negatively charged nutrients get caught up in the web of life, death, ingestion, and reproduction of the underground ecosystem, allowing it to stick around and provide the plants with what they need.

Plants also release carbohydrates, proteins, and sugars into the soil that feeds the microbes underground. Even more interesting is that plants can change the amount or the type of protein, carbohydrates, or sugars they excrete to cultivate a specific breed of fungi and bacteria to support the plant's needs.

It's unique how deep the circle of life goes; at the end of the day, it's all connected and very much necessary. So, to summarize, you want your soil alive!

Growing Soil

Regarding soil, permaculture gardeners focus on enhancing what's already there instead of having to meticulously and routinely add minerals, nutrients, and fertilizers to aid the growing of crops.

The foundation of a self-sustaining garden is cultivating good, healthy soil.

Nature's Way

In a naturally occurring forest, there's no one to water the trees and plants, till the soil, measure the distance between and depth of seeds when planting crops, or pick up debris and excrement from the many animals. Yet, despite this, the wildlife and food culture thrive in a seemingly chaotic fashion, producing more food than any garden ever created.

The soil in forests and natural gardens is rich even though it's completely untouched by human hands. Unfortunately, though, at some point in the past, humans decided that they knew best and created the agricultural industry we know today.

TESTING THE SOIL

Generally, in a typical garden, your first instinct to deal with dying plants is to water them, add some fertilizer, and hope for the best. But more often than not, the declining vegetation has to do with what's happening underneath the earth.

Why You Should Test Your Soil

Unhealthy soil can affect the health of the growing plants, so it's imperative to test your soil to know if it's suitable for growing greenery.

The primary purpose of a soil test is to know the pH level and which nutrients are (or aren't) in it. Suppose the pH and the available nutrients in the soil are not suitable for the vegetation you're planning on cultivating. In that case, you'll have a hard time experimenting and playing guessing games on how to keep your plants alive.

And as you might've guessed, this creates a lot of expenditure in the form of physical labor, resources, and financial loss.

A soil test will tell you precisely what you need to do for the soil to house and maintain the vegetation properly.

When You Should Test Your Soil

There needs to be a more straightforward answer to this. It might take a while to get the soil to the perfect state for planting (depending on how you plan to fix the issues), so the sooner you do it, the better.

As soon as you move to a new house or have found a spot to start your garden, you want to do the tests, so you have the most time left before planting. This timeliness ensures that you can also retest the soil to ensure everything is fit and ready for your garden.

Additionally, soil tests should occur routinely every three to four years to ensure the soil has stayed strong and is still viable and healthy.

How to Test the Soil

Pick a spot in your garden or the site you plan on converting into permaculture, dip a trowel into the ground at least six inches, and scoop it into a clean bucket. Then, move to another area a foot away and repeat the process up to 15 times. This method ensures you get random samples of the entire region, making the soil test results more accurate.

Next, you want to give the bucket a good mix and scoop out about two cups; this is the sample you need to test or get tested.

There should be a variety of reasonably inexpensive DIY soil test kits available at your local gardening supply shop, or you could look for one online. Do some research first to ensure online kits are trustworthy and reputable. However, you can only be partially confident of the accuracy of these testing kits, so the best route is to work with a professional to get detailed, expert results and feedback.

Alternatively, some county extension offices perform soil tests for free. Deliver the sample to the facility and wait a few weeks for the results.

IMPROVING SOIL QUALITY

Once you know in what condition your soil is courtesy of the soil test, you can work on ways to improve the soil quality (even if it's in pretty good shape, to begin with) that will benefit your future garden and the subsurface ecosystem underneath it.

The best way to improve soil quality is by implementing methods based on permaculture ethics and principles. For example, you are utilizing organic, eco-friendly, self-sustainable fertilization methods to enhance the soil you already have rather than importing or buying expensive healthy soil.

A few ways that improve soil quality without damaging the microbiome contained in it are:

Composting

A composting pile is a must-have for every permaculture garden. It is the best, easiest, and most efficient way to recycle kitchen scraps and other waste products and return valuable nutrients and microbes to the soil.

While there is no correct way of making compost, there are a few guidelines to consider:

- Variety is critical for rich compost. Compost should include kitchen scraps (fruits and vegetables, eggshells, coffee grounds and filters, tea bags, nut shells, bread, pasta, etc.), grass cuttings, leaves, paper and cardboard, and manure from pets and other animals. Remember to cover kitchen scraps with a decent layer of grass clippings, leaves, wood chips, or sawdust to deter insects and reduce odors.
- A ratio of 20% nitrogen to 80% carbon is preferred-meaning; approximately 20% of your composting pile should contain nitrogen, while the rest can be carbon-based. This ratio is because carbon materials are plant-based materials already dead and brown, while nitrogen comes from green and organic materials. For this reason, fresh grass clippings are nitrogen, while old, brown grass clippings are carbon.
- Airflow. If your composting pile or bin has a putrid smell, this could indicate that it needs more aeration. As a rule of thumb, your compost shouldn't repel any human being from getting close to it. It's essential to ensure that the pile doesn't compact, so oxygen can reach every layer to avoid creating anaerobic decomposition. If you notice it starting to smell, turn it to allow for better airflow.
- Watering compost. The compost shouldn't be soggy but relatively moist. Give your compost pile a quick hose down once a week in humid, wet climates and twice a week if the temperature is hot and dry.

- Turn it over frequently if your compost needs to be "ready" sooner. Turning the compost more often allows the microorganisms to break down the materials quickly. However, turning is optional if there are no time constraints.
- Compost is ready when it has turned black, resembles soil, and smells like earth on a rainy day.
- It's advisable to keep a few compost piles going at various stages of decomposition so you can have harvestable compost all year round.

There are many ways to build a compost bin, but the ones you want to implement are the ones that allow the easiest and quickest access to usable compost.

Uncontained compost heaps or piles in the corner of the yard isn't necessarily the wrong way to go about it—in fact, it's the easiest— but it's much harder to harvest the finished compost at the bottom of the pile.

A round-wire compost bin is excellent for beginner composters. Using fencing wire, you create a tube out of the wiring that holds all the materials. Then, harvesting ready-to-use compost is as easy as knocking the container over and collecting it. The problem with this way of composting is that you might run out of space eventually, though this is an easy fix as you can make more composting 'tubes.'

One very effective way of composting is the three-bin turning unit. Three composting units right next to each other (or a long bin divided into three sections) allow you to have three compost piles in varying stages of readiness.

It works by continuously adding new compostable materials and kitchen scraps to the bin on the left (or the 'add-in bin'). Once complete, move the contents to the middle bin; this also turns the compost, making it ready quicker. Then, transfer the contents of the middle bin to the next container on the right (the 'finished bin').

When the add-in bin is filled up and has to be moved to the middle bin, the compost in the finished bin should be ready to use.

Worm farming

Worms eat every and all organic matter and turn it into humus. They are easy to manage and don't require any maintenance except for providing them with organic matter in the form of kitchen scraps to eat.

You can technically use the worms you find in your garden beds for composting; however, they only eat about half their body weight in food per day. Therefore, you'll need two pounds of worms to consume a pound of kitchen scraps daily. Depending on the output from your kitchen, you should look at worms that can eat more.

Worms that are excellent for turning organic matter into worm castings (or humus) for use in the garden are Tigers, Reds, and Blues. These worms can eat their entire body weight in food per day, meaning you'll need half the number of worms to compost the same amount of food as if you were to use regular earthworms.

You only need a handful to start with, as they reproduce at a rate that would put rabbits to shame. Next, you can use a large, old bin or trash can and poke a few holes in the lid for ventilation and a hole in the bottom for drainage.

A typical worm farm setup consists of two trays that divide the top and bottom parts from each other with a mesh liner of sorts. You can buy a worm-farming bin or make one yourself.

The top part houses the worms, and the bottom part drains liquids, so the worms don't drown or get waterlogged. On the mesh divider (you can use shade cloth or window screening on top of chicken wire), you should have some bedding for the worms (coconut fiber or compost works well). The kitchen scraps are on top of the worm bedding, then a worm blanket rests (you can use a hessian sack or even more newspaper for this), creating a cool, dark environment for the worms.

The bottom part of the worm bin collects the liquids that siphon from the top. Place a bucket under the draining hole to catch the drainage.

Make sure you're not adding so much food scraps that the worms can't eat up in a few days—you don't want food rotting away for days or weeks and potentially infecting the worm castings with mold or other pathogens.

To harvest the humus, add food to one side of the bin and return a few days later when the worms would have migrated to the side of the container that contains the food, making it easier to collect the humus from the opposite side. However, you'll likely still have to sift through the castings and deal with some lost worms here and there.

Transitional Ground-Cover for Soil Preparation

Since it can take a while to get your soil to be the healthiest and most fertile, it can be, the time it takes for this to happen can vary depending on the current state of your soil. Therefore, introducing transitional ground-covering plants, mulch, and nitrate-fixing trees a year in advance holds multiple benefits for permaculture gardens and food forests.

To do this, you could opt to till the soil (only once and never again) and cover the entire area in sheet mulching. After about six months, the mulch should have broken down or composting enough to start planting. This timeframe is when you can introduce ground-covering plants such as crimson clovers or even legumes (peas, peanuts, cowpeas, beans, etc.), which release nitrogen into the soil.

Introduce Fungi

Fungi have a bad reputation since some species are toxic to humans and animals. However, most fungi play a significant role in your soil's health and the underground food web. Decomposing and mycorrhizal are two categories of fungi that are extremely important and beneficial to the ecosystem, which is why you should strongly consider introducing them into your garden.

Decomposing fungi are already widespread fungi we humans have been growing and cultivating for consumption. Examples of these fungi are mushrooms such as shiitake, oyster, reishi, lion's mane, Chaga, and more.

This delicious fungi mainly grows on the surface of trees or other woody plants. They decompose dead material that falls off trees and other plants and recycle the carbon, hydrogen, nitrogen, and phosphor into minerals and nutrients that the surrounding ecosystem then uses. It's also very efficient for building soil and turning mulch and other organic materials into nutrient-rich compost.

Mycorrhizal fungi are more on the down-low by working in conjunction with the roots of all plants on earth; without them, plants wouldn't be able to survive.

The relationship between mycorrhizal fungi and plants is mutually beneficial; the plant provides carbon-rich sugar to the fungi. In return, the fungi decompose organic material and soil and rock particles, allowing the plant a continuous supply of water and essential nutrients.

These fungi networks have long, threaded hyphae that extend in all directions, allowing the plant's roots access to 100,000 times more soil than the root network of just the plant alone. Surrounding plants can also tap into this network, and the fungi can distribute resources such as water and nutrients to where it's needed while also allowing plants to communicate with each other (to a certain extent).

Every plant connected to the extensive network of mycorrhizal fungi is better able to resist many environmental changes and stressors, such as drought, root pathogens, and other diseases that can destroy the plant's root system.

The quickest, easiest, and most sustainable way of introducing fungi into your garden is by following these simple steps:

1. Create a favorable environment.

Fungi thrive in shaded, moist environments, so crop-covering the area with clover, oats, or even tillage radish is a good starting point and will act as a food supply for them.

2. Find fungi sources.

While you're waiting for your ground-covering plants to grow, take the time to visit local or regional forests and look for both decomposing and mycorrhizal fungi.

Only harvest the mycelium or spawns once the environment in your garden is favorable and ready.

Decomposing fungi are easy to spot and transplant to your permaculture site (any decomposing organic material on the ground of a forest setting will have these fungi on it).

On the other hand, mycorrhizal fungi are a bit more complicated. You will find ectomycorrhizal fungi under rotting logs or leaf piles. To harvest endomycorrhizal, you'll have to dig deeper (literally). To find the right type and mix of endomycorrhizal fungi spores, you must search at least four inches into the ground close to a wild fruit tree or berry bush.

Though, if you plan on planting nut trees, you should look specifically for wild nut trees and harvest the endo and ectomycorrhizal there since nut trees prefer only certain fungi.

3. Introduce the fungi to your garden.

Once your garden and ground-covering crops thrive, you'll want to return to the wild forest sites you surveyed in the previous step. Gather decomposing logs, soil (four inches underground) close to fruit trees and berry bushes, and mycelium (root structures of ectomycorrhizal fungi) to bring to the site of your garden.

Fungi are incredibly resilient, and by simply strewing all that you've gotten from the wild into your garden, they will start to reproduce and rejuvenate your soil for as long as the site provides them with the right environment.

Composting Tea

Besides water, sufficient airflow, and essential nutrients-healthy soil needs the rest of the microbes that make up the underground food web, namely beneficial bacteria, protozoa, nematodes, microarthropods, etc., all of which play vital roles for nutrient cycling and the health of the plants.

This point is where composting tea comes in. Composting tea is like a liquid fertilizer and an inoculant and is easy to make. All you need is a bucket, some healthy soil from a permaculture setting (like a local forest), a mesh bag, an air pump, and a food source for the microbes to be able to reproduce (molasses work well).

To brew the tea, fill the bucket with water and place the mesh bag containing the soil from the forest inside. Then you want to turn on the pump and add the molasses. After 24 hours, the tea is complete.

NO-DIG GARDEN

Also known as the no-till method or a "lasagne" garden, this gardening method doesn't use any digging or tilling methods. As a result, a no-dig garden can situate on completely barren soil, stripped of nutrients, and unfit for growing anything, but also on top of concrete!

You can establish a no-dig garden in a few easy steps:

1. First, pick the location and size of the garden bed.

You can draw a square on rocky or concrete surfaces in chalk, a raised garden bed, or wooden pegs in the ground in all the corners of the area you wish to use.

The area should be as level as possible and receive at least five hours of direct sunlight daily.

2. Gather the materials for the layering of mulch.

You will need newspaper or cardboard, animal manure or organic fertilizer, straw or alfalfa hay, and compost. Though this is optional, you can also throw in some kitchen scraps, worm castings, or rock dust.

If you're creating a no-dig garden on top of rocks, cement, or paved surfaces, you'll need small, dry sticks, branches, and old leaves for the very bottom of the garden bed.

3. Ground preparation.

No additional prep work is needed if you're starting a no-dig garden bed over existing soil.

On concrete, rocks, or paving, you'll have to add a layer (at least three inches thick) of dead sticks, branches, and leaves before continuing.

When starting on grass, fertilize it with nitrogen-rich, organic fertilizer and lime and spray it with ample water before moving on to the next step.

4. Add the first layer.

Right after you have prepared the ground (or concrete), you can add a layer of newspaper or cardboard (if using cardboard, soak it in water for a few minutes before layering).

This layer should be about a quarter of an inch thick to prevent weeds from breaking through and allow any organic material underneath this layer to decompose.

Do not use glossy paper or office paper, as these contain harmful chemicals and bleach, which will kill off any bacteria and microbes. Water the layer well before moving on to the next layer.

5. Second layer.

Add a four-inch layer of pea straw, hay, sugar cane mulch, or lucerne, and water the entire area once more.

It's worth noting that any straw or hay material would work; however, lucerne is the best option since it breaks down quicker than any other option. So, depending on your time constraints, keep this in mind.

6. Third layer.

Sprinkle a thin layer—approximately two inches—of some organic fertilizer or compost and water evenly over the entire area.

If you want to add compostable kitchen scraps to your no-dig garden bed, this is the only point where you should add them. Unfortunately, adding it to the layers closer to the surface will attract mice, rats, and other critters looking for food.

7. Rinse and repeat.

After the previous step, you want to start with a four-inch layer of hay or straw again, followed by a two-inch layer of compost (here, you can add animal manure, worm castings, or rock dust as well). You are watering everything again in between each layer.

Finish it with a final four-inch layer of straw and, you guessed it, water it again.

8. Make pockets.

In the layer of straw, create pockets and fill them with compost. Into these pockets, you can then plant seeds or seedlings.

As a bonus tip, you can add seaweed extract into the water you use to water the seeds or plants, providing them with virtually every mineral and trace element they need to survive.

To maintain a no-dig garden when the annual crops of the previous season have been harvested and declined, add a layer of compost and hay (still watering each layer), create the compost pockets, and start planting again. For perennial crops, mulch the area around the plants with compost and hay as needed.

This process is one of many ways to set up a no-dig garden. It's relatively easy and inexpensive to construct, and you can do it even if you don't have a shred of soil in your backyard.

THE 4-1-1 ON MULCH

Mulch this, mulch that. You've heard that word many times, and you know it's vital in gardening, but what is mulch exactly?

Mulch is a layer of organic, biodegradable material that's added to the surface of a landscape to cover it. Its purpose is to mimic the natural process in forests where fallen leaves from trees and other vegetation decompose into the ground, adding back the nitrogen and other nutrients used by plants and trees.

There are many benefits and functions of mulching, so there's no question that it's necessary to maintain a permaculture garden. Here's a list of the essential characteristics of mulch:

- It absorbs rainwater and moisture.
- It prevents erosion and compaction from rain and other forms of irrigation.
- It turns into humus which is the main ingredient of healthy topsoil.
- It serves as a steady nitrogen supply in the soil as it decomposes, acting as organic fertilization.
- It suppresses weeds.
- It creates a favorable environment for the underground food web and ecosystem.

Mulching for Different Climates

How you mulch—or rather, how you should mulch—will depend on the climate and season.

In a hot and dry climate, your mulch layer should be thick to provide the soil with as much sun protection and moisture retention as possible. In cold and wet environments, the mulch should be thin to prevent erosion from heavy rainfall and allow the excess to evaporate. If it snows in winter, a thick layer of mulch will protect the soil from frost.

You should also take into account the seasonal changes. For example, if you have humid and wet springs, followed by hot and dry summers and freezing winters.

Mulching Techniques

Many different mulching techniques make use of various organic or biodegradable materials. The method or type of mulch you use will depend on a few factors, including the climate, season, your budget, and the resources available to you.

In permaculture, you want to use as many free and natural resources as you can. However, as nonsensical as it might sound, not all organic matter can or should be used for mulching.

Mulching material that has been tried and tested to use for permaculture gardens safely are as follows:

• Living mulch.

Ground-covering crops or vegetation can be either annual or perennial underneath a primary crop, such as a fruit tree or bush. In this scenario, not only are you eliminating the need for manual mulching, but you also receive the benefit of extra produce.

Annual living mulch like borage, calendula, nasturtium, sweet alyssum, and perennial mulch like comfrey, oregano, rhubarb, thyme, and white clover, are commonly used as living mulch.

Keep in mind that living mulch can smother the primary crop if misused. Therefore, you should also adapt the living mulch to the climate and seasons. For example, plant the living mulch closer in hot and dry seasons or climates and remove some of it in wet winters to allow the excess moisture to escape.

To prevent the primary crop and the living mulch from competing for nutrients, ensure the root systems are different (one with a shallow and fibrous root and the other with a narrow and deep basis).

- Green mulch.

This mulching method uses fresh, green plant matter to mulch your garden. Typically, the plants used for green mulch are grown in the same spot where you plan to lay the mulch; hence the commonly used term for this is also 'chop and drop.'

In a sense, green mulch starts as a living mulch. Chickweed, chives, dandelion, parsley, rhubarb, clovers, and yarrow are planted around the garden bed and allowed to grow freely. Then, to prevent them from overshadowing the primary crop, you can cut them down—leaving the root intact—and drop the leaves on the ground. The roots will continue to protect the soil from erosion, while the green mulch will retain moisture and humidity.

If you already have an abundance of weeds, such as dandelion, yarrow, or clovers, you could use them as green mulch since weeds are great for soil health.

When cutting down the green mulch, cut them down at the stem close to the ground. Also, if you've cut down over three inches, you'll have to cut them down more before dropping them.

Typically, permaculture gardeners will chop down (at the base, leaving the root intact) whatever remains of their annual crops and use that as the mulch—in addition to compost or manure—after harvesting all the produce. Then, if they wish for it to look more aesthetically pleasing, they'll follow this layer up with another thin layer of either straw or wood chips.

Most weeds or vegetation can double as green mulch; however, there are a few exceptions. For example, plants of the brassica or mustard family, such as cabbage, cauliflower, turnips, radishes, mustards, etc., can stop other seeds from germinating and inhibit the growth of other plants when rotting down. So, if you're planning on planting something in that area once they've completely decomposed, it can be used as green mulch; otherwise, you should remove them and add them to your compost bin.

- Leaf mulch.

Not only is leaf mulch an attractive dressing for your topsoil, but a pound of leaf mulch also contains almost twice as many minerals as manure, making it a valuable resource for your soil.

You can use the lawn mower to shred large leaves and keep them in a wire bin to spread around the garden throughout the year.

- Wood chips.

This mulch is another excellent option regarding aesthetics, practicality, and finances. In addition, you can get wood chips delivered from a local tree service for a reasonable price (some will even give them to you for free).

Wood chips that have been decomposing for a few years are a great source of nutrients and minerals for your garden. So use them without caution, as they provide excellent ventilation while protecting the soil and retaining moisture.

- Combining mulches.

When you combine mulching materials, you can provide an even richer source of nitrogen and other nutrients to your soil which your plants will thank you.

A practical example of this is combining leaf mulch with green mulch. Leaves do not do much for suppressing weeds, fertilization, or covering the ground since a strong wind might be enough to expose some of your precious soil. However, by layering shredded leaf mulch on top of green mulch, such as grass clippings, you get the nitrogen from the green mulch and the aesthetics of the leaves while still offering sufficient soil protection.

Mulching Do's and Don'ts

However simple it sounds, mulching can harm the plant. So here are some tips on what to do and what not to do when it comes to mulching:

Do:

- Make a donut shape around the plant's trunk with the mulch, covering at least a three-foot radius around the plant, leaving a three-inch distance from the stem of the plant to where the mulching starts.

Do not:

- Make a volcano where the mulch is too close or even overlaps with the stem of the plants. This method causes excess moisture to build up, causing root rot, and deprives the roots of oxygen, effectively smothering the root system.

- Mulch more than three inches.
- Mulch with an inorganic material such as rocks.
- Mulch with colored or dyed material, even if it's organic.

So, you've surveyed and know the area like the back of your hand, figured out and implemented a plan for water management, and are now waiting impatiently for your soil to get into tip-top shape over the next few seasons. But before you can do the planting of any kind, you need to decide what vegetation you want in your garden and whether they're compatible with each other so your garden has the best chance of being self-sufficient.

Improving the Environment Through Permaculture Gardens

"You can solve all the world's problems in a garden."

— *GEOFF LAWTON*

People who are interested in permaculture gardening have one thing in common: They understand the importance of protecting the environment, and they want to do their best in their own gardening practice to ensure it.

Every permaculture garden makes a difference, small though it may seem in the context of the big, wide world... but the more gardens like this there are, the bigger an impact they have on the environment as a whole.

My goal in writing this book was to lead people toward a rewarding lifestyle that would sustain their families and bring joy and fulfillment with every new plant that blossomed... but it is also my hope that the more people who find their feet in this way of living, the better our environment will become. Now that you're well on the way yourself, I'd like to invite you to join the cause.

There are many gardeners out there who are looking for practical information about turning their space into a permaculture haven, and by leaving your feedback online, you can make it easier for them to find it.

By leaving a review of this book on Amazon, you'll help new readers access all the information they need to start a thriving permaculture garden of their own.

Every new permaculture garden that springs up makes a difference to the world around us, and it brings joy and happiness to those who enjoy its bounties. Together, we can help even more gardeners access this joy, and make a huge difference to the environment.

Thank you so much for your support. Just like your garden, it makes more of a difference than you realize.

Scan the QR code below to leave your review:

7

STEP 4—GUILDS AND COMPANIONS

 A forest ecology is a delicate one. If the forest perishes, its fauna may go with it.

— URSULA K. LE GUIN, *THE WORD FOR WORLD IS FOREST*

Take a step back for a second and remind yourself why you want to start a permaculture garden. It might be because you want to save money on food, you're desperately trying to escape the materialistic way of life, or maybe you're just really into gardening but lack the time or energy it takes to devote to a traditional garden.

Regardless of why you buy this book, please write it down to remind yourself of the vision you had the first time you heard about permaculture gardening.

FUNCTION, SPACE, AND TIME

Permaculture is "lazy gardening" because it's known for its low-maintenance, function-focused, and space-sensitive principles and attributes. However, as much as it may seem "lazy," it's not just a matter of simply strewing seeds haphazardly and hoping for the best.

A successful, thriving, self-sustaining garden requires thoughtful planning concerning function, space, and time. With the correct execution, you can eventually get to a point where you can sit back and enjoy your permaculture oasis with little interference.

Let's further explore the layers of these three essential aspects of a permaculture garden.

Layers of Function

There's no such thing as a single-function plant in permaculture; every single seed you plant, propagate, and nurture has many functions to various degrees. So while aesthetics can still be part of your garden, pretty flowers shouldn't be the primary goal of wanting a particular plant.

Vegetation that delivers edible produce is usually one of the main functions of permaculture. In addition, many herbs double as medicines for alleviating symptoms of minor illnesses such as colds, flu, headaches, allergies, muscle pain, toothache, constipation, and the like.

A diverse garden with many different plant species that work well together can also provide you with some money-making opportunities in the form of crafts. For example, some fiber plants, such as bamboo, are suitable for weaving baskets you can use or sell, and particular straws make great hats.

Furthermore, some plants make great mulching material as well as provide nitrogen and detoxification to the soil.

Another vital function of any plant you want in your garden is the insects they attract or repel. By planting the proper vegetation, you can draw a diverse range of beneficial insects and pollinators while repelling harmful pests.

Layers of Space

Polycultures are the be-all-end-all of permaculture. By establishing a polyculture where many different plants occupy every available layer of space, you make the most out of the space you have, feed the ecosystem, and have more produce to harvest. However, a diverse garden doesn't equal a cramped garden, and, once again, you'll have to ensure all plants have enough room to grow.

Earlier, we discussed the different layers of space, including tall trees, small trees, herbs and vegetables, shrubs, vines, ground covers, roots, and water plants. Using all these layers, you can grow a large variety of vegetation in a relatively small area.

Tall trees provide a habitat for wild animals and serve as a windbreak, shaded canopy, and mulch for the surrounding garden. However, big trees take the most time to grow and live the longest. Regardless, you should plan your garden according to the size of the tree (or plant in general) at its maturity, even though it might be many years before it reaches that state.

In the meantime, you can grow herbs, berries, or vegetables around the sprouting that you can later remove as the growing tree takes up the space.

Small trees are the go-to trees of choice if you have limited space. It serves a tall tree's functions while providing food like fruits and nuts. While smaller trees still take a lot of time to mature and bare produce, they're also around for a long time, meaning they'll continue providing future generations with food.

Most herbs and vegetable plants need full or partial sun, so keep this in mind when you get to the actual designing part of your garden. Also, most herbs are perennial, while vegetables are often annual or biennial that will need planting every season. Finally, this option makes vegetables an excellent choice for planting close to small or larger trees since they provide shade and mulch for growing trees.

The shrub layer consists of fruit and berry bushes and fiber plants. They are typically perennials and, once matured, need only the occasional mulching and pruning to continue to thrive. Shrubs need sun during the initial growth period, but once they develop, they are content with being shaded and are pretty drought-tolerant.

Shrubs are very important in a young permaculture garden, while the small or more significant trees still need to be fully grown and able to supply the necessary shade and windbreak for the other plants. So, start your permaculture garden by establishing the shrubs before anything else since the shrubs will protect the more minor crops.

Vining plants take full advantage of the remaining vertical space, which is excellent for smaller gardens. Vines don't mind shade, but they will need it to bear fruit or flowers. In addition, you can also use vines to create a windbreak or microclimate when trellised; otherwise, if left un-trellised, they also serve as an excellent ground cover crop. Finally, they make perfect homes for insects and spiders alike, furthering the diversity of the ecosystem.

Trimming vines are optional, and many climbing legumes are also nitrogen-fixing plants, making them a great addition to your garden.

Ground-covering plants serve as a living mulch, protect the soil from exposure to harsh sun and erosion from flooding, and suppress unwanted weeds. Therefore, it would be best to plant ground-covering plants while other crops are still seedlings. Since living mulch will need sunlight until mature, they grow perfectly well in shaded areas and can even be encouraged to extend to other garden areas—if that's what you wish to do.

That leaves us with the root systems. Some plants are grown mainly for their edible roots, such as potatoes, carrots, beets, etc. Though, of course, all plants have roots since that's how they gain access to all the nutrients and water from the soil they need to survive. To avoid having your plants compete for root space, you should always assume that there's at least as much growth going on underground as above ground and space them accordingly.

It would help if you always considered the roots of the plants and how much space they'll need, and plant complementing crops with different root structures—a balance of shallow and deep-rooted crops.

Suppose you have a natural water feature in your permaculture garden. In that case, you'll need to consider plants on several layers to cleanse and aerate the water and provide food, shade, and a healthy ecosystem for fish and other aquatic animals.

Layers of Time

Like you want to use all the available space you have by using all the different layers of a permaculture garden, you want to take advantage of growing various crops throughout the year. This way, your garden always serves you, the ecosystem, and the underground food web.

Besides having fresh produce every year and keeping the soil fertile, you diversify your garden by planting an array of annual or seasonal crops combined with perennials.

Most climates will allow you to grow and access fresh produce throughout the year, except if you're in an area where it snows during winter, making it exceptionally harder to grow anything.

While thinking of all the plants and vegetation you want in your garden, note their planting and harvesting times, so your garden is always full. Have at least three different crop types for every season, along with how much time it will take them to grow to maturity and yield produce.

Try to include self-perpetuating plants, meaning they leave behind seeds that naturally fall off or spread underground via their rooting systems. But plan for this in your vision for your future garden.

Building a greenhouse or cold frame can also extend most plants' growth and harvest season.

CHOOSING THE RIGHT PLANTS

When choosing the right plants for your permaculture, you must be realistic and keep the layers of function, space, and time in mind. What you don't want to do is spend every spare moment you have trying to keep a plant alive because you're trying to adapt the environment to the plant instead of the other way around.

Picking the correct plants can be tricky because there are many factors to consider, such as your climate, biome, soil type and condition, sunlight needs, water needs, and hardiness zone.

But before you close the book and give up on permaculture, there's an easier way involving something we've discussed already: Observation. Adding on to the information from site surveying in step one—which you might or might not have done already—you can use that to be sure to pick the suitable crops for your permaculture garden.

Here's what you do:

- Where you've noted down the names of the vegetation types, you can add what layer it occupies. Also, note what the specific plant prefers regarding sun, nutrients, and location with other plants. You might have to revisit the site you scoped out in step one a few times.
- Plenty of mobile applications allow you to take a picture of the plant in question, which will then analyze it and tell you what it is (*iNaturalist* and *PictureThis* are two examples of apps that identify plant species from a photo with great accuracy).
- When in doubt, google it out; that is how the saying goes. Then, research a specific plant that occurs naturally in your area. Find out its root structure, functions, soil and sunlight preference, the insects or animals it attracts and repels, and even the beneficial relationships it can have with other plants.
- Please think of the present and future concerning the sun patterns and how much your garden will get when you first start your garden and when all the crops mature and create canopies or shade for other plants around them.

With the combined knowledge of the existing trees, shrubs, herbaceous plants, vines, root vegetables, and ground-cover crops in your area, we can move on to the fun part of selecting the types of plants for your guild.

Choosing Trees

If you do have the space for it, taller trees can be very beneficial to your garden. You can look towards the extended area around your home to find the right tree to flourish in your space. Though, even if taller or bigger trees don't provide fruits or nuts, they can still contribute to your permaculture's ecosystem in other ways, as discussed prior.

Permaculture-preferred trees that thrive in colder climates are apple, crab apple, cherry (sour and sweet), plum, damson, pear, medlar, mulberry, persimmons, quinces, and greengages.

In hotter, more humid (or Mediterranean) climates, trees like eucalyptus, juniper, oak, pine, mango, avocado, olive, fig, citrus (lemon, oranges, nectarines, etc.), pomegranate, walnut, and even almond are all great options.

It would be best to plant some fruiting trees in pairs of two since they don't self-pollinate. Though, almond, walnut, cherry, plum, peach, apricot, pear, nectarine, and some apple trees are self-fertile and will produce fruit without a second tree nearby.

Choosing Shrubs

Most smaller trees, shrubs, and bushes will grow just fine—after they're established and mature—under large trees with only partial sun and can be grown in most climates. However, blueberries and cranberries tend to do better in colder climates.

Berry bushes are perennials and need little maintenance, such as classic, easy-to-grow raspberries, blackberries, gooseberries, strawberries, elderberries, and even currants.

Choosing Herbaceous Plants

The layer of plants underneath shrubs and berry bushes cater towards benefiting all the other layers of a permaculture garden. However, you can still reap some benefits from herbs and brassicas (broccoli, cauliflower, kale, chard, spinach, brussel sprouts, etc.).

The herbaceous layer can also include flowering plants and herbs that attract beneficial insects and pollinators. They also fertilize the soil by replacing the nitrogen and bringing nutrients from deep underground to the surface for other plants to use (examples include comfrey, yarrow, dandelions, and red clovers).

Almost all herbs originate from Mediterranean climates where it tends to be on the more hot and dry (as well as humid) end as far as temperature goes. So, if your area is prone to dry heat, herbs such as chives, oregano, sage, thyme, and even lavender are heat-resistant and can all be great additions to your garden space.

You can still choose from a selection of cold-resistant herbs in highland or cool climates with a mild summer, such as curry leaf, rosemary, mint, lemon balm, parsley, dill, fennel, horseradish, and caraway, which can survive cold winters.

Choosing Roots and Vines

Common root vegetables—called alliums—such as carrots, onions and shallots, garlic, potatoes, beets, parsnips, radishes, and turnips do better in colder climates. However, in hotter climates, they usually do just fine when planted in shady areas.

Vine crops that do well in milder or colder climates are tomatoes, peas, cucumbers, squash, pumpkins, chayote, and beans. Beans are also nitrogen-fixing plants and are an excellent natural fertilizer for the soil, making them one of the best options for your permaculture garden.

Grapes prefer longer summers and a lot of rain; however, there's likely to be a variant of grape in whichever climate you find yourself in that you can grow.

Choosing Ground-Cover Plants

As previously established, ground-cover crops play a vital role in the protection of the soil from sun exposure, drying it out as well as heavy rain eroding or compacting it. But besides that, ground-covering plants also provide an opportunity for more fresh produce in the form of fruits and low-lying herbs.

Ground-cover crops include strawberries, clovers, vetches, land cress, lamb's lettuce, arugula, and comfrey.

DESIGNING A GUILD OF YOUR OWN

Your specific combination of plants in your permaculture garden will depend on your climate and biome. However, you should always consider these two significant factors when creating a plant guild of your own.

While you may be familiar with companion plantings such as tomato and basil, or carrots and onions, a guild is more complex.

The question here is, what's the essence behind a good guild?

Guild Theoretics

A guild is a group of plants of different types and species that work together on all seven layers of permaculture—providing physical support and protection. They also swap nutrients and resources to enhance the entire system's health, enabling the whole thing to thrive independently with little help.

But besides diversity and only growing the plants that work well with the climate you're in, let's look at a guild in more detail.

- A centerpiece.

In a big, open forestry setting, there are usually impressive, tall trees spread around that almost create a ceiling for the understory. However, in smaller, backyard-scale permaculture, you should still have a centerpiece of sorts in the form of smaller trees that the rest of the guild will situate around.

Whether the trees are big (apple, mango, macadamia, pears, pecan, mulberry, chestnut, carob, avocado, or dates) or smaller (papaya, hazelnut, guava, citrus, almond, peach, or cacao), they represent the primary yield.

- The lifeblood.

At the beginning of planting and growing your permaculture garden, a large percentage of your crops are nitrogen-fixing, which will reduce in time but should always consist of about 10% of your garden in total—spread throughout the entire area, of course.

Nitrogen-fixing crops of varying growth times are pigeon pea, ice cream bean, lupin, clover, vetch, groundnut, kudzu, locust, and carob.

- Accumulators.

This characteristic refers to plants with a deep root structure that penetrates the soil and uses nutrients inaccessible to other plants; this also means that they aren't competing with surrounding plants for nutrients.

These nutrients can also be deposited into the topsoil when the accumulator plants utilize trimmings as a green mulch. However, accumulator plants produce medicinal or edible fruits or leaves, such as comfrey and dandelions, but most are typically only used as mulching material.

Examples of accumulator plants are borage, comfrey, chickweed, yarrow, nettles, chicory, amaranth, lamb's quarters, and even the leaves and branches of moringa and mulberry trees.

- Ground protection.

While some weeds are an eye-sore, others might be more aesthetically pleasing and benefit your permacultures, such as clovers and dandelions. Although, if you prefer not to have weeds in your garden, there are other ways of protecting your soil, creating a favorable environment for beneficial insects, and retaining moisture, all while keeping unsightly or invasive weeds to a minimum.

The trick is not to leave any soil bare, which leaves room for weeds to cultivate in your garden beds, especially in the starting stages of your permaculture garden.

Some great options for ground-cover crops are sweet potato, salad greens, parsley, peanuts, rhubarb, and strawberries.

- Pest control and pollination.

You need to control the type, kind, and number of insects in your garden to avoid pest problems.

Plants that attract pollinators have a flower such as lavender, cone-flower varieties, cosmos, daisies, marigolds, milkweeds, and snap-dragons. This feature is vital if crops require cross-pollination to yield produce (bees and other insects must pollinate many fruit trees, berry bushes, and vegetables). Therefore, it would be wise to have a couple of flower bushes that attract pollinators.

A combination of aromatic herbs such as mint, dill, and even sunflowers can help maintain the balance of insects in your garden. The strong scents confuse invasive and damaging insects while simultaneously attracting predatory bugs that eat them, keeping the pest population under control.

Examples of plants and herbs that act as pest control are mint, peppermint, basil, dill, marigold, sunflowers, lemongrass, citronella, lavender, and coriander.

Have at least a couple of variants of plants that cater to each of the criteria mentioned above, so you have a backup plan if something were to damage or ruin one of the plants that serve a specific function.

Why a Guild?

Not only does a guild make the best usage out of the available space and maximize the amount of product you're able to grow, but it also reduces the amount of maintenance and attention the garden needs.

Furthermore, a guild can improve the quality and flavor of the fruit and vegetables you harvest because the soil is healthy, thanks to the diversity of the ecosystem. It also creates microclimates that are good for your plants and the beneficial critters in your garden.

A diverse guild can also ensure you have harvestable produce for you and your family throughout all seasons, or at least most of them.

Keep in mind that, at this point, the space you have to work with will alter your original vision to some extent.

8

STEP 5—PERMACULTURE GARDEN SPACE DESIGN

 Life begins the day you start a garden.

— ANCIENT CHINESE PROVERB

Everyone reading this book and wanting to start permaculture will have different needs, resources, and spacing available. While some people may have wide open spaces to transform into majestic food forests, others might have a small area of grass in their backyard, maybe you have no grass at all, and your entire yard is concrete.

Permaculture is about using what you have first and foremost and expanding if and when you can.

MAXIMIZING GARDEN SPACE

If you're fortunate enough to have access to a lot of room for your permaculture, this section might not be applicable. However, helpful tips could come in handy along the way, even with acres upon acres of land at your disposal.

Less Walk, More Grow

Every time you step on perfectly healthy soil, you compact it, obliterating underground air pockets vital for plant roots and the soil's ecosystem. The obvious solution here is to designate areas specifically for planting with only small walkways between the garden beds so you can access all plants when needed.

Ensure your garden beds are marked, so no one accidentally steps into them. You can do this by framing the beds with rocks, using stakes in the corners, and using twine to mark the borders.

To determine the size of your garden beds, you should be able to stand in the walkway and comfortably reach the center of the bed from at least two opposite sides. This layout means your garden bed can be as long as you want it to be, as long as you can reach the middle from two sides perpendicular to each other.

Feed Soil, Not Plants

Suppose you plan so your soil is rich and healthy and use the techniques we've discussed (mulching, nitrogen-fixing plants, composting, proper water management, companion planting, etc.) Then, chances are you won't have to buy fertilizer or harsh chemicals to fight weeds or kill pests. In addition, if you set up your permaculture right, your soil quality will improve with every season instead of declining.

When your soil has enough organic material—and you keep feeding it via compost, mulch, and worm castings—and a thriving food web, the ground will continue to feed and nurture the growing plants.

Don't Do Lines

Ignoring the title's double entendre, when have you seen nature form perfect lines or distinguish between trees, bushes, and foliage?

That's because straight lines aren't very natural and can cause problems such as soil erosion and flooding in the lowest points of the landscape because runoff rain has nothing in its path that's slowing it down and allowing it to absorb into the soil evenly.

Staggering your plants will increase the number of plants you can grow in your space. In addition, this technique benefits companion planting, where every plant still needs a certain amount of elbow room but requires planting together.

Be Creative

There are many ways that you can maximize your garden space by using designs that are specifically for permaculture. For example, make a garden bed that's a semi-circle, so you're able to enter it, work, and move about effortlessly without disturbing the soil you're planting in. Again, as long as you can access all the plants, you can get creative with the shape or size of your garden bed.

DECIDING ON A LAYOUT

Once you have a good idea of what you want to grow based on your needs, climate, and space, you need to figure out the best layout so all of your crops get the right amount of sun or shade, beneficial insects, pest control, and water.

More space means more options for potential designs, and less space means you will have already determined your plan to an extent. The following three steps will help you choose the perfect layout for your space and design it correctly.

1. The garden bed.

There are many garden beds, but we'll focus on the three most common ones and their functions for this exercise.

In-ground beds are when you create a garden bed directly on the soil of an existing piece of land. These are common and functional for home gardens but work well with larger-scale farming. They're considered the easiest and most cost-effective beds to establish. You'll need to ensure the soil is in good condition with adequate drainage.

Raised beds are elevated and supported by a frame or enclosure (usually wood) that you can build yourself. This method is excellent if you have low-quality soil that will take a very long time to fix or no dirt (paved outside flooring). Raised beds are a great option since they warm up quicker (creating a microclimate), drain well, and are easier to manage. The only downside is that constructing a raised bed can be labor intensive, and the material to build it costs money.

Hügelkultur is, at the core, a raised garden bed filled with organic, biodegradable material such as rotten wood, branches, leaves, and twigs. Hügelkultur beds are a great way to start a permaculture garden since they provide long-term fertilization and adequate drainage and irrigation; however, building it can be pretty labor-intensive, depending on the size.

2. Garden bed orientation.

How you orient your garden bed is of no significance, but there are three factors to consider concerning this: sun, rain, and slope.

It would be best if you oriented the garden bed so that all the crops get equal sunlight when the sun passes over it.

If your area gets heavy rain or is prone to flooding or runoff water, your garden bed should be oriented along the slope of the land to avoid soil erosion.

In hot and dry areas, orient the bed so that taller crops create shade when the sun passes over them.

3. Work in sections.

Whatever the size you have to work with when designing a permaculture garden, you should break up the space into a few sections that are roughly the same size.

For example, you can create a section with year-round greens and companion plants, another with kitchen staples and companion herbs, and a third section with primary fruits and their complementary crops. I suggest having an area for rotation as well if or when it's needed.

GARDEN BEDS

The three most common garden beds you can use in most spaces (briefly mentioned before) can significantly benefit you depending on your particular set of circumstances of your climate as well as the area and resources available to you.

Let's expand on these garden bed options' benefits, drawbacks, and specific uses.

In-Ground Garden Bed

This setup is the go-to option for the no-till method. Not only is it relatively easy to restore barren, lifeless soil to its former glory, but it's cost-efficient. The only thing you need to do is prepare the soil, as explained in step three.

If you have a proper soil structure and live in a hot and dry climate, in-ground garden beds are the best option—as opposed to raised garden beds.

When your water management, harvesting, and storing system are adequate, the soil can hold on to a lot of water, which is helpful in a dry climate. There's less cost and labor involved with an in-ground garden bed, and you can use machines or more significant equipment if needed.

However, suppose the soil you want to grow a garden in could be more suitable due to heavy foot traffic. In that case, it can be hard or even impossible to reverse, hurting the plants, discouraging the underground food web microbiome from developing, and nursing the soil back to health.

If your climate is wet, the soil has a higher chance of eroding, becoming waterlogged, or flooding from heavy rainfall, which can have devastating effects on a permaculture garden.

The soil will also take longer to thaw after cold or frozen winters, which means you have to wait longer before being able to plant annuals, and perennials will also take longer to produce.

Raised Garden Bed

A raised garden bed is an excellent option if you're renting a house or apartment but still want to grow a permaculture garden. You can also get to planting much quicker by choosing or buying healthy, organic soil.

Soil compaction is a non-issue with raised garden beds since no one walks over them. It also offers better drainage so your plants will never flood or sit in waterlogged soil, which can cause mold and root rot along with many other plant diseases.

If you have back problems or other accessibility issues, you can customize the height of your garden bed, which means less bending and squatting. And the natural insulation and heat retention of a raised garden bed means the soil thaws quicker, and you can plant earlier after winter.

However, raised garden beds have a few disadvantages, such as the initial construction. You're also limited to using your hands and other small garden tools for maintenance, though this isn't usually a problem with smaller gardens. Also, the material of the garden bed might degrade over time, especially when using wood, which might need repairing or replacing after a few years.

Hügelkultur

The name hügelkultur is German and translates to "hill culture" in English. It refers to creating a garden bed by filling up a trench, raised garden bed, planter, or piling organic material straight onto soil and covering it with compost to plant on top of it.

A hügelkultur (pronounced huggle-culture) has many benefits, the biggest one being that it encourages biodiversity in the soil. In addition, it provides a long-lasting (up to 20 years) source of nutrients and water storage for the plants to tap into even if your existing soil isn't quite up to par or contains too much clay or sand.

Hügelkulturs are both budget and eco-friendly and provide the soil with more than enough aeration—no tilling necessary!

The decomposing material inside the hügelkultur also defrosts quicker and provides natural insulation.

The downside to constructing a hügelkultur is that you will need to acquire a fair amount of natural materials depending on how big you want the bed to be, not to mention you'll have to assemble everything yourself, which can be labor-intensive. In addition, the mounded garden bed may also settle and will likely need to be topped up with additional soil and compost every year or so.

You also have to ensure that the organic material used for your hügelkultur is pest and disease free since any of these will transfer to your garden. There's also a chance that a hügelkultur can experience something called nitrogen lock, which is when small wood chips, branches, and other natural debris prevent the plants from accessing the nitrogen in the soil. However, this typically goes away after a few years and can be avoided using large pieces of organic material such as tree stumps.

HEDGEROWS

Previously, we've discussed the importance of the "edge effect" in forests and nature. The edge is where two different landscapes or habitats meet and serve animals, insects, and critters from both habitats, making it an incredibly diverse ecosystem.

A hedgerow can accomplish a small-scale edge effect in a small permaculture garden. In addition, a hedgerow can benefit your garden by providing privacy, water storage and conservation, and a buffer for noise, wind, pollution, harsh sun, and more.

Depending on your garden's needs, the plants in the hedgerows can also vary. They tend to be perennials, can take a while to become established, and will need frequent maintenance and attention. Still, annuals can serve as a temporary hedgerow until the permanent one is mature.

Designing a Hedgerow

Hedgerows aren't only on the outer edges of your garden. They can consist of various perennial herbs, flowers, and other low-lying vegetation that extends well into the rest of the area and different layers (assuming they'll get the necessary amount of sun they need).

Typically, a hedgerow is about 10 feet wide, but a smaller one will do if you have several rows of different plants that attract and support insects and critters of many kinds.

With this in mind, depending on the amount of space you have, your entire garden might be a hedgerow since a hedgerow's main idea is to provide shelter for beneficial animals that further the health of your garden (which most smaller permaculture gardens do anyway).

Preparations for a hedgerow are the same as for the rest of the garden; aerating the soil, layering different mulch, and then either waiting a few seasons for it to decompose or immediately topping the mulch with healthy soil and compost and waiting two weeks before planting.

A hedgerow should be compact and cover all the soil via taller shrubs or herb plants as well as understory or ground-cover plants.

The definition of a hedgerow is a polyculture of plants that run along the outer edge of a garden. However, it can be present in all seven layers of permaculture. It is multifunctional and can serve many purposes.

Suffice it to say; hedgerows are very important in a larger permaculture setting such as a food forest. Still, for smaller gardens, a hedgerow can be as simple as setting up a fence or trellis with vining plants growing up the side of it to serve as a windbreak or a contour garden to manage runoff rainwater.

ESPALIERS

In ancient Rome, gardeners "trained" trees to grow a certain way, typically against a flat surface such as a wall, fence, or trellis in small spaces where the tree would otherwise be too big.

Growing fruit trees against a south-facing wall absorbed heat during the day and used it as thermal insulation—similar to a greenhouse—extending harvest periods beyond their season.

Other benefits of this technique include saving space and creating living fences that are functional but also yield produce.

You can train virtually any plant this way by encouraging growth along a two-dimensional surface, and you do this by pruning away any development that you can't correct.

You can make your espalier by either planting the plant in question right up against a wall or making a trellis to support it. If doing it with a wall, the wall should receive full sun daily.

TRELLIS

Climbing plants such as grapes, pumpkins, beans, and tomatoes will need support to grow to their full potential.

A simple trellis structure can utilize star pickets, plastic-coated or galvanized wire, bolts, nuts, and washers. Regarding tools, you'll need a turnbuckle or some other way of tensioning the wire, a hammer, drill, and pliers (the ones that can also cut wires).

You're aiming for a ladder-like structure with the star pickets hammered into the ground (forming a frame) deep enough so they don't move and the wire spanning a few inches apart. It doesn't have to be perfect, but it does have to be stable, so make that your main goal.

If you don't have the tools or skills to pull this off, buying a trellis might be a quicker, easier, and fail-safe way to go about it.

With your garden fully designed, the time has come to put all the theoretical knowledge you have gained into practice.

9

STEP 6—PLANTING AND PROPAGATION

 The glory of gardening: hands in the dirt, head in the sun, heart with nature. To nurture a garden is to feed not just the body but the soul.

— ALFRED AUSTIN

Whether you've been taking action at every step or aren't planning on doing anything until you've finished the book, you'll probably be revisiting some—if not all—of the nine steps before you propagate or plant your first seed.

I can't stress enough how vital the preparations are before you can continue with this next step. Double-check your initial site surveys, plans for water management (including harvesting and storing water in the soil), soil preparation, your plants, and the design of your guilds and permaculture in general (make sure you're planting vegetation that's right for your climate).

PLANT SOURCING

Depending on your budget, you have several options for sourcing the plants you intend to grow in your permaculture. You can buy them from an established nursery or wander the wild and source them yourself.

Considering permaculture principles, you should grow them by yourself, regardless of your budget. This process is a great learning opportunity and an essential skill for a beginner permaculture gardener to acquire.

Suppose the task of propagating and planting everything in your garden sounds too intimidating. In that case, you can buy the young (already grafted and established) trees for your garden and produce everything else.

Doing everything at once is an option, but you don't have to. For example, you can plant your garden in sections if you have a thought-out layout and design.

PROPAGATION 101

Plant propagation is when you grow new plants from existing plants via their seeds, roots, stems, or leaves. Propagating plants is relatively easy to do and inexpensive.

Buying established trees from a nursery can cost upwards of $20 a pop. However, this method is satisfactory if you only grow a small garden with one or two smaller trees.

On the other hand, why spend money if you can do it for free?

As much as I want to, I can't go over the propagation and planting methods of every single plant in the world. So depending on the specific plants you want to grow, you'll have to do further independent research on the proper way to propagate them.

Propagation Methods

Propagation includes two categories: sexual and asexual. Both these propagation methods have their benefits and drawbacks; however, you must decide which will work best for you.

Sexual

Sexual propagation is when you grow a plant from a seed. It's how nature has been doing it for millions of years and is the most straightforward way to grow plants. First, however, you'll have to look into the proper conditions for every seed to germinate successfully and create the right environment. Since every plant species has different moisture, oxygen, temperature, and even light requirements, it makes sense that their seeds will too.

With sexual propagation, there's a lot of uncertainty about the fruit's quality and potential genetic mutations that might be present. You could also damage the unviable or dormant seed, which could be difficult or impossible to propagate.

Asexual

Asexual propagation is when grafts or cuttings are taken from a "mother" plant and make a replica of the original plant. Meaning you can be sure that the new plant you're growing will yield fruit that is the same quality as the mother plant.

For this reason, most experienced gardeners prefer to clone a plant asexually to avoid the uncertainty of sexual propagation.

Remember that some plants like herbs and leafy vegetables (spinach, lettuce, and such) would need to propagate asexually, though it's way less complicated than grafting one plant onto another.

PROPAGATING PLANTS

You can grow anything from the seeds in the mother plant's fruit. However, if a tree or plant is not self-pollinating, there's a high chance that the seeds might not be replicas. This uncertainty is because a plant that requires cross-pollination will fuse with whatever pollen attaches to it.

Imagine an apple tree, but a plant of a different species pollinated the flowers. The result is an apple containing seeds with half apple tree genes while the other half is from, well, *not* an apple tree. If you were to plant this seed, you would end up with a completely different species of tree that will likely never bear apples or fruit of any kind.

Therefore, if the plant is self-pollinating (and there are no other pollinators near it), your chances of having seeds that genetically match the mother plant are way better.

You can grow trees or other plants through either the natural way (outside) or assisted germination (where the seeds are planted in a controlled environment until they're ready to be transplanted outside).

First, always assume that any seed you want to plant is dormant. Dormant seeds need a period of warm or cold stratification before germinating. Then, depending on which season they produce fruit, research which sources require which stratification method. This variation is because, in nature, the seeds will first go through either a winter or summer before germination can happen.

Natural Propagation

With natural propagation, you can plant the seeds in the spring or fall when they undergo winter or summer before they germinate. However, you may lose many to rodents or other environmental factors this way, so you should make sure you're planting more seeds than you need.

You can do this by filling a large container with potting soil and mixing the seeds so they're fully covered. Then, place the bucket outside in direct sunlight and leave it there throughout winter or summer. Don't worry about the heat or freezing temperatures; that's what some seeds need before they can germinate.

Covering the container with chicken wire can prevent birds and other animals from digging up the seeds and eating them. Other than that, ensure to water the bucket when needed and check back in spring for the seedlings, which you can transplant into small pots or propagation trays. You can transplant them into your garden bed when they're big enough with a sound root system.

Assisted Propagation

Alternatively, propagating the seeds indoors will give you better control over the conditions resulting in more successful germinations. However, some might require scarification, including removing or damaging the hard outer coat so water can penetrate it.

Most seeds will need manual cold or warm stratification with assisted germination. This process includes soaking them in water for up to 48 hours, folding them into a moist paper towel, and placing them in a bag in the freezer for cold stratification.

On the flip side, some seeds remain dormant throughout summer and require warm stratification. The exact process applies as with cold stratification, just with heat. You soak the seeds, fold them into a moist paper towel, and store them in a greenhouse or area above room temperature.

Once germination has started, transplant the seedlings into a propagation tray immediately. Ensure the seedlings are planted at the proper depth (or more than twice the seed's width), as most of them can't grow through deep or dense soil and need light and air.

The process of hot or cold stratification can take anywhere from 4-20 weeks, with an average of 12 weeks.

It would be best if you transplanted the seedlings into a potting mix of three parts peat, one part fine bark, one part perlite, and a small amount of slow-release fertilizer (or compost). Keep the potting mixture moist but not wet until the seedlings are ready to be moved into their final spot in the garden. Seedlings will be sturdy enough to be transplanted into bigger pots after a month and into the garden after three months.

Propagating Softwood Cuttings

Besides seeds, you can also propagate most of the herbaceous plants in your garden through cuttings, from new growth in late spring to early summer.

When taking cuttings for softwood propagation, you should always take them from a matured, healthy mother plant with no dying leaves, pests, or visible diseases. Other than that, you should keep the cutting moist and start the process as soon as possible.

To take the cuttings, make a clean cut at a 45° angle to maximize the rooting surface. The cutting should be between three and six inches in size and should have the tip of the stem and at least two sets of leaves and a few nubs intact—the nubs are where new flowers or growth starts but will be where the roots will sprout from when propagating. Make sure to take at least a few cuttings of the same plant since not all of them will propagate successfully.

Prepare the rooting containers (at least four inches deep) with a soilless potting mix; however, some cuttings will need to be placed directly in water to root. Next, make a tunnel into the propagating medium and put the cutting into it, so the nubs are covered and kept moist.

Some plants are more accessible to propagate than others, and there are a variety of ways in which you can propagate softwood cuttings, but the most common is either in water or with a soilless potting mix.

The newly planted cuttings need to be in a warm area with indirect sunlight. To increase humidity, cover the plant with a clear, plastic bag, but don't seal the bag around the container since this will smother it, and make sure the bag isn't touching the cutting or any of the leaves.

Roots generally take around four to eight weeks to develop, but it may take longer for specific plants. To know whether or not new roots have grown, gently pull on the cutting; if you feel some resistance, your propagation was successful!

Another thing to look for is new growth. Once the roots have sprouted and you can see further development on the cutting visible above the propagating medium, you can transplant it into a bigger pot or directly into your garden.

For water propagation, remove the cutting once the roots are about an inch long, transplant them into a small pot with potting soil, and then mist them with water.

Remember to prune away new growth at the top of the plant for a few months to encourage and establish new development at the base and roots first.

PROPAGATING TREES

Before you decide that cloning—or propagating—trees from cuttings are too advanced for your skill sets, let's look at how you can propagate trees from cuttings and why it's way less complicated than it sounds.

Propagating trees is mainly done by hardwood cuttings since many large trees have difficulty growing roots. Softwood cuttings are reserved for bushes and plants and taken during the growing season when the tree or plant is growing. Keeping these cuttings in humid, moist soil conditions would be best until they form roots to avoid drying out or rotting.

Hardwood cuttings are taken in winter when the tree or plant is dormant and all the leaves have fallen off; therefore, the cutting will be less likely to dry out until the roots have sprouted.

Propagating Hardwood Cuttings

You can propagate many fruit and nut trees, grape vines, kiwi, and currant fruits such as blackcurrant, redcurrant, and even gooseberries from their cuttings.

You can propagate any plant with stems in this way. The propagation medium should be compatible with the requirements of the cutting for propagation to be successful. For example, some cuttings can sprout roots in water; others will rot. Some cuttings do better with a soilless potting mix, and so on.

Here's how to take and graft hardwood cuttings:

1. Select suitable plants.

We've established that propagating cuttings is typically used with fruit and nut trees but can also be done on flowering and vegetable plants such as roses, tomatoes, and grapes.

Hardwood cuttings are from trees and plants that lose their leaves in the winter and become dormant. But before you start cutting down branches, you must establish that the two plants you want to merge are compatible. A quick google search will tell you.

Once you know which plants you want to graft together, the best time to collect the cuttings is from early autumn to late winter when all the leaves have fallen. Take pencil-width cuttings from the current season's growth that are mature and woody, and cut off any soft, green growth that might be present on the tip of the branch.

2. Making the cut.

Cut where the small branch has grown from a large branch. The smaller is the current season's growth, whereas the big branch is the previous season's growth.

The branch will have many buds where future branches will form. Cut through horizontally about a quarter inch below the bud closest to the base where the small branch joins the big.

Measure 6-10 inches from the cut toward the tip and find the nearest bud to that measurement. Now, a quarter inch away from this bud, cut at a diagonal that slants away from the bud.

3. Wounding the cutting.

Some species of trees are more challenging to root than others, "wounding" the cutting can encourage it to form roots. You can do this by scraping the layer of bark off at the base of the cutting with a knife—just enough to expose the green cambium that's right underneath the brown bark layer.

Cuttings from trees that don't form roots might need dipping in a rooting hormone powder. This step is only sometimes necessary, but it does give you a higher chance of successfully propagating the branch.

4. Propagation medium.

The medium that is best to use will depend on the type of plant.

If a cutting needs to be in the soil, you can use the slitting method to plant it until it has formed roots. The slit method is when you make a slit by jabbing a spade into the ground and moving it back and forth to create an opening for the branch. If the soil doesn't have good drainage, add sand to the slit.

Alternatively, you can fill a container with a propagating medium, such as a mix of peat and perlite or peat and sand (equal parts of each).

The cutting needs planting two-thirds of the way into the soil so that only a third sticks out above the ground.

Planting and establishing your permaculture might happen over months or even years, but with time, you'll see your garden transform into a living entity with its ecosystem.

10

STEP 7—CREATING A BIODIVERSE ECOSYSTEM

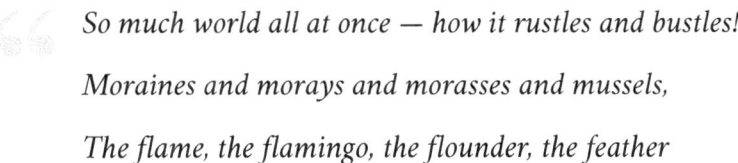

So much world all at once — how it rustles and bustles!

Moraines and morays and morasses and mussels,

The flame, the flamingo, the flounder, the feather

— WISŁAWA SZYMBORSKA, *BIRTHDAY*

Permaculture is deeply rooted in applied ecology, conservation biology, wetland management, natural resource management, soil formation and protection, climate regulation, infrastructure, community health, and economics, based on fundamental and applied science.

But permaculture is not just about furthering food security and longevity for humans but for the environment and ecosystems, including all life forms. The systems permaculture puts in place are dynamic, functional, and productive.

Without biodiversity, we'd have massive mono-cultured, industrialized land that's misused and stripped of resources and nutrients until there's nothing left and no way for any ecosystem—or the planet—to benefit from or benefit us.

AN ECOLOGICAL HEAVEN

An abundance of biodiversity has never been the issue; the fact that humans decided it was, is. Wildlife being present tells us that a planet is healthy, habitable, and providing. Why else would we get so excited when they discovered single-celled organisms on Mars?

Some pests can carry and introduce diseases into the environment, so we invented chemicals to eradicate them, effectively introducing dangerous and harmful chemicals into the diets of everyone on earth. But there's an easier and safer way of dealing with these pests, and it all starts with creating an ecological heaven.

Another mistake we, as humans, have made is to divide forestry and agriculture and promote monoculture crops that could be more appealing to wildlife or the underground food web. We shouldn't have the power—or motivation—to eradicate an entire species of living creatures from existence just because they're an inconvenience to us.

In permaculture, you work with the plants and the animals, not against them. And biodiversity is necessary for a rich ecosystem, including various cultures, crops, and wildlife in your garden. An abundance could be harmful only if it's an abundance of a single species (too many snails, not enough ducks, remember?). You need to consider all aspects of nature to keep the balance between prey and predator, with the help of companions—and diverse—guilds.

COMMON COMPANION PLANT COMBINATIONS

Like some plants do extraordinarily well together, there are combinations of plants that can damage each other. But there's no need to reinvent the wheel. Instead, by drawing from the experience of other established and knowledgeable permaculture farmers of the past, we can gain access to their shared findings and be sure that what we're growing together will work.

Therefore, I present a list of typical vegetation you'd likely want in your garden, along with the best and worst companion plants for them. Think of it as planning the seating chart for a wedding; you want to seat the guests who get along together, away from the guests that don't get along. This approach will make designing your permaculture garden easier.

- Asparagus.

Asparagus need full sun (at least eight hours a day), so it should be planted near the edge of the garden or away from shaded areas, tree canopies, or anything that might prevent them from receiving full sun for most of the day.

Asparagus pairs well with marigolds and herbs like basil and parsley but is a good match for tomatoes since the asparagus repels nematodes while tomatoes repel asparagus beetles. Marigolds, herbs, and tomatoes also require full sun, making them the perfect "edge" for your permaculture garden.

On the flip side, you shouldn't grow asparagus with garlic or fennel since they deplete sulfur from the soil rapidly.

- Basil.

Basil matches well with tomatoes and lettuce and improves the taste of these companion plants. Basil also deters mosquitoes, which are more to the benefit of people than plants.

Basil is like that aunt everybody loves and is safe to put next to virtually any crop (though they prefer the company of vegetables over other herbs) except for rue and sage because they will inhibit the growth of basil.

- Beans.

Beans need full sun and grow well with cabbage, beets, carrots, cauliflower, potatoes, strawberries, and marigolds. Marigolds and potatoes, in particular, repel beetles that tend to infest beans, making them great companions.

It would be best if you did not plant beans near onions, shallot, garlic, or anything in the same family as onions. Onions and related vegetation produce too much nitrogen.

- Beets.

Beets need at least six hours of sunlight per day and are excellent companion plants for garlic, onion, broccoli, cauliflower, cabbage, and brussels sprouts. The beets mine minerals and nutrients underground, which are deposited into the topsoil when the beet leaves. Other plants use this as a green mulch. In return, garlic and onions serve as a pest repellant for the beets.

However, beets don't get along with beans, field mustard, or charlock, so keep that in mind.

- Borage.

Borage isn't typical in any ordinary garden, but it can benefit the area by planting near squash, tomatoes, eggplants, and strawberries. Borage repels tomato worms and other damaging pests and serves as rich green mulch feeding the topsoil.

- Broccoli and cauliflower.

Broccoli and cauliflower are cold-weather, or winter crops and typically do well with other winter crops, along with marigolds that repel moths that like to feed on broccoli, cauliflower, and other cabbage-like vegetables.

In addition, broccoli and cauliflower particularly benefit from aromatic, pest-repelling herbs such as chamomile, dill, mint, sage, rosemary, thyme, and calendula, which produces a sticky compound on the stalks that attracts and traps aphids. Dwarf zinnias are also suitable for attracting ladybugs that eat pests associated with broccoli and cauliflower, which makes them great for planting in between broccoli and cauliflowers.

However, broccoli and cauliflower should situate somewhere other than near strawberries since they all attract similar pests.

- Cabbage.

As mentioned above, marigolds, sage, dill, and thyme are great companions for cabbage since they repel moths. Furthermore, tomatoes keep diamondback moth larvae at bay, whereas dill attracts predatory wasps that enjoy feeding on cabbage worms.

Growing clovers around cabbage will replenish nitrogen that the cabbage would otherwise deplete.

It would be best if you didn't plant cabbage near strawberries because they attract similar pests.

- Cantaloupe.

Cantaloupe needs full sun (eight to ten hours per day) and a trellis or other climbing support.

Dill, fennel, and parsley attract pollinators for cantaloupe and are, therefore, great companions that will result in a larger yield. Marigolds are also a great choice since they will ward off nematodes that feed on the cantaloupes.

Cantaloupe leaves are an excellent mulching material as well. Though, you should avoid planting cucumbers, watermelons, or squash in the same area since they also attract the same kinds of pests as cantaloupes.

- Carrots.

Plant carrots near their fellow cold-seasoned vegetables, with the addition of sage, rosemary, and chives which all keep carrot flies at bay.

However, it would help if you didn't plant carrots near dill or celery.

- Chives.

Chives make an excellent ground cover crop that you can plant all along the garden bed. In addition, they greatly benefit fruit trees, bushes, and other vegetables by improving their flavor and deterring pests.

The only plants that aren't particularly fond of chives are beans and peas.

- Cucumbers.

Another vining plant that thrives in full sun-cucumbers both provide and receive benefits from cabbage, beans, sunflowers, and radishes. Marigolds offer excellent habitats for spiders that keep the beetle population under control.

However, sage and potatoes can cause early blight (a fungal infection that can destroy the plant) in cucumbers, so make sure to separate them as much as possible.

- Dill.

Dill can enhance the flavor of any fruit or vegetable near it and does exceptionally well with cabbage, broccoli, and cauliflower.

Dill is known to stunt the growth of carrots, so you should avoid planting them together.

- Echinacea.

This flower does best in cool climates and enjoys partial shade. Many over-the-counter medicines use it, but it attracts predatory insects in the garden that help with overall pest control and cross-pollination.

- Eggplant.

Eggplant can grow in virtually any climate, although it, unfortunately, can't withstand frost. It attracts the same insects and pollinators as tomatoes, potatoes, and peppers. Eggplant repels certain beetles that feed on many garden crops and are safe to plant near most other fruits and vegetable plants.

Though, you should avoid planting eggplants near fennel which is known to stunt the growth of most other plants.

- Fennel.

Speak of the devil, and you step on his tail! Fennel is a tricky plant to have in your guild since it inhibits the growth of most other garden crops. The only exception is dill and kohlrabi.

If you want to grow fennel in your garden, you should only cultivate a couple of fennel and dill (or kohlrabi) plants. Situate them away from the main guild since fennel will cross-breed with celery, carrot, and parsley (along with any other plant that shares their genera) and stunt the growth of nearby plants.

- Garlic.

Garlic is an excellent plant companion and can be safely grown with most crops (except for peas and beans); that's also extremely easy to grow. In addition, garlic deters onion flies, aphids, moths, and some beetles in addition to rose pests.

While garlic works well with most crops, it's worth mentioning that they prefer fruits, roses, tomatoes, and cabbage over other crops.

- Kale and kohlrabi.

Both these plants belong to the cabbage family and can be coupled with garlic, onions, dill, sage, thyme, and rosemary. They particularly enjoy minty herbs (all except basil).

Kale and kohlrabi can, however, inhibit the growth of a select few crops, namely tomatoes, beans, and strawberries, so you should avoid planting them close to each other.

- Lettuce.

Lettuce can be grown alongside carrots which both serve as weed suppressants. When you add mint to the mix, you repel slugs that can damage both crops.

Lettuce also tenderizes and improves the quality of radishes but can also be planted with beets, parsnips, and strawberries.

It would be best to avoid planting lettuce with crops from the cabbage family (cabbage itself, broccoli, cauliflower, brussels sprouts, kale, or kohlrabi) since the root secretions of cabbage plants will prevent the lettuce from germinating or growing well. It also doesn't like onions or garlic.

- Marigold.

If you haven't picked up on it by how many times it has appeared in this list, marigold benefits every crop in your garden besides cabbage and beans.

It encourages growth in many plants, deters various pests, and attracts pollinators and predatory insects that further keep pests away and help pollinate crops for a larger yield.

- Mint.

Mint is arguably the best pest control plant and is considered one of the easiest herbs to grow. In addition to repelling most pests and attracting beneficial insecs, it also attracts earthworms which we know are great for the underground food web and natural fertilization.

The only downside of mint is that it can take over and spread throughout your entire garden in the blink of an eye; however, it can be "chopped and dropped" to serve as a readily available mulching material if it starts to grow out of control.

The only reason mint can be a bad companion is when it becomes invasive; it can steal nutrients from other plants and smother them. If you want to avoid this, consider keeping mint around the garden in pots instead of directly in the ground.

- Mustard.

Mustard is a tasty addition to the kitchen while encouraging the growth of other plants around the garden. Mustard especially does well with cover crop plants, fruit trees, legumes, and alfalfa.

The only plants that shouldn't be near mustards are sunflowers, soybeans, and dried bean varieties since they all attract the same pests.

- Onions.

Another kitchen staple that is easy to grow, onions are great companion plants for other root vegetables such as beets and carrots, as well as other crops like tomato, cabbage, and eggplant.

When planted alongside chamomile, the flavor and quality of onions improve. Onions also deter pests.

Beans, peas, and asparagus are the only garden crops incompatible with onions.

- Oregano and parsley.

These two herbs can be grown with other garden crops and deter maggots and flies.

- Peppers.

Peppers grow well with tomatoes, eggplants, basil, parsley, and carrots but should be separate from fennel and kohlrabi.

While it's not particularly hard to grow peppers, they are climate sensitive and cannot survive frost or extreme cold.

- Potatoes.

As long as potatoes get ample sun, they can grow almost anywhere in any climate. They're also a staple in many diets, making them a good choice for any permaculture garden.

Potatoes benefit from being planted near marigolds and basil, which help keep nematodes and potato beetles at bay, respectively. Also, horseradish can improve potatoes' resistance to disease.

Other than that, planting potatoes near cabbage vegetables, corn, peas, beans, and sweet alyssum attracts predatory insects that feed on potato pests.

Keep potatoes away from tomatoes, sunflowers, raspberries, pumpkins, cucumber, apples, cherries, and birch since they will either compete for soil space and nutrients or attract the same type of pests.

- Rosemary and sage.

Rosemary and sage are compatible with beans, cabbage, and other cabbage-family vegetables, tomatoes, and carrots. These aromatic herbs also serve as pest control for bean beetles and other common pests.

It would help if you did not plant cucumbers near rosemary and sage.

- Spinach.

Spinach thrives when planted with cauliflower, eggplant, celery, and strawberries. Peas and other legumes also benefit from spinach.

It would be best if you didn't plant spinach with potatoes since their respective root systems will smother each other. The potato leaves might also shade out the spinach.

- Strawberries.

These juicy, irresistible berry-like fruits are considered the easiest plants to grow and establish in virtually any sunny climate. They do exceptionally well when planted near beans, lettuce, spinach, and borage.

Since they attract similar pests, keep strawberries away from vegetables in the cabbage family (including broccoli, cauliflower, brussels sprouts, etc.).

- Sunflowers.

They're a great option to bring color, partial shade, or windbreak to any crops in your garden that might need it, but they're also great for drawing in pollinators.

They work well with cucumbers and squash but planting them with something other than potatoes is recommended.

- Thyme.

Thyme will not harm any of your other crops and will enrich the soil and deter cabbage moths. This herb is a tolerant and beneficial plant to add to your permaculture garden.

- Tomatoes.

Tomatoes get along with almost every crop except for black walnut trees, corn, potatoes, eggplant, and kohlrabi. Something important to note is that you should rotate tomatoes yearly since larvae and other harmful microbes that may have infiltrated the soil can stick around for a long time—rotating the crops prevents this from happening.

For the best results, plant tomatoes with various other crops and herbs to deter pests and contribute to the flavor of the tomatoes (basil, sage, and rosemary are great options for this).

- Yarrow.

Yarrow is an effective pest management system that breaks down easily, making it an excellent mulching material for your entire garden. Though, be warned that if not appropriately managed; yarrow can invade your garden and smother other crops.

It might feel overwhelming when you have to consider all the different types of plants and figure out how to arrange them so that they will benefit and not kill or damage each other, as well as attract the proper ratio of biodiversity.

Attracting Wildlife

Animals are simple creatures; all they need to survive is food, water, and shelter. Cover all these bases; they'll inevitably find it and make a home in your garden.

The types of creatures that will inhabit your garden will hugely depend on its size and setup and your area. For example, if you only have a small garden bed or live in the city, realistically, you won't see larger wildlife in your garden. Also, if there aren't any squirrels or rabbits roaming your neighborhood, it wouldn't make sense to try and attract these types of animals.

However, smaller insects and birds are everywhere, and you can still create a biodiverse habitat that will benefit your garden substantially.

Identify

First, research the type of animals that could visit your garden so you know what to expect and how to attract them.

Larger wildlife, most common in urban and suburban areas, are raccoons, foxes, squirrels, skunks, possums, rabbits, bats, birds and birds of prey, rats, mice, and even coyotes.

Smaller wildlife most common in urban and suburban areas are insects and bugs such as butterflies, moths, spiders, lizards, beetles, weevils, ladybugs, bees, wasps, grasshoppers, crickets, worms, gnats, ants, termites, flies, mosquitoes, and aphids.

Most bugs mentioned above are known to be pests, and while they can damage plants when their population growth is exponential, these pests serve as food for larger animals and other beneficial insects. You can control the population of nearly any pest that threatens your garden by researching their natural predators and adjusting to attract them.

Additionally, you want to keep a journal of all the animals making a home in your garden once it's maturing. Remember to update the list every season since different seasons attract bugs and potential pests. Take photos if you need to figure out the type of bug or pest in your garden so you can research them (this is also where those *iNaturalist* or *PictureThis* apps can come in handy).

Food

Once you have a good grasp of the type of animals that will likely visit your garden, you want to ensure a steady supply of food for them so they don't look for greener pastures—or in this context, greener gardens.

Flowers and herbaceous plants are an excellent food supply that attracts beneficial insects like butterflies and bees. However, most other beneficial insects, such as spiders, beetles, ladybugs, and praying mantis enjoy munching on pests—or the eggs and larvae of pests—like aphids, scale insects, flies, mosquitoes, and mites.

In essence, your garden will inadvertently attract damaging pests; there's no getting around it since your garden in and of itself provides food and shelter for them. However, they provide a food supply for beneficial, predatory insects and animals, so all you might have to do is make sure the environment is fit for them to take up residency.

Water

Even though there might be a body of water, such as a pond, lake, or river, not far from your permaculture site or garden, supplying fresh water in the actual garden will further encourage beneficial insects and animals to return or even stay.

You can do this by leaving a few bowls of water out around the garden or building a birdbath or pond that's easily accessible for birds and other small animals such as rabbits and squirrels.

However, birdbaths are too deep for insects and bugs and might pose a drawing risk. To make an 'insect fountain,' fill a bowl with sand or small rocks and pour in the water to create a puddling dish with lots of islands for the bugs to crawl onto if they accidentally fall into the water.

Shelter

Animals and critters need shelter to hide from predators and foster their offspring. In addition, they need to feel safe if you want them to return often or take up permanent residency in your garden.

You must include as many hiding spots around your permaculture as you can. The shelter can be in the form of birdhouses in trees, large rocks stacked so there's an entrance with a "cave" underneath it, or a pile of logs would also do the job. Insects appreciate loads of foliage and bushes as well.

It doesn't have to break the bank; you can create shelter out of almost anything if you think creatively and use whatever materials you have available.

Plants That Attract Wildlife

It's essential to have as much of a variety of plants in your garden as you can house. However, the selected plants should all work together to foster the bugs and insects that you would like to attract since, as we know, some plants can deter some bug species.

For small gardens, animals like birds and small mammals might only pass through occasionally, whereas insects will decide to stay in the garden if it meets all their needs. So while you want to attract larger animals, insects and other bugs can serve as the main focus of your ecosystem network.

Attracting pollinators into your garden is the best way to encourage diversity because if the habitat is suitable for them, chances are, it's right for other insects as well. Unfortunately, no specific guilds work to attract pollinators, so you might have to revert to using native plants that typically attract bees and butterflies.

Furthermore, insects and lizards will create their homes in the cracks of large trees with rough or shedding bark, whereas birds will occupy the canopy. Small bushes, shrubs, and vines are great for other insects.

Again, looking to your local environment to find inspiration to attract insects and small animals to your garden is best.

FARMING ANIMALS

We've previously discussed how farm animals like chickens and guinea pigs can contribute to your garden. Although having a couple of chickens or even goats isn't necessarily feasible or necessary for your permaculture garden (depending on the scale of it), it makes managing and maintaining one a whole lot easier.

For larger-scale permaculture and food forests, you can implement a variety of typical farm animals that can immensely reduce the manual labor that goes into managing them. For example:

- Bees might not be the easiest to farm, but they can significantly impact your garden—in a good way. Besides the honey and beeswax they produce, they can pollinate your entire garden for you, increasing and improving the quality of your yield.
- Chickens are excellent for clearing pieces of land of weeds while turning the soil and producing manure. They also feed on bugs, maggots, flies, and kitchen scraps and have an output of eggs.
- Rabbits can double as an efficient lawnmowers by placing them in a cage without a bottom on the lawn and moving it around regularly. Simultaneously their manure serves as fertilizer.
- Goats help trim shrubs, eradicate weeds, and produce delicious goat's milk for consumption and manure that works excellently as fertilizer.
- Ducks don't cause as much damage to your garden as chickens do, though they enjoy eating cabbage and snails that typically infests cabbage. They produce feathers and meat as an output.
- Cats don't have any output; however, they do a fantastic job controlling the various rodent populations.
- Dogs make excellent companions for humans on top of protecting by alerting us of intruders or suspicious behavior.

- Pigs will eat everything you put in front of them and turn it into fertilizer in the form of manure. They can also dig up stubborn weeds, prepare a space for planting, and provide meat as another output.

Do Not Disturb

Disrupting your garden's ecosystem often will be detrimental to the insects and animals since their instincts force them to run away as soon as you approach. If you are always in your garden for extended periods, the insects and animals will assume it's not a safe place to be.

Your garden shouldn't be close to an area that receives much foot traffic from humans or pets. So, a fenced or trellised area in the back garden away from the patio where you entertain guests regularly is preferred.

Eventually, visiting wildlife might get used to the occasional appearance of yourself and see that you don't pose a threat; however, you should still keep disturbances to a minimum.

BENEFICIAL WILDLIFE

A thriving garden will automatically attract wildlife of all kinds. This attraction is a good thing and means your garden is diverse and provides everything it needs to sustain life. As a result, the plants will benefit from the animals and insects and vice versa.

Insects

Any insect or animal can become a nuisance to your garden if the population grows out of control, so attracting a diverse range of wildlife is the best action. Common pests that can cause damage and destruction to your garden are mites, scales, thrips, earwigs, aphids, snails, and some beetles and caterpillars.

Beneficial insects prey on pests that can harm your garden, spread diseases amongst your plants, and help fertilize and pollinate your garden.

However, if you're unsure whether a particular insect classifies as "good" or "bad," here's a list of the most common beneficial insects to have in your garden and why you'd want to keep them around.

- Soldier beetles help pollinate your garden and are attracted to blossoming flowers such as marigolds and zinnias. Soldier beetles feed on aphids and caterpillars. as well as the larvae of moths and grasshoppers.
- Geocoris (also called big-eyed bugs) have an insatiable appetite for mites in addition to aphids and caterpillars. You can attract these beneficial bugs with marigolds, cosmos, fennel, and mint.
- Hoverflies are pollinators attracted to cosmos, zinnias, Queen Anne's lace, dill, lemon balm, mint, parsley, and yarrow. They enjoy feeding on aphids, mealy bugs, scale, and thrip and will often lay their eggs amongst aphids that supply the hoverfly larvae with food.
- Ladybugs may look sweet and innocent, but they are considered predators in the bug realm. Like hoverflies, they feed on the same pests and are attracted to the same plants, meaning that if you have hoverflies in your garden, you will likely have ladybugs.
- Rough stink bugs might cause you to grimace due to their potent stench; however, they are not pests like the invading brown marmorated stink bug. Instead, rough stink bugs are drawn to areas by trees (particularly fruit trees of all varieties) and are known as friends of the

garden because they enjoy feasting on aphids, beetles, and caterpillars.

- Lacewings are nocturnal and—despite their delicate appearance—they are vicious predators of aphids, mealy bugs, mites, thrips, and white flies. You can invite lacewings into your garden with sunflowers, cosmos, tansy, yarrow, dill, fennel, and ornamental onions.
- Dragonflies and damselflies are mainly attracted to bodies of water (including small to medium water features in your garden) and will gobble up flies, gnats, and mosquitoes.
- Braconid wasps pollinate to an extent, though they could be more efficient than honeybees. However, these wasps make a great addition to your garden since they feed mainly on beetles, hornworms, squash bugs, stink bugs, and caterpillars. They will lay their eggs on hornworms which serve as a living nursery and food supply for the wasp larvae. Braconid wasps are attracted to flowering plants, catnip, chamomile, dill, fennel, feverfew, sweet alyssum, and even carrots.
- Native bees help pollinate your garden and feed on the nectar of flowering plants. You can invite them into your garden with coneflowers, evening primrose, basil, dill, oregano, mint, rosemary, cucumbers, and peas.
- Butterflies are also pollinators and feed on sap and nectar from flowers. They are attracted to cone flowers, goldenrods, zinnias, milkweed, butterfly weed, fennel, and parsley.

Understanding that the food web (both under and above ground) is a circle is essential; this means that there will inevitably be an overlap at some point where beneficial insects may feed on or kill other beneficial insects. Therefore, as counterproductive as it may seem, the population control of beneficial insects is just as important and necessary as pests like aphids, mites, scales, etc.

Birds

Birds are great for entertainment, bird watching, comic relief, listening to their songs, and so on, but they can sometimes bring about the destruction of fruit and other produce in your garden. So, you might be curious as to why someone would want to invite them to the permaculture party.

And the answer is relatively simple. Permaculture principles encourage us to work with nature despite the problems that some animals might bring to the table. Now, you don't have to exclusively design your garden with the accommodation of birds in mind, but these winged creatures do offer some benefits in small numbers.

For starters, they are a part of—and therefore contribute—to the ecosystem. They help with pollination, pests, and rodent control to a certain degree and can help gently and naturally till the topsoil of your garden.

Something to keep in mind is that the only reason birds might destroy your entire berry harvest for the season is that when the garden isn't meeting their needs sufficiently, they will make do with what's available.

The needs of birds are the same as with any other living creature: food, water, and shelter. Supply all three of these, and you will prevent the birds from taking their frustrations out on your berry bushes.

Water and shelter are relatively easy to supply; keep the birdbath full and either make bird nests and hang them up or wait for them to build some in a large tree if you have one in your garden.

Now, if the only food source for the birds is a couple of berry bushes, your berries will be the primary target. However, supplying a variety of fruits for them to choose from makes the chances of them destroying an entire harvest of anything rare.

You can also provide sunflower seeds in a bird feeder to cover all grounds and extend their feed options.

You know all about the necessity of diversity; in the next step, we'll be going into more detail on integrated pest management without using harmful chemical insecticides that ruin the integrity of the soil.

11

STEP 8—PEST MANAGEMENT

 Agricultural science is largely a race between the emergence of new pests and the emergence of new techniques for their control.

— ALDO LEOPOLD, *THE LAND ETHIC, ESSAYS FROM A SAND COUNTY ALMANAC*

P est management is crucial to protect your garden and the produce it bears. Harmful chemical pesticides such as DDT absorb into the ground, where it not only destroys the underground food web but also get soaked up by the roots of any plants that inhabit the soil.

For effective chemical-free, permaculture-approved, integrated pest management, it is vital to approach it from an ecological point of view.

INTEGRATED PEST MANAGEMENT

Integrated pest management uses observation and creative thinking to control pests instead of chemicals that kill the entire ecosystem.

Chemical pesticides kill most—if not all—biodiversity in the local ecosystem and can even damage your crops. If you ever wanted a reason as to why we shouldn't ever use pesticides as a way to control pests, here are several:

- At best, chemicals offer a temporary fix, and the pests will return the very next season, if not earlier.
- Pesticides kill natural predators of pests, and since they often get resistant to chemical pesticides, the pest population continues to thrive while the population of natural predators dwindles.
- Besides contaminating the soil and the harvest, it contaminates the water that flows into rivers and dams, exposing aquatic ecosystems to dangerous chemicals.
- Chemical pesticides require continuous rotating to prevent resistance building and re-infestations, which can be expensive.

Integrated pest management (IPM) means considering the types of animals that might take up residence on your site or in your garden—even before planting—and putting measures in place to repel or reduce the number of unwanted or harmful ones in a natural, non-chemical way.

IPM Techniques

Integrated pest management is more than just planting aromatic herbs or attracting natural predators. There are four categories under IPM that permaculture farmers use: physical controls, biological controls, cultural controls, and chemical controls.

Physical Controls

This method of pest control is done manually or with mechanics. It involves controlling the population of pests by physically removing them or preventing them from accessing your garden.

Examples of physical control elements for pest management are:

- Closing up a hole in the wall, so cockroaches are less likely to infiltrate the kitchen.
- Setting up rodent traps in your garden or pantry.
- Building enclosed greenhouses so larger pests have a more challenging time getting to the crops.
- Removing larger pests by hand.
- Calcined kaolin is an organic spray made out of clay that forms a white film barrier on the leaves and stems of plants, protecting them from sunburn and particular pests.

Biological Controls

Biological control elements for pest management are mostly centered around controlling the population with natural predators such as ladybugs, wasps, beetles, and even bacteria that feed on pests.

Cultural Controls

This method of pest management involves purposely disrupting the environment and making it harder for the pests to establish, reproduce and survive in your permaculture.

Examples of cultural control elements for pest management are:

- Crop rotation.
- Changing irrigation of fertilization methods frequently.
- Choosing mostly pest-resistant plant varieties for your garden.
- Proper sanitation and hygiene of your garden (removing fallen fruit and debris that can house and feed pests).

Chemical Controls

Chemical controls are often the last resort for permaculture gardeners and farmers. Only when all other methods have been exhausted do they turn to certain chemical pesticides in conjunction with different ways to reduce pest infestations.

Using the least toxic pesticides in ways that are safest for the surrounding ecosystem and biodiversity. In addition, using only selective organic pesticides to target specific pests exclusively instead of everything in sight. These organic pesticides include:

- Horticulture oils
- Neem oil-based products
- Copper fungicides
- Sulfur fungicides
- Plant oil-based herbicides

Soil preparation also goes a long way with the ecosystem's ability to resist pests and survive even when attacked or infiltrated. In addition, the microbes present in healthy soil will contribute to population control.

IPM Components

Integrated pest management revolves around systemic, scientific, and ecological approaches to prevent, monitor, and control pest populations. It focuses on minimizing the damage that pests cause rather than eliminating them.

Let's discuss the three components of IPM in more detail.

Prevent

By changing and managing the ecosystem, you are implementing measures that prevent or limit pest infestations long-term.

This process will involve a proactive response as well as knowing and understanding the environmental factors that come into play regarding specific pests and their ability to survive and procreate. When you create an environment that is less favorable or safe, they are less likely to stay.

As discussed previously, preventive measures can involve planting companion guilds, attracting predatory insects, or non-living pest control techniques.

Monitor

To take the proper precautions when dealing with pests, you'll need to know as much about the pest as possible. This monitoring will require you to assess the scale of the damage or pest population and correctly identify the type of pest you're dealing with before determining the best way to correct the issue.

Don't react when spotting a pest, but monitor the situation to see if it will be a problem and whether any action is required. Always do further research to find out what the pest's ideal environment is, what crops they're attracted to, what type of plants repel them or what their natural predator is.

Control

Considering the pest, you're trying to control and its specific needs and lifecycle, you can combine several IPM techniques to increase the effectiveness rate and, therefore, the chances of your implementations being successful.

You should always rely on various control methods for pest management, evaluate the progress, and assess the feedback from your garden to determine if your processes are working.

WHOLE SYSTEM IPM

While pests are pesky and can pose a real risk to your garden, it's essential to recognize that they're simply doing what they've evolved to do. You can't blame them for trying to survive like everything else on earth.

Nature always finds a way to keep the balance, though this process isn't linear and often comes in waves of abundance. Using the example of having too many worms in your garden and attracting birds to thin out the population, let's look at how this will play out in real life:

The birds will flock to your garden and start to guzzle down worms left and right until the worms are at minimal capacity, after which the birds will eventually go to look for greener (more worm-infested) pastures. The worms will then reproduce until they are overpopulated again, at which point the birds will return (potentially with your help).

Whether you attribute this to the "circle of life" or just 'supply and demand,' it's how nature keeps the balance—by correcting when the scales tip either way. The idea is to create a balance where pests are still there, not overtaking them to a degree where they destroy everything in sight.

How do you create your entire design around IPM?

Diversity! Yes, that's all it takes. As long as you're not growing a monoculture, many different animals and creatures will visit your garden and do what they do best—keep the balance.

Make sure there's a selection of food, water, and shelter for as many beneficial animal and bug species that your garden can comfortably provide for and allow nature to do its thing.

After this step, your permaculture should be set up and ready to thrive independently. Now all that's left to explore is how you can help maintain a mostly self-sufficient garden.

12

STEP 9—MAINTENANCE AND ZERO-WASTE PRACTICES

We have no right, nor any ethical justification, for clearing land or using wilderness while we tread over lawns, create erosion, and use land inefficiently. Our responsibility is to put our house in order. Should we do so, there will never be any need to destroy wilderness.

— BILL MOLLISON, *PERMACULTURE: A DESIGNERS'*
MANUAL

As we know by now, permaculture isn't just about "lazy gardening." Instead, it has several principles that advocate for zero-waste practices because permaculture genuinely has the future and the planet's health in mind.

It's about forming a connection with nature, respecting the ecosystem and all creatures that inhabit it, and not polluting their homes. After all, they were here first.

THE CONNECTION

Gardening and permaculture will help you cut down on wastage, even if you don't go all out with the idea. For example, food and herbs from your garden aren't wrapped in plastic or drenched in chemicals and are readily available outside your back door or on your windowsill.

And while composting isn't a strict requirement for permaculture, it's easy, doesn't have to take up loads of space, and benefits the planet and your garden in many ways.

Zero-Waste Lifestyle

Transitioning to a zero-waste lifestyle can be challenging and requires a lot of adjustments, creativity, and patience.

You don't have to beat yourself up over any waste you produce, and you don't have to be zero-waste by tomorrow, either. It's a process, and every action you take considering the planet is a step in the right direction.

Living a zero-waste life may sound intimidating and even impossible in modern times, where everything is industrialized and packaged. However, it's not about how regularly you sort your recyclable materials but rather about reducing the overall waste you produce—recyclable or not.

It all starts at the grocery store. Before purchasing any item, consider how it may contribute to your garbage output. This methodology applies to food, clothing, electronics, toys, etc. More often than not, packaging materials are not recyclable or compostable.

Also, consider how much use you'll get from your purchase, and always donate or upcycle old appliances, clothing, and furniture rather than throw it away.

While sustainable or zero-waste living on a global scale might not come to fruition any time soon—if ever—don't lose hope in humanity just yet. Starting a garden or living with sustainability in mind can still benefit you and the environment on a small scale.

Some things you can do to transition to a more environmentally conscious and sustainable in your own home are:

1. Reduce, Reuse, Recycle.

I'm sure you've heard this term; it's hardly a secret. But it would be best to remember the simple things you can do to help the environment.

Reducing your waste is the most important and impactful thing you can do for the environment. Composting kitchen waste, buying second-hand furniture, donating unwanted items, avoiding single-use items or items wrapped in plastic, and buying non-perishables in bulk are all simple ways to reduce the amount of waste in your home.

Reusing something you would normally throw away is another great way to reduce overall waste and give it a new purpose. For example, there are many ways you can reuse plastic bags to make things like tote bags and rugs. Please don't throw away glass containers; instead, reuse them in your pantry for spices or other food items or turn them into decor by spray painting them or turning them into candle jars. Please don't get rid of old tires; use them as a planter box. It might take creative thinking to reuse items for a completely different purpose, but it's always worth it.

Recycling should be the last resort if you have waste that can't be reduced or reused. But recycling it's still better than having it end up in the ground at a landfill.

2. Purchase wisely.

What we buy can significantly impact the environment and our carbon footprint. It may take some initial investment on your part to purchase items that are sustainably sourced and made since these items are often more expensive, but they also last much longer.

Try to avoid purchasing products where the primary packaging material is plastic. However, it might be challenging since most manufacturers still use plastic or non-biodegradable packaging materials.

Avoid using chemical cleaners and opt for natural or homemade cleaners such as baking soda, vinegar, lemon juice, salt, and water (not all combined, of course). You might be surprised at how well they work.

3. Grow your food.

Of course, you won't be able to grow everything you need for every meal, but having a selection of fresh herbs and maybe a tomato plant is a good start.

Not only is gardening a fun, productive hobby that will make you feel more connected with nature, but it might even encourage you to adopt more sustainable ways of living.

4. Permaculture landscaping.

This ties in with the previous point as it encourages gaining knowledge of local greenery and how they contribute to the living space of humans as well as animals and insects.

An example is growing some strawberries in a patch of garden that was previously covered or not in use—replacing suburban flower beds with herbs that can be equally as visually pleasing and way more practical.

5. Water conservation.

Using fresh, drinkable water to water inedible plants and grass is not sustainable. Instead, there are many ways to conserve water, such as installing rain barrels and planting foliage that loves water in spots where water usually accumulates. This process will allow the rainwater to absorb into the ground better instead of entering the sewer system.

6. Organic fertilizers and pesticides.

Harsh chemicals in pesticides and even some fertilizers can harm the soil and the creepy crawlies in it and pollute the underground waterbed. However, organic fertilizers and pesticides can keep your lawn and garden looking great without the negative impact of chemicals on the ecosystem.

Permaculture

Zero-waste ties into the first prime derivative of permaculture; care for the earth. Reducing waste is as beneficial to us as it is to the environment and ecosystems.

MAINTAINING A PERMACULTURE

The dichotomy of having to do maintenance on a self-maintaining garden does not escape permaculturists; it's an oxymoron that requires a bit of explanation on our part.

While a permaculture garden builds on the idea of emulating or mimicking nature to get the most produce from a harvest, you'll need to offer some help since some environmental factors in an untouched forest can negatively impact a plant and how much fruit it bears. And while this isn't an issue when no one is harvesting the produce, when you're relying on your garden to provide sustenance, you have to do some—not much—maintenance.

Though, once your garden matures, the maintenance decreases even further.

Seasonal Maintenance

The initial maintenance you have to do for the first few seasons—or until your garden matures—can be surmised into the following:

Weeding

Young plants and guilds are susceptible to competition, so you should put measures in place to reduce the number of weeds or manually extract them until they're mature and bearing produce.

Weed your garden at least once a month. You can "chop and drop" annual weeds that will serve as mulch; however, perennial weeds, seed-carrying weeds, or root weeds should be removed from your garden or composted.

Mulching

We have gone into intricate detail on why mulching is necessary for your garden. This step is one of the few things you'll probably have to do every so often for quite a while or even indefinitely.

Even if you have big trees that naturally provide mulch for the understory, you'll have to continuously ensure the layer is thick enough to suppress any weeds and protect your soil.

Pruning

Pruning your plants while growing is crucial since it will help establish the roots and result in better yields and resistance to environmental factors such as pests, disease, cold, etc.

Pruning is done yearly (in late fall and throughout winter) to either form or maintain the tree's shape. Furthermore, when pruning, you should remove or cut away any dead, diseased, or broken branches and remove weeds from the base of the tree. Only trim up to 25% of the canopy at a time. Only cut new growth to half the newly formed branch's length, and always make a clean, 45° angled cut a quarter of an inch from an outward-facing bud.

Lazy Gardening

After following all the steps to creating permaculture and nurturing it to maturity, there is only a little maintenance involved. But I thought I would leave you with a few more tips for achieving a "lazy" garden:

- More diversity and companion guilds will reduce maintenance.
- Never have bare soil. Ever!
- Don't fight nature; use it to your advantage.

- Think long-term regarding solutions and planning.
- Caring for the soil is caring for your plants.
- Harvest water and store it in the soil.
- Plant more perennials than annuals and choose low-maintenance plants.
- Listen to the feedback and respond actively.
- Consider your climate and local ecosystem.
- Design your garden with easy access in mind.
- Stagger your harvests for year-round produce.
- Consider composting or worm farming.
- Only disturb or interject when necessary.

Consider a Calendar

A calendar can help keep track of all the planting, growing, and harvesting timelines, helping beginners and veteran permaculture gardeners.

First, write down all the plants you want to include in your garden when they should be planted (or propagated), how long they take to reach maturity, and when is the best time to harvest.

Next, use a calendar either specifically for planting or a regular one and write all the information down in the corresponding months or specific dates—you can also use your phone for this.

The benefits of a calendar like this are that you can also jot down other reminders, such as when you need to prune, mulch, weed, etc.

Enjoy It

Permaculture isn't just about creating a means to an end. It's about fostering a connection, an understanding, and a relationship with nature and your garden in particular.

Respecting nature and all the creatures we share this planet with is the pinnacle of what permaculture stands for. So, enjoy the beauty, serenity, and knowledge that the earth, your future children, and even grandchildren will benefit from the fruit of your labor.

Spread the Joy!

Once you start your adventure with permaculture, you'll never look back… and this is your chance to help someone else out on their journey.

Simply by sharing your honest opinion of this book and a little about your own experience, you'll help new readers find everything they need to get started.

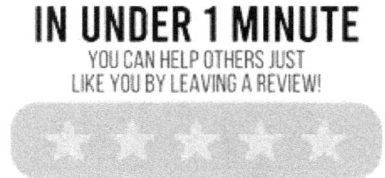

Thank you so much for your support. Together, we can make an enormous difference.

Scan the QR code below to leave your review:

CONCLUSION

When you look to the future, what do you see? I'm talking about more than what you plan to have for dinner tonight. Think about the future of the planet, the people, the animals, and the plants. Based on our current trajectory and past statistics, agricultural farming is not a long-term solution.

Your permaculture garden alone will not revolutionize farming, reverse pollution and global warming, or change how the world approaches feeding everyone on earth. But it still has a better chance of doing so than not doing anything.

Permaculture is rooted in caring for the planet and the people and sharing and re-investing the abundance. I can't think of a better way to live than being able to count on a community that genuinely cares about the world and the mark we're leaving.

Nature has had millennia to perfect its survival mechanisms, so it's pointless to try and fight against it for our benefit or convenience. Furthermore, humans have been around for less than a blink of an eye, whereas plants and microorganisms have been here since the very start.

The world will be fine without us, but without the world, there's no us.

Whether your reasons for starting permaculture are profound or shallow at best, it contributes to the overall message: There's a better way!

Not only that, but with a bit of knowledge, patience, and creative thinking, it's doable for everyone, regardless of education, age, or the environment, because mother nature always finds a way.

Please take the initiative to further your knowledge and understanding of permaculture. While following this nine-step process is easy enough for a beginner, it's impossible to fit everything you need to know about permaculture for your specific climate, ecology, and available resources in a single book.

Using *your* surroundings as a guide for *your* permaculture garden is essential.

It doesn't matter how much we know about science, ecology, and the environment. Planning for water management, soil replenishment, mutually beneficial biodiversity, and pest management is a delicate art that can make or break an ecosystem. It's okay to research something if you are unsure or need further information or elaboration.

There will be trials, sweat—possibly some tears—and even failure. But to be good at something, you must first be bad at it. Either way, you will have to do it.

Whether you're designing a food forest or planning to start with tomatoes, basil, and marigold in a small garden bed made out of an old tractor tire, the principles of permaculture—along with this nine-step guide— still apply.

Many things in life are uncertain, but I can guarantee that you will never regret starting a permaculture garden!

If you found this book helpful, please consider leaving a review on the site of purchase.

REFERENCES

Amber. (2022, April 13). *Life begins the day you start a garden.* Biodynamic Land Trust. https://biodynamiclandtrust.org.uk/life-begins-the-day-you-start-a-garden/

Amy. (2015a, January 29). *Make a worm bin for composting food scraps.* Tenth Acre Farm. https://www.tenthacrefarm.com/worm-bin/

Amy. (2015b, April 27). *Building a compost bin (5 ways).* Tenth Acre Farm. https://www.tenthacrefarm.com/building-the-right-compost-bin/

Amy. (2020, January 10). *How to build a rain garden to capture runoff.* Tenth Acre Farm. https://www.tenthacrefarm.com/build-rain-garden/

Angelo. (2009a, September 25). *How to build a grape vine trellis.* Deep Green Permaculture. https://deepgreenpermaculture.com/2009/09/25/how-to-build-a-grape-vine-trellis/

Angelo. (2009b, September 29). *How to build an espalier support trellis.* Deep Green Permaculture. https://deepgreenpermaculture.com/2009/09/29/espalier-supporttrellis/

Angelo. (2012, June 29). *Propagating plants from hardwood cuttings.* Deep Green Permaculture. https://deepgreenpermaculture.com/2012/06/29/propagating-hardwood-cuttings/

Angelo. (2019a, August 18). *How to prune a fruit tree, step by step.* Deep Green Permaculture. https://deepgreenpermaculture.com/2019/08/18/how-to-prune-a-fruit-tree-step-by-step/

Angelo. (2019b, November 19). *What is integrated pest management (IPM).* Deep Green Permaculture. https://deepgreenpermaculture.com/2019/11/19/what-is-integrated-pest-management-ipm/

April. (2016, February 12). *Biomimicry & permaculture today.* Permaculture Visions. https://permaculturevisions.com/biomimicry-permaculture-today/

Ashwanden, C. (2020a, June 22). *Integrated pest management – part 1.* The Permaculture Research Institute. https://www.permaculturenews.org/2020/06/22/integrated-pest-management-part-1/

Ashwanden, C. (2020b, July 6). *Integrated pest management – part 2.* The Permaculture Research Institute. https://www.permaculturenews.org/2020/07/06/integrated-pest-management-part-2/

Austin, A. (n.d.). *Alfred Austin*. En.wikiquote.org. Retrieved November 17, 2022, from https://en.wikiquote.org/wiki/Alfred_Austin#The_Garden_That_I_Love: _Second_Series_(1907)

Bailey, P. (n.d.). *10 benefits of urban permaculture*. Agritecture. https://www.agritecture.com/blog/2019/5/28/10-benefits-of-urban-permaculture

Barth, B. (2016, April 19). *Permaculture: You've heard of it, but what the heck is it?* Modern Farmer. https://modernfarmer.com/2016/04/permaculture/

Bartleby.com. (n.d.). *V. education. Ralph Waldo Emerson. 1904. the complete works.* Www.bartleby.com. https://www.bartleby.com/90/1005.html

Bell, G. (2017, March 23). *Why do we need wildlife?* The Permaculture Research Institute. https://www.permaculturenews.org/2017/03/23/why-do-we-need-wildlife/

Bradley, K. (2015, November 8). *Permaculture design process 2: Making a base map.* Milkwood: Permaculture Courses, Skills + Stories. https://www.milkwood.net/2015/11/09/permaculture-design-process-2-making-a-base-map/

Davey. (2019, April 9). *How to perform a soil test (and why you need one!)*. Davey tree. Blog.davey.com. https://blog.davey.com/how-to-perform-a-soil-test-and-why-you-need-one/

Deep Green Permaculture. (2010, August 24). *Permaculture ethics.* Deep Green Permaculture. https://deepgreenpermaculture.com/permaculture/permaculture-ethics/

Deep Green Permaculture. (2011a, May 23). *2. each element performs many functions.* Deep Green Permaculture. https://deepgreenpermaculture.com/permaculture/permaculture-design-principles/2-each-element-performs-many-functions/

Deep Green Permaculture. (2011b, May 23). *Permaculture design principles.* Deep Green Permaculture. https://deepgreenpermaculture.com/permaculture/permaculture-design-principles/

Deep Green Permaculture. (2011c, August 5). *Permaculture design principle 3 – each important function is supported by many elements.* Deep Green Permaculture. https://deepgreenpermaculture.com/permaculture/permaculture-design-principles/3-each-important-function-is-supported-by-many-elements/

Deep Green Permaculture. (2012a, January 4). *4. zones and sectors – efficient energy planning.* Deep Green Permaculture. https://deepgreenpermaculture.com/permaculture/permaculture-design-principles/4-zones-and-sectors-efficient-energy-planning/

Deep Green Permaculture. (2012b, May 29). *7. small scale intensive systems.* Deep Green Permaculture; Deep Green Permaculture. https://deepgreenpermaculture.com/permaculture/permaculture-design-principles/7-small-scale-intensive-systems/

Deep Green Permaculture. (2013a, February 5). *Permaculture design principle 9 – diversity.* Deep Green Permaculture. https://deepgreenpermaculture.com/permaculture/permaculture-design-principles/9-diversity/

Deep Green Permaculture. (2013b, October 1). *No dig gardening, sustainable gardening with less effort.* Deep Green Permaculture. https://deepgreenpermaculture.com/2013/10/01/no-dig-gardening/

Deep Green Permaculture. (2014, September 23). *The complete guide to worm farming, vermicomposting made easy.* Deep Green Permaculture. https://deepgreenpermaculture.com/2014/09/23/worm-farming/

Deep Green Permaculture. (2019a, February 6). *The 12 principles of permaculture.* Live-Native.com. https://www.live-native.com/the-12-principles-of-permaculture/

Deep Green Permaculture. (2019b, June 11). *Chop and drop gardening (sheet composting).* Deep Green Permaculture. https://deepgreenpermaculture.com/2019/06/11/chop-and-drop-gardening-sheet-composting/

Desan, J. (2017, April 2). *Permaculture & biomimicry - global ecological humanities.* Duke Green Classroom. https://sites.duke.edu/lit290s-1_02_s2017/2017/04/02/permaculture-biomimicry/

Doug. (2019, March 9). *Creating A permaculture pond.* Highland Titles. https://www.highlandtitles.com/blog/creating-a-permaculture-pond/

Earth Ways. (n.d.). *Observation routine in permaculture: The sit spot.* Www.earth-Ways.co.uk. Retrieved November 4, 2022, from https://www.earth-ways.co.uk/sit-spot/#.Y2TIN3ZBzIW

Engels, J. (2015a, May 14). *Why permaculture isn't just organic farming.* One Green Planet. https://www.onegreenplanet.org/lifestyle/why-permaculture-isnt-just-organic-farming/

Engels, J. (2015b, July 13). *Permaculture and soil: How to follow nature's lead to grow amazing produce.* One Green Planet. https://www.onegreenplanet.org/lifestyle/permaculture-and-soil-how-to-follow-natures-lead-to-grow-amazing-produce/

Engels, J. (2015c, October 23). *Piecing together a guild of your own.* The Permaculture Research Institute. https://www.permaculturenews.org/2015/10/23/piecing-together-a-guild-of-your-own/

Fabiano, C. (2017, June 21). *Moving towards a zero-waste life: The basics.* The Permaculture Research Institute. https://www.permaculturenews.org/2017/06/21/moving-towards-zero-waste-life-basics/

Flores, H. J. (2020, April 5). *If You Guild It, They Will Come: How To Grow A Permaculture Food Forest.* Permaculture Women. https://www.permaculturewomen.com/grow-a-permaculture-food-forest/

Folk, E. (2020, November 4). *How to turn your backyard into a certified wildlife habitat.* The Permaculture Research Institute. https://www.permaculturenews.org/2020/11/04/how-to-turn-your-backyard-into-a-certified-wildlife-habitat/

Food Forest Plants. (2019, August 12). *5 steps to maintaining an edible food forest garden.* Food Forest Plants NZ. https://foodforestplants.co.nz/5-steps-to-maintaining-an-edible-food-forest-garden/?sfw=pass1669104799

Free Permaculture. (n.d.). *Bugs, bees, integrated pest management and organic pest control.* Free Permaculture. https://www.freepermaculture.com/integrated-pest-management/

Free Permaculture. (2020a). *Closing the loop towards A goal of zero waste.* Free Permaculture. https://www.freepermaculture.com/zero-waste/

Free Permaculture. (2020b, December 27). *Shrubs, hedges, and hedgerows.* Free Permaculture. https://www.freepermaculture.com/shrubs-hedges-and-hedgerows/

Free Permaculture. (2021a, March 29). *Patterns in nature and biomimicry.* Free Permaculture. https://www.freepermaculture.com/patterns-in-nature/

Free Permaculture. (2021b, June 10). *Permaculture sector analysis & mapping.* Free Permaculture. https://www.freepermaculture.com/sector-analysis/

Free Permaculture. (2021c, September 10). *How to grow a permaculture food forest.* Free Permaculture. https://www.freepermaculture.com/food-forest/

Gardenerdy. (2011, September 29). *What are the benefits of permaculture? You'll be amazed to know.* Gardenerdy. https://gardenerdy.com/what-are-benefits-of-permaculture/

Good Life Permaculture. (2015, November 10). *Water archives.* Good Life Permaculture. https://goodlifepermaculture.com.au/category/water/

Goodreads. (n.d.). *A quote from A history of western philosophy.* Goodreads. Retrieved October 26, 2022, from https://www.goodreads.com/quotes/607880-the-search-for-something-permanent-is-one-of-the-deepest

Goodreads. (2019). *A quote from an airman's odyssey.* Goodreads. https://www.goodreads.com/quotes/19905-perfection-is-achieved-not-when-there-is-nothing-more-to

H, M. (2016, January 7). *Why is sustainability important?* The Permaculture Research Institute. https://www.permaculturenews.org/2016/01/07/why-is-sustainability-important/

Holden Forests and Garden. (n.d.). *The do's and don'ts of mulching.* Holden Forests & Gardens. Retrieved November 12, 2022, from https://holdenfg.org/resources/the-dos-and-donts-of-mulching/

Homestead and Chill. (2022, May 18). *Hugelkultur: A natural, cheap way to make or fill garden beds.* Homestead and Chill. https://homesteadandchill.com/hugelkultur-garden-beds/

Jenkins, E. (2018a, August 5). *9 steps to create a permaculture garden.* New Life on a Homestead. https://www.newlifeonahomestead.com/steps-to-a-permaculture-garden/

Jenkins, E. (2018b, August 23). *7 ways to harvest rainwater for your (permaculture) garden.* New Life on a Homestead. https://www.newlifeonahomestead.com/harvest-rainwater-for-your-permaculture-garden/

Jerad, A. (2014, August 4). *Soil science basics for beginners.* The Permaculture Research Institute. https://www.permaculturenews.org/2014/08/04/soil-science-basics-beginners/

Keela Yoga Farm. (n.d.). *Integrating animals on a permaculture farm.* Keela Yoga Farm. https://www.keelayogafarm.com/permaculture/integrating-animals-on-a-permaculture-farm/

Le Guin, U. K. (1972). *The word for world is forest.* The Anarchist Library. https://theanarchistlibrary.org/library/ursula-k-le-guin-the-word-for-world-is-forest-1

Leichty, C. (n.d.). *Are raised garden beds better than in-ground garden beds?* Do Not Disturb Gardening. https://donotdisturbgardening.com/are-raised-garden-beds-better-than-in-ground-garden-beds/

Leopold, A., & Schwartz, C. (n.d.). *Essays from a sand county almanac.* http://www.umag.cl/facultades/williams/wp-content/uploads/2016/11/Leopold-1949-ASandCountyAlmanac-complete.pdf

Live-nation. (2019, February 6). *Permaculture - what is permaculture?* Live-Native.com. https://www.live-native.com/what-is-permaculture/

Lynne, K. (2010, February 2). *Companion planting - the ultimate guide.* New Life on a Homestead. https://www.newlifeonahomestead.com/companion-planting/

Manu Saunders. (2019, May 14). *Birds, bees and bugs: Your garden is an ecosystem, and it needs looking after.* The Conversation. https://theconversation.com/birds-bees-and-bugs-your-garden-is-an-ecosystem-and-it-needs-looking-after-65226

Marx, M. (2019, March 5). *Permaculture principle 1 - observe & interact.* Gympie District Landcare. https://gympielandcare.org.au/permaculture-principle-1-observe-interact/

Mason, M. (2014). *What is sustainability and why is it important?* https://www.environmentalscience.org/sustainability

McLaughlin, C. (2009, September 29). *What is sustainable gardening?* FineGardening. https://www.finegardening.com/article/what-is-sustainable-gardening

Missouri Botanical Garden. (n.d.). *Rooting cuttings in water.* Www.missouribotanical-garden.org. Retrieved November 18, 2022, from https://www.missouribotanicalgarden.org/gardens-gardening/your-garden/help-for-the-home-gardener/advice-tips-resources/visual-guides/rooting-cuttings-in-water

Nemett, A. (n.d.). Permaculture maps #4 and 5: *The zone map and master plan.* Thunderbird Disco Homestead. Retrieved November 4, 2022, from https://www.thunderbirddisco.com/blog/permaculture-zone-map-master-plan

Open Source Ecology. (2011, March 12). *Inputs and outputs in permaculture.* Wiki. open-source ecology.org. https://wiki.opensourceecology.org/wiki/Inputs_and_outputs_in_permaculture

Orwell. (2019, December 29). George Orwell: *A good word for the vicar of bray.* Www.orwell.ru. https://www.orwell.ru/library/reviews/vicar/english/e_vicar

Penn State Extension. (2016, March 29). *Soil testing.* Penn State Extension. https://extension.psu.edu/soil-testing

Permaculture Apprentice. (2015a, May 10). *How to start a small permaculture nursery and grow 1000s of trees by yourself.* Permaculture Apprentice. https://permacultureapprentice.com/how-to-start-a-small-permaculture-nursery-and-grow-1000s-of-trees-by-yourself/

Permaculture Apprentice. (2015b, July 29). *How to design your property - the process of permaculture design explained.* Permaculture Apprentice. https://permacultureapprentice.com/how-to-design-your-property/

Permaculture Apprentice. (2015c, October 9). *The definitive guide to building deep rich soils by imitating nature.* Permaculture Apprentice. https://permacultureapprentice.com/building-soil/

Permaculture Apprentice. (2016, February 12). *Everything you need to know about growing trees from seeds.* Permaculture Apprentice. https://permacultureapprentice.com/permaculture-growing-trees-from-seeds/

Permaculture Apprentice. (2017a, April 17). *Water management for every permaculture farm.* Permaculture Apprentice. https://permacultureapprentice.com/permaculture-water-management/

Permaculture Apprentice. (2017b, May 5). *Creating a food forest - step-by-step guide.* Permaculture Apprentice. https://permacultureapprentice.com/creating-a-food-forest-step-by-step-guide/

Permaculture Apprentice. (2018, January 11). *How to use native fungi to improve soil quality and bulletproof your food forest against disease.* Permaculture Apprentice. https://permacultureapprentice.com/food-forest-fungi/

Permaculture Apprentice. (2020, May 19). *Crisis garden layout: The three-step permaculture design method.* Permaculture Apprentice. https://permacultureapprentice.com/crisis-garden-layout/

Permaculture Apprentice. (2021, June 11). *How to choose the most suitable plants for your food forest.* Permaculture Apprentice. https://permacultureapprentice.com/choosing-plants-food-forest/

Permaculture Food Forest. (2016, April 13). *CLAY POT IRRIGATION.* Permaculture Food Forest. https://permaculturefoodforest.wordpress.com/2016/04/13/clay-pot-irrigation/

Permaculture Quotes (109 Quotes). Goodreads | Meet Your Next Favorite Book. Accessed December 15, 2023. https://www.goodreads.com/quotes/tag/perma culture

Project Gutenberg Australia. (2002, February). *Gone with the wind.* Gutenberg.net.au. http://gutenberg.net.au/ebooks02/0200161h.html

Quote Investigator. (2021, September 10). *If there is magic on this planet, it is contained in water.* Quote Investigator. https://quoteinvestigator.com/2021/09/10/magic-water/

Resilience. (2010, July 19). *Permaculture ethics: Why permaculture is different.* Resilience. https://www.resilience.org/stories/2010-07-20/permaculture-ethics-why-permaculture-different/

Ritar, N. (2015, May 31). *Design basics: Mapping the sun on your site.* Milkwood: Permaculture Courses, Skills + Stories. https://www.milkwood.net/2015/06/01/design-basics-mapping-the-sun-on-your-site/

Roberts, T. (2017, October 13). *A primer on creating soil.* The Permaculture Research Institute. https://www.permaculturenews.org/2017/10/13/primer-creating-soil/

Sayner, A. (2021, June 24). *How to propagate plants: A guide to plant cuttings.* GroCycle. https://grocycle.com/how-to-propagate-plants/

Schiller, N. (2022, January 1). *23 beneficial insects & creepy crawlies great for your garden.* Gardener's Path. https://gardenerspath.com/how-to/disease-and-pests/beneficial-insects/#What-is-an-Insect-Pest?

Studylib. (n.d.). *Wislawa szymborska - poems.* Studylib.net. Retrieved November 18, 2022, from https://studylib.net/doc/8370911/wislawa-szymborska---poems

Tallarico, G. (2018, June 4). *We believe in abundance.* World Permaculture Association. https://worldpermacultureassociation.com/permaculture-is-applied-ecology/

Telkamp, M. (n.d.). *What is permaculture?* HGTV. Retrieved October 28, 2022, from https://www.hgtv.com/outdoors/gardens/planting-and-maintenance/what-is-permaculture

Tenth Acre Farm. (2013, July 18). *Mulching in the permaculture garden.* Tenth Acre Farm. https://www.tenthacrefarm.com/mulching-in-the-permaculture-garden/

Tenth Acre Farm. (2015a, March 23). *How to plant a hedgerow.* Tenth Acre Farm. https://www.tenthacrefarm.com/how-to-plant-a-hedgerow/

Tenth Acre Farm. (2015b, April 21). *What is permaculture? Design a garden that works with nature.* Tenth Acre Farm. https://www.tenthacrefarm.com/what-is-perma culture/

Tenth Acre Farm. (2015c, August 19). *7 ways to improve the quality of your soil.* Tenth Acre Farm. https://www.tenthacrefarm.com/improve-soil-quality/

Tkaczyk, F. (n.d.). *Permaculture food forest.* Alderleaf Wilderness College. Retrieved October 29, 2022, from https://www.wildernesscollege.com/permaculture-food-forest.html

Traynor, J. (2019, March 20). *How often should you water your plants?* Start a Food Forest. https://www.startafoodforest.com/how-often-should-you-water-your-plants/

Trinklein, D. (2016, July). *Plant propagation.* Extension.missouri.edu. https://exten sion.missouri.edu/publications/mg3

Tropical Permaculture. (n.d.). *Permaculture design principle 2 - multiple functions.* Www.tropicalpermaculture.com. Retrieved November 2, 2022, from https:// www.tropicalpermaculture.com/permaculture-design-principles-2.html

University of Alberta. (2013). *What is sustainability?* In McGill (p. 1). University of Alberta. https://www.mcgill.ca/sustainability/files/sustainability/what-is-sustainability.pdf

Waddington, E. (2019, September 29). *How to make a forest garden.* Happy DIY Home. https://happydiyhome.com/forest-garden/

Waddington, E. (2020, July 3). *20 tips for A beautiful & productive low-maintenance garden.* Rural Sprout. https://www.ruralsprout.com/low-maintenance-garden-tips/

Waddington, E. (2021, March 4). *The role of water in a forest garden design.* Treehugger. https://www.treehugger.com/water-management-forest-garden-design-5095576

Wikiquote. (n.d.). *Bill Mollison.* En.wikiquote.org. Retrieved November 21, 2022, from https://en.wikiquote.org/wiki/Bill_Mollison

Yellow Birch Hobby Farm. (2018, April 13). *Maximize your garden space with perma-culture.* Yellow Birch Hobby Farm. https://www.yellowbirchhobbyfarm.com/maximize-your-garden-space-with-permaculture/

THE COMPLETE BEGINNERS GUIDE TO SEED SAVING

A HASSLE-FREE JOURNEY TO SELF-SUFFICIENCY, SUSTAINABILITY AND BIODIVERSITY IN YOUR GARDEN

INTRODUCTION

In 1903, you would've had just under 500 varieties of lettuce plants to choose from, but by 1983, that number had depleted to 36. In general, we've lost about 93% of our unique seed strands just in the 20th century (Fast Company, 2012). Unless we step in and reverse this trend, that's just a glimpse of what we can expect going forward.

But first, why is this depletion happening? Well, genetic modification. It's the squash that can withstand a drought and whose seeds will sowed next season. The most enormous, sweetest watermelon seeds survive, while the rest aren't worth keeping. The sweet corn that produces four times as much come harvest time will move up the priority list of preferred crops to replant for next year.

We want the best results for our time and effort. However, there's power in numbers, and nature prefers diversity—that's how we've all survived this long in the first place. We can look at the human gene pool and see that more diversity is beneficial in preventing autoimmune diseases or fatal genetic mutations. We can also look at monocultures—how they strip the soil and require more intricate care to keep alive—and see that *this* method isn't sustainable. We can acknowledge that we can't bend nature to our will without severe consequences. We can look at nature's most steadfast rule, "survival of the fittest," and deduce that the strongest, fastest, most resilient life forms result from biodiversity, not despite it.

You've decided you want to get your hands dirty (literally) and start your garden. Whatever pushed you toward growing your food, whether it's the cost-of-living crisis or the eco-sustainability movement, it doesn't make sense if you still depend on buying your seeds in the store. The costs of buying seeds, seedlings, and whole plants, in addition to all the other expenses and resources that go into a healthy garden, quickly add up and become unaffordable and unrealistic.

Being raised on a farm with implementations of permaculture principles (living off the land sustainably, composting, working with nature instead of against it, and, of course, seed saving), you quickly learn that it is truly the best way to live, not only for us in the present and future but for the environment. Did I have my doubts? Did I complain about some of the "luxuries" I missed out on as a grumpy teen? You bet!

But the older I got, the more I started appreciating nature and experiencing every consequence our actions have on the land. We get so caught up in things that don't matter that we don't realize we're neglecting (and, in most cases, ruining) the one thing that continues to give us life. At one point, I could think about one question day and night: *How much more are we going to take, and how much longer is nature willing to give?*

That's my origin story in a nutshell. It started with adapting our farm to be even more eco-conscious and sustainable. I didn't expect it would grow into a deep-rooted (excuse the pun) passion of wanting to teach others that it's possible to make a difference, even on a small scale. We can take care of this floating space rock so it can keep on giving back to us for generations to come.

But learning wasn't without its challenges. The more I researched, the more I became aware of everything I didn't know yet or hadn't even considered. It's overwhelming. However, the Dunning-Kruger effect wouldn't stop me from going on my journey. The Dunning-Kruger effect is a cognitive bias that suggests that the more you learn about a particular subject, the more you will doubt your knowledge, competence, or capabilities.

Think of learning everything there is to know about a subject. It is like an ice cube in water, with only 10% showing above the surface. Many people will stop at 10% and be done (and wildly overestimate their knowledge), but the deeper you go, the more there is to discover, making you doubt your ability to learn and retain the other 90%.

I'm glad I didn't let the mental barrier of having a lack of knowledge stop me. I have never felt more content than when strolling through the farm and being present in the ever-giving haven we built with our hands. It took me years to learn as much as I know now, and I still don't quite understand everything. But what got me this far is my willingness to learn and to do it one step at a time.

When you start or manage your garden, you will undoubtedly be faced with obstacles (some worse than others), such as pest and disease management without depending on chemical fertilizers, limited garden space (because who can afford to own land these days?), unpredictable weather and seasonal changes, on top of an already busy lifestyle. But here's the thing: permaculture makes gardening more manageable, not harder. So, if you have a garden and want to implement permaculture gardening, I have a handbook dedicated to what it is and how to do it.

If you want to be at the forefront of the sustainability and eco-conscious movement, name a better place to start than an in-depth guide on how to save seeds—and potentially save the dwindling numbers of unique strands of fruits and vegetable varieties in the process. It all starts with gathering the knowledge, absorbing it, practicing it, and not being afraid of failing or making mistakes (and learning from them).

My background taught me how vital seed saving is in permaculture gardening practices. Additionally, knowing how to save seeds to remain stable and viable for as long as possible is crucial. Whether you're a complete beginner or already have a thriving food forest, it's always early enough to learn the value of seed-saving and how it can promote biodiversity, improve food security, and leave you feeling fulfilled by your role.

As you learn various seed-saving techniques, drastically reduce your reliance on store-bought seeds and seedlings, and improve your gardening practices, you will gain the confidence to take your backyard garden to a new level. No contribution to increasing the number of plant varieties and biodiversity is too insignificant.

By the end of this book, you will have all the knowledge you need to step forth and cultivate a diverse and resilient garden from the seeds you save and grow yourself in perpetuity. It's a closed circle of resilience and self-reliance.

You'll save money and life's most precious resource—time. You'll wake up one day and realize you've become that person. You know? The person you've always wanted to become: self-sufficient, knowledgeable, resourceful, eco-conscious, and with a garden that thanks you in abundance.

1

SEED SAVING BASICS

Consider that a single tomato has, on average, between 150 and 300 seeds inside it. That's one tomato with the potential to grow more than 100 other plants. But what do you do with so many seeds? And how do you store them?

Slow down—this guide will answer all your questions in good time. In this chapter, we'll go over the basics of seed saving, why you should do it, and what you should consider first and foremost.

WHAT IS SEED SAVING?

As the name suggests, seed saving (also known as brown bagging) is the act of saving seeds to plant them again or to increase the number of plants you have (and therefore increase your yield). Saving seeds also involves storing other reproductive material from fruits, vegetables, grain, herbs, and flowering plants (cuttings, tubers, roots, etc.).

The seed-saving process is more nuanced than just putting seeds in a plastic jar. We want the best possible harvest next year—

because why wouldn't we? So, you select the best plants—the ones that are the most healthy and resilient. Then, you collect seeds from various produce of the same type (not just from one plant). You then need to process and store the seeds correctly to use them the next time you want to plant them.

The main objectives of seed saving are to preserve heirloom seeds (which we will discuss thoroughly in the next chapter), preserve open-pollinated seed varieties (diversity within the genetics), encourage self-reliance, and save rare or endangered plant species from looming extinction.

A BRIEF HISTORY LESSON

Seed saving has been traced back as far as 30,000 years ago (Allaby et al., 2017). Granted, back then, we humans were still mainly reliant on hunting and gathering our food rather than farming it. Evidence suggests that crop cultivation started roughly 11,000 years ago; at around the same time, the domestication of cattle and various other farm animals became all the rage. You know what they say: work smarter, not harder.

The exact reason why farming and seed saving became the logical thing to do isn't known, but it's likely due to a variety of factors: the climate shifted, which led to a decline in food sources and availability, animals migrated, and steady human population growth didn't exactly help. At the same time, the new climate brought about the perfect conditions for annual vegetation. With some observation, they likely started to recreate the conditions under which crops grew. They could successfully own wheat, rice, corn, fruits, and vegetable fields with some practice and even keep animals for meat.

One thing is sure. Farming was necessary for survival for a long time, so people had to figure it out. So what happened? Why is no one growing their food and saving seeds anymore?

The answer is, of course, capitalism, consumerism, and corporate control. After the colonization of America, Europeans ran into some issues when the seeds they brought from the other side of the world failed to grow or produce a sufficient yield. In light of this problem, the US formed a patent office for agriculture. 1862, the United States Department of Agriculture (USDA) was born. Their plan was simple and effective: hand out free seeds to farmers to grow and adapt to different climates so there's more food.

Private sectors thought this solution was a waste of a great opportunity, and in 1883, the American Seed Trade Association (ASTA) was established. Less than 50 years later, ASTA convinced the government to stop this nonsense—no more free seeds for anyone. To add insult to injury, ASTA also developed and implemented intellectual property rights and patents that made it illegal to save seeds that belonged to these private corporations.

Mega agricultural corporations own over 67% of seeds worldwide as of right now. Any seeds you buy at the garden store are held and patented. Not only that, but they're also most likely treated with harsh chemicals and genetically modified to depend on pesticides (regardless of what the packaging says).

That is how you kill over 11,000 years of history and life-giving tradition in less than a decade. Today, home gardeners do most of the seed saving and what's left of the nomadic tribes in some parts of the world.

TYPES OF SEEDS

Knowledge is indeed power, and before you go and start gathering seeds, there are a few things you need to know. There are three main types of seeds: open-pollinated, hybrid, and GMO. Each type has its benefits and drawbacks, and the seed you choose to grow and save will depend on your specific needs and goals.

Open-Pollinated Seeds

When a plant or flower is fertilized through natural means by insects, birds, rain, and wind by a plant of the same variety, the seed is genetically similar to its "parents" with only slight variations. These variations in the genetic makeup of the seed offspring are how plants gradually adapt to environmental changes.

Keep open-pollinated seeds separate from other varieties of the same family or genus. Otherwise, cross-pollination between two variants of the same plant species can happen naturally, so you will no longer have open-pollinated (or heirloom) seeds but hybrids.

Hybrid Seeds

Hybrid seeds are when two varieties of plants cross-pollinate (organically or manually), resulting in seeds with a much more diverse genetic makeup. For example, suppose you fertilize a disease-resistant tomato plant with a drought-resistant tomato plant of a different variety, and you continue to save and plant these seeds. In that case, you will eventually end up with seeds with positive characteristics of both varieties (a disease- and drought-resistant tomato plant). This process is a form of genetic engineering and modification.

However, the seeds you get from crossing two different crop varieties are highly unpredictable, and, in many cases, they're not even viable (because they're infertile) and won't germinate or survive for very long. But even if you manage to get past all that, this new variation of the plant you created will only be stable and predictable for a very short time. You need to know what you're doing if you want to make an entirely new species of crop.

GMO Seeds

As I'm sure you're familiar with, GMO stands for Genetically Modified Organism. But unlike hybrid seeds, where cross-pollination is still somewhat natural, GMO seeds are made in a controlled environment (a laboratory), involve expensive and complex technology and engineering, and utilize gene splicing (the stuff you read about in sci-fi novels). These seeds are most commonly made for large-scale commercial use only since you need a license to grow these "Frankensteined" seeds. The seeds you buy at the store are not this modified, but they might still be hybrids.

Heirloom Seeds

Heirloom seeds aren't a type of seed on their own, but it's worth mentioning what they are and how they come to be. Almost any seed can be an heirloom seed. The category means that the seed has a long history of being open-pollinated. An heirloom seed, through years of cultivation (a minimum of 50 generations), likely has had many desirable traits passed down to it, such as hardiness, better nutritional value, flavor, productivity, and resistance to pests and diseases. It's also perfectly adapted to the climate it's in.

THE SEED-SAVING CYCLE

In gardening, both heirloom and hybrid seeds have their place. Heirloom seeds ensure that every generation of seeds results in better-quality plants—the genes both improve and get "solidified," meaning that the chances of it failing for any reason and going extinct are less, and we get better quality food from them. Hybrid seeds ensure a more extensive variety of species to choose from, grow, and enjoy.

However, cross-pollination is only sometimes successful, especially if you let it happen naturally. If you want to create a stable hybrid variety, you will likely run into some issues in the future. But it *is* doable.

Before starting your seed-saving journey, you must know how the cycle goes. Some of it is self-explanatory, but some involve nuance and many things to remember—as you'll see.

Planting

Whether you already have a thriving garden or are just starting, the first step is to have or grow healthy, open-pollinated plants. Ensure that plants of the same species or varieties are isolated in some way so they don't cross-pollinate when the time comes. You also want to ensure that you're providing the proper care to your plants and garden regarding water, soil quality, and sun requirements.

Pollination

As mentioned, you want only to create and harvest hybrid seeds if you already have hybrid plants that made it through the first generation of replanting. However, even with hybrid plants, you want to ensure pollination by other plants with the same genetic variety. In short, don't breed two different types of hybrid plants.

Remember that some plants are self-pollinating and will pollinate themselves before the flowers open up. However, self-pollinating plants are not immune to cross-pollination, as insects can still crawl into the flowers and pollinate them. You need to know which plants are more likely to cross-pollinate and which aren't so you can take the necessary precautions to minimize the possibility (which we will discuss later).

Seed Maturity

The produce is often ready for picking and eating long before the seed matures. It's essential to allow the seed to develop and grow on the plant before it gets harvested. Do some research on the plants in your garden to ensure you're not picking the produce and saving underdeveloped seeds.

Underdeveloped seeds can still germinate. However, they might be weak and end up not surviving for very long, unable to withstand harsh weather, and producing a small or underperforming yield.

You should always leave a few fruits or vegetables on the plant until the seed has fully matured before picking them and moving on to the next step.

Harvesting

Crops can either be dry-fruited or wet-fruited. It's pretty simple to distinguish between these two types of seed: if the seed is inside the fruit, it's wet-seeded (tomatoes, squash, watermelon, peppers, etc.), and if it's not inside a fruit, it's dry seed (usually inside a pod, tract, capsule, or seed head).

The fruit has to be fully ripe or overripe with wet seeds to ensure they are mature before you can harvest and process them for storage. Dry seeds should remain on the plant until they're mature enough (you can look up what color or texture dry seeds from specific crops should look like when matured) before harvesting and storing them.

Processing

Wet seeds often have pieces of fruit pulp or jelly stuck to or surrounding them (like tomato seeds surrounded by a jelly-like sac). Even dry seeds might have some moisture even when they're mature and the seed head is wholly dried out. For this reason, you should always ensure the seeds are sufficiently dried if you want to save them for long periods (otherwise, they might sprout prematurely or decay).

For wet seeds with lots of pulp or jelly sacks surrounding them, there are several ways to make separating them more manageable. You can put the seeds in a container and place them in a dark but warm environment away from sunlight so they can ferment. After a few days, mold will form on top. At this point, you can add water and, with gloves on, squish everything together so the seeds get released from the pulp or goo surrounding it. The moldy pulp or jelly will float to the surface while the seeds fall to the bottom. This process makes it easier to separate the jelly bits from the seeds by scooping out (or pouring off) the top layer of gunk.

From here, you can strain, rinse, and dry the seeds. For dry seeds (after you've separated them from seed pods and plant debris), you can spread them thinly on trays and leave them to dry. The drying process for wet-fruited and dry-fruited seeds can take up to three weeks.

Storage

Seeds processed and dried can be stored in airtight containers in a cool, dark, dry place such as a closet or basement for up to a year or two. For several years, you can keep the seeds in airtight containers in the fridge or freezer. However, some seeds are notoriously known to have a shorter "shelf life" and won't last as long, so be sure to use them before they "expire."

Always label your seed containers with the crop type, variety name, date of harvest, and any other information that might be useful, such as how long you can store the seeds or how many plants you harvested from.

THE BENEFITS OF SEED SAVING

Many traditions don't serve the human race. Throwing them away would benefit society immensely—like consumerism and sketchy marketing strategies. But seed saving has so many benefits that it's hard not to consider doing it.

It would be best if you honored this significant old tradition for the following reasons:

- It's free.
- It's relatively easy after learning the basics.
- It results in more resilient and bountiful crops every year.
- It results in better produce every year.
- Home-saved seeds have higher germination rates.
- You're contributing to your independence instead of capitalism.
- You are contributing toward and improving genetic diversity.
- You're in control of your food supply.

- You learn a valuable and essential skill.
- Eventually, you have heirloom seeds to pass on to the next generation.

CHALLENGES FACING THE SEED-SAVING MOVEMENT

The number one problem the seed-saving movement is trying to solve is the need for more diversity regarding the rate at which fruit and vegetable varieties are declining. Seed Savers Exchange (SSE), a non-profit organization in Iowa, has done a fantastic job preserving these dwindling statistics by growing their vegetable seed bank to over 20,000 varieties.

With the economy hanging on by a thread, more people are now turning to grow their food out of desperation. Of course, this process highlighted how much control big corporations have over the seed industry and the legal implications on the public's ability to save and share seeds.

The seed-saving movement has gained much traction, but it's still mainly comprised of small players (such as school and home gardens, a handful of small-scale commercial farms, and a few non-profits). This fact means that funding and resources are limited.

And since seed saving isn't a common tradition anymore, the lack of knowledge breeds doubt, uncertainty, and apprehension in even the keenest gardeners. Moreover, urbanization led to a significant loss of space to grow enough food to feed a family, and 40-hour work weeks leave us exhausted. So many people who want to join this movement need to learn how, don't have the space, and need more time or energy to do much of anything. Even when working themselves into the ground, many people need more financial wiggle room to donate to the cause.

But an even bigger issue that the seed-saving movement—and most of us—is trying to outrun is the adverse effects of climate change. While politicians debate whether it's real, the people growing our food must deal with the ever-growing proof (and threat) of its existence.

Don't fret. The seed-saving movement has been steadily growing for many years, and although the movement spent many of those years growing in silence, there will be a storm. Mark my words.

SEED SAVING MYTHS AND MISCONCEPTIONS

Seed saving has existed longer than we can conceptualize. However, our ancestors went through much trial and error to learn how to do it properly. Based on them passing on their hard-earned information and knowledge, we have the luxury of buying and reading books about it and looking it up on Google.

However, there's also a lot of misinformation about seed saving out there—some of which might've even played a role in your ambivalence. Let's clear up some of the most common myths and misconceptions about seed saving right now:

You Don't Need Any Special Knowledge

While seed saving is more complicated than you might think, it's not common knowledge either. There is a lot of information, and there are a lot of things to remember. For example, different seeds require different processing and storage needs. Some plants are more likely to cross-pollinate than others, and so on. It's more than just bottling up some seeds; you must know its specifics. But it's completely doable.

Heirlooms Are Always Best

This statement is only sometimes true. Some heirlooms have a shorter shelf-life and require more specialized care than hybrids. This fact is especially true for heirlooms that cultivate asexually (they grow a new plant from a fragment of the mother plant), meaning they are genetically identical to their parent, which increases their risk of infection and disease.

All Seeds Can Be Saved

Within each plant's genetic makeup, there are beneficial and harmful traits that survive to the next generation. Valuable traits are usually dominant, meaning the chances of getting a diseased or mutated plant are less, but it still happens. Diseased, weak, or mutated plants need to be "thinned out" (in other words, removed and preferably composted) with every new generation without saving the seeds; otherwise, you risk these traits surviving.

You Must Isolate All Crop Varieties

It depends on your goals, honestly. If you plan on selling or sharing seeds, you must avoid cross-pollination. If you're creating your variety of fruit or vegetable, and that variety's existence depends entirely on you, then you should also be careful that the "bloodline" is not contaminated. But if you have a decently sized seed bank and you're not too concerned with cross-pollination in your backyard, you can afford to take the risk (you might even end up with an improved variety).

It Takes No Extra Effort

Hey! I said it wasn't that difficult, not that it doesn't take time and effort. Of course, picking, cleaning, processing, labeling, and storing the seeds take time. And then there's a certain amount of time you'll spend researching, gaining practical experience, and learning from mistakes. You'll need to know how to tell which plants are the best from a genetic standpoint (it's not only about the size of the fruit or how much the plant produces) and many other factors that go into seed saving. But it's a necessary learning curve. I call it school fees—the price you pay for knowledge.

SOMETHING TO CONSIDER

To determine whether seed saving is your practice, reflect on your gardening goals for a few minutes. Ask yourself why you started gardening in the first place and how saving and using your seeds could contribute to those goals.

Is the goal to become more self-sufficient or eco-conscious, save money on groceries, and have fresh herbs to supplement your cooking, or is it more of an eccentric hobby now? Or do you have a different goal in mind? Remember, even if you're not yet sharpening your shovel to join the seed-saving movement, saving and using your home garden's seeds can still benefit you on a personal, small-scale level (as well as the environment in the long term).

Now that you know the history and bare basics of seed saving, what it entails, the types of seeds and how they come about, and the impact your seed-saving journey can have on the environment, we will use this information moving forward. In the next chapter, we'll discuss heirloom seeds and their importance.

2

WHY HEIRLOOM SEEDS MATTER

Heirloom seeds are the antique furniture of the gardening world. In the previous chapter, we mentioned that heirloom seeds can be finicky and don't always result in the most resilient plants, but they're still important for many reasons. And just like baggy jeans, they're making a comeback!

DEFINE HEIRLOOM

Heirloom plants (also known as heirloom varieties or heritage plants) are plants grown and maintained by gardeners and farmers (usually in isolated communities) for generations via open pollination. This process isolates them to prevent cross-pollination, and every time the plant leaves behind seeds, those seeds are saved and used in the next growing season. However, heritage plants can also be cultivated and maintained through grafts and cuttings.

For a plant to be considered an heirloom plant, the specific variety of plant needs to be at least 50 years old. Heirloom seeds usually have apparent, desirable traits that have been passed down and reinforced. A plant doesn't just survive that long without picking up some superhuman (or "super-plant") genetics. But again, this concept doesn't mean they can't or don't put out some less-than-optimal seeds now and then.

The bottom line is that heirloom seeds are old, open-pollinated, non-hybrid, and something so valuable that they get passed on to the next generation of trustworthy gardeners. They're a big reason why we had so many varieties of fruits and vegetables to choose from in the past.

However, it's more than the age, rarity, and exceptional genetics that make these seeds so unique. It's the culture surrounding them as well, the stories they carry with them, and their uniqueness that adds to their inherent value and importance.

Their Significance

While hybrid seeds play a significant role in expanding variety and genetic diversity, it's always a gamble; crossing two varieties of corn will result in offspring that have a genetic mix of the two plant parents, but there's no telling what would happen if you save those hybrid seeds and plant them next season. Will you get the same results in the second generation as in the first? You'll end up with infertile seed at worst and diminished returns at best.

This information means that if you plan on creating a variety of your own through cross-pollination, you shouldn't count on these plants to feed you and your family. It also means that if you want to play mad scientist and recreate your original results (because you liked the resulting fruit or vegetables and want another successful yield), you must cross the original two varieties repeatedly from scratch or keep buying hybrid seeds yearly. You can only save hybrid seeds once the genes become stable (meaning the resulting plants and produce of hybrid seeds no longer have any outliers when replanted), which takes an immense amount of time and patience.

Heirloom seeds ensure that variety survives the test of time, and they grow stronger with each generation because they acquire natural resistance to pests, diseases, and climate changes. Heirloom seeds always produce fruit and vegetables that are true to type. Hence, the tomato you pick today from a heritage (or heirloom) plant has the same genetic code that your great-grandma harvested before World War II (give or take a few beneficial mutations as it continually adapts to the environment). We can save the seeds of an heirloom without fear of unpredictable results. And that's why they're so important: preservation of species.

All this talk is about preserving biodiversity, but why is preserving biodiversity so essential? Well, when you only focus on cultivating one variety of fruit and vegetables and have fields upon fields of the same crop type, it only takes a little to destroy an entire harvest and wipe out a whole country's food supply. For example, the Irish potato famine led to the death of a million people because their primary food source was compromised. They grew one variety of potatoes (Irish Lumpers), and the yield succumbed to a blight.

That's the problem with putting all your eggs in one basket; it topples easily and leaves you with no backup plan.

FINDING AND SELECTING HEIRLOOM SEEDS

Heirloom seeds are known because they taste better, have better nutritional value, and are hardy. And yes, buying heirloom seeds to fill up your entire garden can be expensive (unless you inherited some from your parents or grandparents). Still, if having heirloom varieties in your garden is something you want, the investment is worth it.

You can get heirloom seeds or even seedlings from your area if you have reputable garden stores. But research where they get their seeds and ensure they're chemical-free. Also, farmer's markets, garden centers, and seed swap communities are all fantastic options for sourcing heirloom seeds.

Getting seeds in or around your area (non-commercially) is the best-case scenario since that's your best chance to ensure the seeds (or seedlings) are locally sourced and grown. Plus, they've adapted to the climate you reside in.

Otherwise, you can order the heirloom seeds online or through catalogs. Just do your research and make sure whatever website you buy them from is legitimate. Here are a few examples of trustworthy websites that sell quality heirloom seeds at great prices:

- True Leaf Market
- Baker Creek Heirloom Seeds
- Seed Savers Exchange
- Eden Brothers
- Select Seeds

You should do extensive research and decide beforehand what type of heirloom fruits and veggies you want to grow, how many varieties you want, and their requirements and maturing times.

Don't be afraid to experiment with unique varieties—did you know there's a variety of purple tomatoes? No one said gardening has to be boring. I encourage you to go after unconventional fruit and vegetable varieties since this choice will do even more to preserve genetic diversity.

Now you know where to find heirloom seeds, but what do you look for or consider when selecting them? Besides looking for the word "heirloom" or the abbreviation OP, which stands for open-pollinated (which may not be heirloom at the time of purchase, but they *can* eventually become heirloom in your garden), most of it is personal preference. However, some limitations might prevent you from growing your desired plants. The space you have available, the amount of sunlight your garden gets, your specific climate, and existing companion guilds that might be negatively impacted by certain plants will shorten your choices for heirlooms.

The most crucial factor is whether the seed will fit your needs or goals. Don't plant something you don't want or that doesn't benefit you or your garden.

A pro tip: don't wait until spring is knocking on your door to purchase heirloom seeds because the best varieties sell out quickly, and if you wait until May, you might miss out on the ones you had in mind. You can stock up on seeds months or years in advance if you store them properly.

To store your purchased heirloom seeds, you can remove them from the original packaging and place them in an air-tight container with a packet of silica gel (which will absorb any moisture). Keep the container in a cool, dark place or the freezer for long-term storage. Label them with the proper information (year collected, date stored, and variety).

GROWING HEIRLOOM PLANTS

For the most part, growing heirloom plants are like growing any other plant. The requirements are typically the same. The only difference is you will get attached to your heirlooms—of all your plants in your garden, you don't want your heirlooms to die.

As mentioned before, you need to choose the variety of heirloom vegetables carefully based on the climate you're in and the conditions of your garden. Know your soil type and quality (or grow your heirlooms in containers or raised garden beds so you have complete control over this aspect), and consider the unique or beneficial traits you need or want and research which variety has them (hint: pick those!).

Remember that no plant (no matter its lineage) is resistant to all diseases. You still need to practice good gardening hygiene, crop rotation, soil management, and cover cropping to prevent diseases from wreaking havoc on or destroying all of your hard work.

Using organic mulch (and fertilizer) and knowing how to water your garden correctly and consistently will prevent fungal diseases, root rot, and a host of other issues from occurring. Supporting your plants with stakes or trellises where necessary is also a good idea. Furthermore, you should monitor your plants regularly for pests and signs of potential health problems and deal with them before they spread or kill the plant. The best cure for diseases or pests is prevention, and you can do this by using pest-repellent plants or other natural methods.

If you find dead or diseased plants, remove them immediately and sterilize all your garden tools. Overcrowding your garden will also contribute to diseases and pests and might cause plants to under-produce and die. Stick to the recommended spacing distances and bear in mind the root systems of your crops.

Some garden produce (like lettuce, spinach, and other tender crops) are best eaten shortly after harvesting. Please feel free to harvest all fruits and vegetables at once; instead, harvest and use or eat them as needed. This method is also why you should space out germination and planting (succession planting) so that everything isn't ripe and ready for picking simultaneously.

Allow the produce to ripen before you pick them to ensure you get the best flavor. Remember to allow some fruit and vegetables from different (healthy) plants to become overripe on the plant so you can save those seeds for next year!

HEIRLOOMS AND COMMUNITY

What do you get when people with similar goals come together? A community. Seed saving doesn't have to be something you do alone. It's far more fulfilling and helpful if you do it in unity as part of a much larger circle of passionate individuals.

Before people bought seeds in supermarkets, they were traded and swapped between communities and neighbors. Keeping that sense of community alive is essential, not only because it brings people together but also because it keeps the practice alive. It circulates the knowledge of how to do it so future generations can continue the legacy of saving seeds. It enables local gardeners and smaller agricultural centers to swap seeds instead of buying them.

Seed saving, swapping, and passing down heirloom seeds to your children keep the culture alive and enrich the stories connected to these seeds. Even if you're not interested in a seed that dates back to the 1800s, you must admit it's pretty cool to think about every-thing this plant's lineage has been through, the different hills and backyards it grew on, and what it survived. If only plants could talk!

And you can be part of that history, too. You can become part of a community that helps and supports one another in a collective mission, even if your main goal is to have great-tasting (or interesting-looking) lettuce and tomatoes for your garden salad.

REMEMBER

Your gardening objective is unique to you. No rule says you need to grow heirlooms, but you have to admit the benefits of doing so are undeniable. You get to help the environment, preserve the variety for future generations, and enjoy superior quality fruits and vegetables. You become part of the already rich history and can pass the seeds down and tell the stories to your children or grandchildren.

Heirlooms are an essential aspect of gardening. In a way, it's less effort than buying and growing hybrid seeds every year because you can save the seeds, swap or sell them, or expand your garden when you're ready and able to do so.

In either event, there's a lot more to saving seeds and how to do it properly so you don't risk the integrity of (or accidentally killing) the seed. In the next chapter, we will detail how to store seeds for both the short and long term.

3

SEED PRESERVATION 101

At the risk of sounding a bit dramatic, seed saving is like preserving or capturing time in a bottle to experience in the future. But if you're going to do it, it needs to be done correctly. In this chapter, we go into more detail about storing seeds, including why it's important, the different methods, testing viability, tools you'll need, how to avoid common mistakes, and more.

WHY PRESERVATION IS KEY

To a gardener, nothing is quite as fulfilling as raising a plant from a seed into a thriving and bountiful plant. To continue that lineage with every passing year, they hold a very high regard. It is indeed something to be proud of.

Without the seed, we have no harvest to enjoy. Saving seeds is a way to honor the hard work and dedication of our predecessors in addition to feeding our bodies. It's a commitment to carry on their legacy because a gardener's impact lives on with every passing generation.

Another, and perhaps more important, reason why the preservation of seeds is essential is what's known as "domestication." Over the millennia, we've turned plants that were once able to thrive in the wild into plants utterly dependent on us for survival. For example, sweeter and larger fruit-bearing plants survived over plants that could withstand harsh climates. Resilience was less important than a bigger harvest.

Nowadays, domesticated plants can't survive without constant pruning, weeding, and irrigation because that's what we agreed to provide them with thousands of years ago. From a permaculture point of view, seed saving is non-negotiable since the goal is to work with nature instead of against it and to reduce our negative impact on the ecosystem. But we must recognize that it must make sense financially and for personal gain.

Preserving your seeds is an assurance policy. Sometimes, certain seed varieties are in short supply because big corporations corner the market and condense the supply or availability of some varieties (they only keep the most profitable seeds around, and each year, more and more unique varieties are discontinued or aren't worth restocking). Saving and preserving your seeds gives you more control of your supply and varieties and allows you to swap with others.

Preserving your seeds also means you have more control over the quality and quantity of seeds you have at no additional cost. Most importantly, you can decide which seeds to save based on selective breeding and superior traits. Your garden will be stronger and better with each generation of seeds you save.

METHODS OF PRESERVATION

If you're starting with saving your seeds, start conservatively (with only one or two types of crops) and with self-pollinating varieties since they are more likely to bear open-pollinated (or "true to type") seeds instead of hybrid seeds. As for what comes after, here's what you should know.

Cleaning Seeds

Once you've harvested the seeds, you must immediately clean them to remove dirt, dust, and soil residue. You can use a clean, damp towel. Some seeds will require you first to remove seed coatings, shells, husks, pods, gel sacs, pulp, or other forms of plant matter and debris. You can usually use your hands, fingernails, or tweezers.

You need to ensure you know the proper way to clean and process the seeds you have before moving on to drying them.

Drying Seeds

Spread your now clean seeds thinly onto trays (or plates), which you can line with dye-free paper towels, wax paper, parchment paper, or a screen or mesh. Don't use newspaper, as the ink might seep into the seed, reducing its viability or germination rate. Some people use ovens or food dehydrators set to the lowest heat to speed up drying, but this method can potentially damage the seed.

Ventilation and air movement are the safest and most convenient ways to dry your seeds. Stirring the seeds now and then (even if they're spread thinly on the trays) ensures that all the seeds—and all sides of all the seeds—receive thorough ventilation so they dry evenly. If you live in an area where it rains frequently or is always humid, having the seeds stay in front of (or even just in the same room as) an electric fan will prevent them from taking too long to dry (and either growing mold or accidentally germinating).

The optimal moisture content in seeds for storage is between 5% and 10%. However, since the typical home gardener will need more resources or tools to measure this percentage, it usually takes one to three weeks. You'll know when the seeds are properly dried when they're hard and don't give when squeezing them, bend, or leave an indent when pressing your fingernail into them (this test is called the fingernail test).

Controlling and Monitoring Storage Conditions

During seed storage, you must avoid four things: moisture, air, warmth, and light. Humidity and warmth can both result in rehydration of the seed (causing mold or bacteria growth or premature germination in storage). In contrast, air and light will cause the seed to deteriorate quickly ("expire" or lose viability sooner than usual).

Seeds do best when stored between 32°F and 50°F, but it's even more important to keep the temperatures as constant as possible (no sudden temperature spikes or drops). If you're storing them in fridges or freezers, they should be in ones that aren't going to open regularly.

Furthermore, it would be best to store seeds in air-tight packaging (such as opaque plastic or glass jars, resealable plastic bags, aluminum foil packets, or paper envelopes) away from sunlight. Additionally, you can make use of silica gel, charcoal, or rice to minimize and control the humidity levels inside the containers, as well as cushioning material (crumpled-up paper towels or cloth) so the seeds don't get damaged by smacking into each other or the sides of the container.

Short or Long Term Solutions

For short-term storage (less than two or three years), you can keep the seed containers refrigerated or in a dark, cool cupboard or closet if you live in a cooler climate. You may freeze them for long-term storage (more than three years). If you plan on storing the seeds for over three years, consider investing in a vacuum sealer to seal your seeds before freezing. Remember to label them appropriately.

Storing your seeds in a fridge or freezer is unnecessary, but it helps keep the conditions consistent when your climate is unpredictable. Not to mention, bacteria and mold are much less likely to grow on your seeds if you store them in the fridge or freezer. As long as your seeds are thoroughly and properly dried and in airtight containers, they only stand to benefit from this storage method.

You'll also want to check in on your storage environment now and then (once or twice a month at least) to ensure the containers or bags are still intact, no light is getting to them, and the temperature and other storage factors are staying consistent.

Monitor Viability

It's essential to keep in mind that some seeds have a very short life expectancy or "shelf-life," meaning they can only be stored for a few months at most before they deteriorate (examples of seeds with short expiration dates include chives, onions, garlic, leeks, parsnips, and turnips). However, when stored properly, most seeds have three to five years of shelf life.

Seeds with a medium to extended life expectancy, like brassicas, cucumber, tomatoes, melons, and pumpkin, can be stored for up to five years. However, germination rates will naturally decline the longer they are stored, so you should test the viability of these seeds every year. You do this by taking a sample of seeds (a minimum of 10) out of storage, letting them come to room temperature, and rehydrating them. An effective way to rehydrate your seeds is to soak them in water overnight before placing them between a folded paper towel (to keep them moist). Then, place the paper towel in a Ziploc bag and leave it somewhere humid (I find the kitchen works well for this process).

To avoid having to remove an entire container of seeds from their proper storage conditions (and potentially contaminating them by opening up the container and exposing them to humidity or pathogens) to acquire a sample, you can isolate and sort all seeds into groups of ten by using smaller Ziploc bags within a more extensive, labeled container.

Using a sample of 10 seeds to test viability makes math simple. Every seed represents 10%. So if, for example, all ten seeds sprout, the germination rate is 100%, but if only four sprouts, it's 40%. As a general rule of thumb, you want to discard stored seeds if the germination rate for that "batch" is lower than 50% since this percentage could indicate the seeds are either too old, have genetic defects, or were stored under improper conditions (which might negatively affect the longevity, production, and hardiness of the plants in that specific group of seeds).

Tools You'll Need

Before you panic and think you'll have to make an expensive trip to the garden store, most of the things you need for harvesting and storing seeds you might already have or will easily be able to substitute or make yourself for way cheaper.

Here's a detailed list of everything you need to harvest, process, and store seeds:

- Blossom bags: Blossom bags are necessary if you're tight on space and need help isolating self-pollinating crop varieties by the appropriate distances. Blossom bags prevent similar crops from cross-pollinating; if you plan to save the seeds, you can't have them cross-pollinating. You can substitute blossom bags for tulle fabric and string or mesh party favor bags (the ones with the drawstrings). You cover the flower before it opens in spring and remove it once the flower petals fall off or you see its setting fruit. Remember that this method only works on plants that self-pollinate (but still risk cross-pollination). You'll have to hand-pollinate plants that require open pollination.
- Tape or ribbon: Use these items to mark fruits that have been hand-pollinated or isolated with blossom bags so you know which fruits (and therefore which seeds) are for sure open-pollinated and will grow back true to type.
- Scissors or pruners: These items are needed to harvest overripe fruit off the plant before processing the seeds. Some fruits or flowers might have no problem parting with their mothers with a gentle tug; however, you can damage the plant if you have to put some force into every fruit or flower you harvest.
- Gloves, knives, and tweezers: You might have to remove seeds from inside fruit, husks, pods, or shells after they dry. Gloves prevent you from getting cuts or splinters when cracking open dried seed coverings, the knife is for cutting

fruit to get to the seed inside, and you can use tweezers for many functions (such as organizing or planting tiny seeds or seedlings and removing plant matter that's stuck to the seeds).

- Cloth: Use a cloth to clean the seeds. A wipe-down is typically sufficient for cleaning seeds in flower heads or pods.
- Containers: Mason jars work perfectly for some seeds that require fermentation before drying, but you can also use old plastic containers. You'll also need containers (glass or plastic jars or sealable plastic bags) that seal air-tight for storing the seeds after drying them. Paper bags also come in handy when extracting seeds from flower heads (this information will make sense later on). Utilize paper envelopes for seeds that aren't going to be stored long-term.
- Trays and liners: Wax or parchment paper works best to prevent seeds from sticking to the tray and aid in helping them dry uniformly. But you can also use paper towels to line the trays (bear in mind the seeds might get stuck to the paper towel, and you'll need to loosen them and replace them once or twice during the drying process). And, of course, you'll need trays for spreading the seeds thinly and evenly. However, you can substitute trays with old, paper, or serving trays you no longer use.
- Labels, pens, or markers: You'll need to label the seed containers with the date harvested, variety, life expectancy, and other helpful information before storage.
- Silica gel packets: This item is one of the very few things on the list that you might have to buy. Silica packets help keep moisture away from stored seeds, preserving them better for extended periods. The great thing about them is they're reusable, so you only need to buy them once. However, you can collect them in other purchases; you can

find them in shoes or shoeboxes, medicine bottles, purses, boxes containing electronics, etc. Ask your friends and family if they have any lying around and save them for you.

- Fridge, freezer, or a cool, dark place: You don't have to buy a refrigerator or freezer to use specifically for your seeds, but it does help to think of where you're going to store your seeds so they don't get disturbed too much or risk exposure to something they shouldn't (air, light, moisture, or warmth). This location can be at the back of a cool, dark cupboard or drawer if you live in a colder climate or a separate bar fridge or freezer that you use sparingly.

The following list includes things you don't necessarily need, but that would undoubtedly make your life a whole lot easier, especially if you're processing a lot of seeds for storage:

- Seed sieves or screens: These items will help you separate seeds from foliage, husks, or other types of debris instead of doing it manually (which can be quite labor-intensive and time-consuming if you need to debride hundreds of seeds). However, you can make your seed sieve or screen— there are plenty of resources and step-by-step video guides online. Just calculate the prices of the materials and see whether making one yourself will be more cost-efficient than simply buying one. Also, remember that making one (or investing in a well-made one) will most likely be better quality and last longer than buying an inexpensive one. This decision is totally up to you and what you need.
- Electric fan: Again, unless you're in a warm, humid, or rainy climate, a fan is optional. However, it will decrease the drying time needed and ensure sufficient ventilation. A

fan is a good investment here to speed up the process and leave no room for error (mold or germination).

Seeds well-stored in a garden half-planted. There's nothing quite as demotivating and disappointing as putting all your time and effort into harvesting, processing, and storing your seeds to realize the following year (or the next time you plant them) that none of them are viable anymore—or discovering that your next generation of seeds lost their vigor and aren't growing as fast or producing as much as their predecessors.

THE IMPORTANCE OF PROPER STORAGE

How you store your seeds will affect the seed's genetic integrity, quality, and viability. That's why proper storage conditions for seeds are so vital. It's also an insurance policy. Some leftover seeds from a previous, bountiful season or harvest can supplement a current, underperforming one.

Then there's the fact that you save money because you don't need to keep re-buying seeds every year, and you have a better idea of what to expect from the harvest if you know how the parent plants performed. However, all the benefits of seed storage depend on the seed storage conditions. If you're not vigilant, you risk losing or damaging your entire seed bank.

To reiterate, seeds' germination rate and vigor naturally decline over time, no matter how good your storage conditions are. The point of these rather precise seed storage guidelines is to retain the germination rates of the seeds for as long as possible and to ensure the overall quality of the resulting plant and yield in the future.

There are a few things to keep in mind that will ensure seeds survive both short and long-term storage:

- Mature seeds will retain their viability longer than immature ones will.
- The hard shell or coating of the seed increases the amount of time the seed can last in storage (though probably not far beyond its inherent shelf life).
- The colder the better. It would be best to store seeds in a refrigerator or freezer.
- If a seed is severely damaged before storage (if it's nicked or scratched, for example), it will likely not survive very long. A broken seed is not viable at all.

Containers

The containers you use to store the seeds in have a few straightforward objectives: to keep moisture, light, and pests out and to keep the seeds in. However, the type of container you choose will depend on how long you want to store the seeds. It would be best to use only particular containers for short-term storage; others will keep the seeds safer for longer.

For very short-term storage (a couple of months up to a year, maximum), you can get away with using paper envelopes. For several months and up to two years, Ziploc bags or plastic containers will do great. For multiple years (three or more), glass containers like Mason jars or metal tins work best (as long as they're air-tight).

Optimal Conditions

The conditions for storage help slow the aging process of the seed down. The most crucial factor is that the temperatures shouldn't fluctuate too much or too quickly. Keeping the temperature consistent is more important than keeping it cool. So, a temperature range from 50°F to 60°F is optimal versus a range of 10°F to 40°F.

Recommendations to stick to specific temperature ranges differ depending on your source or who you ask. Still, a general rule of thumb is that the temperature (in Fahrenheit) and the relative humidity shouldn't exceed 100 when combined. For example, if the temperature in storage is 60°F, the humidity levels should be below 40%. However, this rule usually applies if you're storing your seeds under room temperature conditions (in a dark cupboard or drawer).

Additionally, it would be best to keep your seeds dry and away from light.

Cataloging

There is some information regarding your seeds that will come in handy. Adequate labeling and organizing saves more time and effort than it takes to maintain. Therefore, each packet or container of seeds needs a label that contains clear, accurate, relevant, and helpful information to avoid potential identification problems in the future.

The helpful and relevant information might not need to be as detailed as the next seed-saving gardener. It depends on the size and complexity of your garden and what you plan to do with the seeds. What I mean by this information is that a person with a more miniature garden who mainly saves seeds for personal use won't need as detailed labels as someone with a large garden with many varieties and who shares seeds with the community.

With that information in mind, here's all the information you want on your labels whether you're a small or large-scale seed saver:

- Name of the species and variety (or the common name if you don't have many varieties).
- Source: where did you acquire the seed from? Personal garden, store-bought, swapped, etc.
- Harvest date (preferable), received, or bought.

Now, if you do want to add more detail to your labels if only to make your life easier, you can do so by adding some of the following information (if you think it will be helpful) in addition to those mentioned above:

- Short description of the physical or biological characteristics (drought or pest-resistant, for example).
- Requirements (sun, water, soil type preferred, etc.).
- Days to maturity (how long it takes to grow into a mature plant from sowing or germination).
- Germination rate.
- Season or months you should plant them in (and if you should germinate them inside beforehand).
- Number of seeds.

If there are too many seeds to count or tiny seeds, weighing them might help with this step. An easy way is to count out 10-100 (depending on their size) and determine their weight. Use the following formula to determine how many seeds you have:

Even number of seeds = X grams

X grams ÷ specific amount of seeds = weight per seed

Weight of all seeds ÷ weight per seed = total seeds

For example, you count and weigh ten pumpkin seeds. The weight of 10 seeds is 2 g. That means every seed weighs about 0.2 g (2 g ÷ 10 seeds). Now, you weigh all your seeds and divide that by the weight of one seed. Let's say all the pumpkin seeds you have weigh 120 g. 120 g ÷ 0.2 = 600. You have 600 pumpkin seeds in total.

As far as how to organize your seeds, there are a few ways you can sort or catalog them so they're easily accessible and arranged functionally. You can sort them alphabetically by name, type, variety, or planting season.

Sorting seeds alphabetically is the least practical way. But who am I to interfere with your system if it works for you? Alphabetically organizing seeds will require another, more detailed way of keeping track of which seeds need to be taken out of storage and sown at what times. You'll likely need to go through your entire collection every few months to find what you're looking for or need.

Sorting by type or variety isn't that much better, either. Sure, you'll know exactly where to find the broccoli or tomatoes, but it still doesn't provide a straightforward sense of what seeds you need to plant next.

The best way to sort seeds is by planting season. There's an apparent differentiation when spring, summer, and fall crops are separated. For starters, it's a much smaller amount to rummage through for the next season, and you can make it even easier by further organizing each seasonal category.

In other words, you can sort all the seeds for every season so that the seeds that need propagating first are in front. This method requires a lot less additional organization and keeping track of. When you open up your seedbox, fridge, or freezer, keep the seeds that need to be planted or propagated for the next season in the very front.

Also, make a spreadsheet to keep track of your seeds by listing each seed variety, the number of packets you have, how many seeds per packet (and in total), and the year obtained (and preferably month). Any other information that will help you know your seed collection inside and out can also be added, such as "expiry" or sowing dates. Keep the inventory updated whenever you remove or add seeds, and closely monitor the viability dates.

Organizing System

If you're going to put this much love and dedication into something, you have to see it through and do it right from start to finish. Knowing how to set up a well-organized seed storage system that is guaranteed to keep your seeds healthy, safe, and accounted for is just as crucial as preserving them beforehand.

Regarding the organizational side of seed saving, you need to find a system that works for you. Simple and functional are the keywords. It won't benefit you if your system is too time-consuming or expensive to maintain.

Organizing your seeds includes keeping track of your seed inventory. You need to know how many types of seeds you have, how many of each variety you have, the harvest date, when you're planning on planting them, and when they need to be used (life expectancy). The goal of your system is to maintain the seeds, planting the oldest seeds first and keeping track of how many seeds you have so you're aware of when it's time for planting again.

This process can be as simple as a notebook and proper labeling. You can also implement strategies like dividing the seeds into categories, using large plastic storage containers (placing new seeds at the bottom and the oldest seeds on top), having a separate holding area for seeds you're planting soon, and notes on crop rotations.

COMMON SEED PRESERVATION PITFALLS

As time passes, you've likely experienced the magic of gardening first-hand. It happens when holding a seedling, harvesting fruit, or simply admiring new growth. You didn't think it was possible to attach this to plants, seedlings, or seeds, but here we are. When you put so much time, energy, and care into your garden, it would be strange not to get attached (even though the average, garden-less person won't understand it).

You've withstood the trials and tribulations of being a beginner gardener, or maybe you're still going through this phase and learning as you go. I want to reassure you that it's okay to make mistakes—overcoming challenges is life's most motivating and educational thing. But it's also perfectly normal and rational to want to avoid running into them. So here are the biggest and most common mistakes people make when starting their seed-saving journey (and how to avoid them):

Saving Hybrid Seeds

Hybrid seeds will most likely either be infertile or result in a mutated plant or produce. Hybrid plants *can* stabilize and result in a new species or variety. Still, this process takes years of adapting, effort, careful selection, and saving seeds over many generations (and failed attempts). Listen, if your life goal is to make a new type of strawberry that's bigger, sweeter, and tie-dyed, don't let me stop you from following your dreams. But the risk and effort aren't worth it if you're gardening to feed yourself or your family.

Not Separating Similar Varieties

You can cross-pollinate plants with similar varieties (in the same family tree). For example, "Sweet Million" and "Sungold" are both varieties of cherry tomatoes. While tomato plants are self-fertile, they can still cross-pollinate if not separated by distance or isolation (blossom bags). You may still get delicious, edible cherry tomatoes, but the resulting fruit will carry hybrid seeds.

Always research the proper isolation distance (which is not 100% fail-safe, by the way) for the varieties you're planning on growing, or take the time to isolate your crops manually—or at least a few flowers on each plant so you can save those seeds without the risk of saving hybrid seeds.

Not Planting Enough of the Same Variety

To preserve genetic diversity and prevent gene bottlenecking, you need to grow enough of the same variety of plants. Otherwise, your plants' genetic stability will eventually deteriorate, resulting in weak, ill, and low-producing plants.

The number of plants of the same variety needed to prevent this from happening depends on the array itself. For example, beans need around 20 plants, while corn needs a minimum of 200 plants to prevent genetic bottlenecking. I advise planting as many plants of the same variety as you can and saving some of those seeds. Then, every other year or so, introduce new genetic variation into your garden by buying the same variety of seeds (or swapping them) from a trusted source and adding a few of those into your garden so they can pollinate each other.

Not Storing Seeds Properly

This problem can include not following the proper steps or procedures beforehand or simply not ensuring the conditions for storage are favorable and consistent. But it can also include not keeping your seeds away from potential pests like rats or mites that can eat or contaminate them. That's why I always recommend glass jars for seed storage (especially if you live in an area where pests are a known issue)—they do a great job of keeping pests out of your seed stashes.

IN SUMMARY

You might only need some of the tools we mentioned in this chapter. Consider your gardening and seed-saving goals before you run out and buy things you don't need. From those goals, you can list tools you will use and need. For example, if you only plan on growing one variety of fruit and vegetables in your garden because you have limited space, you won't need blossom bags.

Seed saving and all the steps and considerations surrounding it can be time-consuming and overwhelming at first. But the steps are there for a reason. The main things to keep in mind are:

- allow the fruit to become overripe on the plant, just to be safe
- collect the seeds
- clean the seeds
- dry the seeds
- package and label the seeds
- store the seeds in proper conditions
- maintain a simple but efficient system of organization
- test the germination rates every year

- introduce new seeds every other year for genetic variation (not necessary for all crops)

Keeping your seeds organized and stored under the proper conditions is vital to retain their germination rates and vigor. In the next chapter, we'll go into more detail on exactly when and how you should harvest seeds so you can be sure you're saving only the best for the next season.

Now that the technicalities are out of the way and you have a better idea of setting up a system that will work for you, we're moving on to bigger things. And by more significant things, I mean big, juicy yields and how to harvest the best seeds!

4

HARVESTING SEEDS LIKE A PRO

Harvesting seeds sounds pretty simple. You pick the seeds; what more is there to do? Well, harvesting seeds is like a treasure hunt for a seed-saving enthusiast. And there's a lot more to it than you might think. Every plant is different, and their seeds are unique, with varied requirements for harvest to give them the best chance at reaching full maturity (and therefore withstanding storage) and resulting in a better next generation.

WHAT YOU'LL NEED

Depending on the crop type you plan on growing, you might only need some things listed here. But to avoid potential injuries (to you or the plant), here's a list of tools you'll need when harvesting seeds:

- Gloves: Protection from potential thorns and spikes to protect you from skin-irritating plants, insect bites, or being cut by leaves or stems.

- Eye protection: You can protect your eyes with items like clear goggles. The last thing you want is to have plant debris stuck in your eye for days, trust me.
- Scissors or pruners: Use these tools to cut stems and seed heads to avoid harming the plant by harshly pulling on it.
- Nutcrackers: If you're growing nuts or need to crack open hard shell coverings or husks, you'll need them.
- Trays, buckets, or bags: Essential for collecting your seed harvest and drying them out.

WHEN TO HARVEST

Timing is everything. One thing all plants have in common regarding harvesting seeds is that it's best to leave the fruit on the plant until it shows signs of being overripe. This stage will look different in each type of crop. For example, peppers shrivel, tomatoes go soft and squishy, and pea or bean pods dry out and turn brown.

A rule you can follow here is that if you need clarification on whether the fruit is ripe enough, leave it on the plant for a few more days. Also, fruit dropping off the plant by themselves indicates that the seeds have reached maturity and are ready to be collected, processed, and stored.

There's some nuance involved in harvesting seeds from different types of crops, such as annuals, biennials, perennials, and self-incompatible crops. Let's first discuss what these different classifications mean.

Annual Crops

Annuals (as you might already know) are plants that don't grow back after winter. Instead, they die off and must be re-sowed or replanted yearly. Self-fertile (or self-pollinating) crops are the easiest to save seeds from. This simplicity is especially true if you only have one type or variety of each plant because the likelihood of accidental cross-pollination (and, therefore, getting hybrid seeds) is rare in self-fertile plants.

This method is where you'll save the most money when it comes to gardening since saving your annual seeds will result in you not having to buy them yearly. As with all seed harvesting, you should allow the fruit and seed to ripen or become overripe on the plant. You can even wait for the plant to turn brown before retrieving the fruit and seeds, though this step isn't necessary.

Self-pollinating crops are known to be the easiest to grow in your home garden. A few examples of self-pollinating annuals you might want to grow in your garden and save seeds from include tomatoes, peppers, lettuce, eggplant, peas, and beans.

Biennial Crops

Biennials are crops that will stay alive for two years and typically won't flower or produce fruit or seeds in the first year. And even if they do show signs of flowering prematurely (within the first year), it's typically advised to pinch or cut these buds off so the plant's energy goes towards establishing the plant in the first year, which results in a much better yield in the second year.

The most apparent issue with biennials is you don't get a yield or any seeds to save for a whole year. That is why, if you want seeds every year from your biennials, you should plant a handful of them every year. This method means that, yes, in the first year, you'll have no seeds to save, but after that, you'll have a loop system where you have fruit and seeds every year. Let me explain:

- First year: You plant the first batch of seeds, and those seeds develop and become established for a whole year. There will be no seeds or produce to harvest this year.
- Second year: You plant another batch of seeds to develop over the next year. The first batch of biennials starts flowering and producing fruit. Once the fruit from the first batch of biennials is ready for harvesting, you can save some seeds. The first batch of biennials starts to die off over the next few months.
- Third year: You plant another batch of seeds to grow and develop over the next year. The second batch of seeds starts flowering and producing fruit and seeds, after which they will die off.
- Repeat this process, planting new seeds yearly and harvesting from last year's crops.

If this process sounds too complicated, or you need more space, save as many seeds as possible from a single harvest every other year. Some common examples of biennial crops are carrots, onions, beets, garlic, and parsley.

Perennial Crops

Perennials are plants with long life spans (more than two years) and do not fall under the classification of trees or shrubs. Perennials might go through a cycle where the plant is inactive in the off-season (usually during the winter), but they come back and produce flowers, fruit, and seeds every year in continuation.

You can aim for a garden with primarily perennial crops and a few annual crops. This strategy reduces the time and effort you need to propagate or sow seeds.

Examples of perennials include strawberries, blueberries, asparagus, chives, mint, and some spinach varieties.

Self-Incompatible Crops

A plant is self-incompatible when it can't be fertilized by itself, not even if it is hermaphroditic (it has both male and female parts on the same plant or flower). This classification means the plant can recognize when fertilized with its pollen and outright reject it. This distinction prevents inbreeding (a loss of genetic variety) and encourages environmental adaptation.

A self-incompatible plant will produce fruit (and therefore seeds) if exposed to pollen from a different plant (of the same variety). In layperson's terms, you need more than one of the same variety of plants to acquire a successful yield.

Most brassicas, such as cabbage, cauliflower, and broccoli, are self-incompatible along with certain other types of fruit, such as pineapples, cherries, citrus fruits, and apples.

HARVESTING FLOWER SEEDS

The key to a thriving garden is adding flowers that attract pollinators and predatory insects (which helps with pest control). You'll also want to save seeds from these plants (even if you only plant perennial flowers such as yarrow or coneflowers).

Harvesting seeds from flowers is a different process than harvesting seeds from fruit. However, it's not difficult at all. You can reap most flower seeds by allowing the flower to dry before clipping it off and shaking it upside down into a paper bag. The seeds should come loose and drop into the bag with minimal effort. If they don't, it usually means the flowers have yet to dry out enough.

Some flower seeds, such as sunflower and calendula seeds, need to be soaked in water for a few days before being dried again (for one to three weeks) for storage.

Seeds are plant embryos, so thinking of the seed-collecting process as collecting tiny gifts of nature is accurate. Many techniques make harvesting these pre-plant babies easy and time-efficient. Some seeds are more straightforward to harvest than others, but once you acquire the knowledge, you can collect seeds like a pro.

BASIC METHODS OF SEED COLLECTION

You'll likely get away with some basic approaches to harvesting seeds for most of your crops. In nature, seeds must fall when the time is ready without much struggle, so a future generation is unavoidable.

In general, seeds from annual crops are more straightforward to harvest than perennials. This statement is accurate because perennial seeds have the luxury of time for the husk or pod to break down before the seeds germinate (usually after being in the soil for several seasons or even years). Meanwhile, with annuals, the seeds need to be readily available so that when the fruit drops to the ground, it will grow a new plant by the following year.

This urgency is also why perennial seeds are more challenging to grow than annuals. Most perennial seeds need to go through specific conditions before they germinate—spending winters in frozen soil, being pecked at, or even being eaten and expelled by animals. These processes break down oils and wax coatings, softening hard shells that inhibit germination. This exposure ensures the seed germinates when the external conditions are just right.

The following basic seed collection techniques can work for both annual and perennial crops:

Hand-Picking

This one is self-explanatory. The process is manual, whether you're picking pods, heads, or the seed itself right from the plant. You already do this with your fruits and veggies if you have a home garden. It's the most basic and straightforward way to gather seeds.

Shaking or Beating

This technique can go hand-in-hand with hand-picking (no pun intended). When it comes to seed capsules and heads, the seed in them will require some form of dislodgement before you can dry and store them. Shaking or beating ripe seed heads over a tarp or large container is efficient. However, this method is best for crops where seeds simultaneously mature since you risk dislodging immature seeds with this method.

A few examples of common garden crops and flowers that hold their seeds in seed heads or capsules include dill, coriander, lettuce, most brassicas or mustard varieties, carrots, onions, coneflowers, marigolds, and alliums.

Threshing

This technique separates seeds from other plant material like stalks, stems, leaves, husks, and even what's left over from seed heads and pods. The harvested plant material containing the seeds is dried before the threshing begins. You can carefully crush seed pods and heads to expose the seeds. You can thresh seeds attached to stems or surrounded by leaves by pulling the stalks through a fork or metal comb.

Threshing is less labor-intensive than shaking or beating individual seed heads, especially if you have a lot of seeds to separate. You can separate several common garden crops by threshing the seeds from plant material, including soybeans, lentils, chickpeas, and sunflowers.

Winnowing

Winnowing is typically the next step after threshing. Once you've released all the seeds from their pods, heads, and capsules or separated them from unusable plant material, the seeds are still typically mixed in with a decent amount of debris. Winnowing is the process of isolating the seeds from everything else. A simple way to do this is to take a handful of your debris and seed mixture, drop it from a few feet above a tarp or large container, and allow the wind to blow through it. The heavy seeds will fall straight down (back onto the tarp or into the large container) while the dry, light plant material will blow away.

To make this process more efficient, or if the wind is lacking, you can use an electrical fan to help things along. It would help if you did this work outside; otherwise, you'll be sweeping up dust and plant debris around the house for weeks.

HARVESTING DIFFICULT SEEDS

As mentioned, most seeds in your garden will be easy to harvest or collect, but some of them can be a real pain in the pod if you know what I mean. Some seeds are incredibly tiny, which makes them harder to harvest and clean (or debride) in preparation for storage.

You must carefully take some seeds out of hard shells or pods, which can lead to physical injuries (to both you and the seed). Some seed heads or pods explode when you break them open. Climbing plants or trees might make the fruit or seeds hard to reach.

Your safety is the most crucial factor when dealing with complex harvesting processes. Here is how to protect yourself from getting hurt when harvesting seeds:

Wear Protective Clothing

This suggestion includes wearing gardening gloves, long-sleeved pants and shirts, closed-toe shoes, masks, and protective glasses (especially when threshing, winnowing, or breaking open pods or shells). Many plant materials can irritate, cut, scratch, or even cause allergic reactions (or rashes) on your skin. Not to mention, there might be thorns or small insects that can bite or sting you.

Use the Proper Equipment

Continuously pulling on the plant to harvest fruit, vegetables, or seed pods and heads can damage the plant and lead to you being cut or hurt. Use pruners or scissors to cleanly and gently cut the stems to separate the fruit or seed heads from the plant. Always be careful when working with sharp tools to avoid cutting or nicking yourself. Also, remember to sterilize your tools between uses (and intermittently while using them) to protect the plants and yourself from getting or spreading potential infections or diseases.

QUALITY CONTROL

Seeds that are too old, were harvested too early, or are missing a live embryo on the inside will not germinate and grow. It's essential to take the necessary steps to ensure the seeds you save are healthy and viable. There are a few ways you can go about implementing quality control before and during the seed-storing process:

- Initial and ongoing germination tests: you need to perform annual germination tests to ensure optimal storage conditions. However, you should also do an initial germination test beforehand. This method is the most accurate way to determine the germination rate of your seeds. It would be best to take the sample (10 seeds minimum) from the same batch and make it a completely random selection.
- According to the water float test, any seed that floats in water after being harvested is considered a "dead" seed. Meaning it has no embryo inside and is not viable to save. However, while there might be some truth to this belief, it is certainly not trustworthy or accurate for all types of seeds. The water float test is only reliable for certain species of seeds within the legume and mint family.
- Physical inspection: Seeds that appear malformed, moldy, or have already started sprouting are not viable and will likely fail to germinate. It's worth mentioning that a variation in seed color doesn't necessarily indicate a dead or damaged seed, so don't discard those but instead investigate further and isolate them, just to be safe—seeds that are a different color than what's considered normal for a specific plant type might be indicative of a fungal, viral, bacterial, or genetic condition.

WHEN IT COMES TO PLANTING

The entire purpose of this book is to provide you with all the necessary knowledge and information you need to harvest and store your seeds effectively. However, some seeds need some "special treatment" before you sow them; otherwise, the germination rate of those seeds will be poor.

Most seeds enter a dormancy phase after they dry out, which enables us to store them for long periods (and a big reason why thoroughly drying your seeds is such a crucial step in the whole process). However, certain seeds have an inherited dormancy to ensure the seed only germinates when the conditions are just right. This phenomenon provides the plant's survival.

There are two main types of pre-sowing treatments: scarification and stratification. These pre-sowing treatments aim to overcome obstacles preventing some seeds from germinating. These obstacles usually include a state of endogenous dormancy (chemicals and genetic factors that affect the embryo itself, which generally requires cold stratification) or exogenous dormancy (a hard seed coating through which water can't penetrate, which requires scarification).

It's important to mention that scarifying or stratifying a seed must be done before you want to plant or sow the seeds. If you do this step before you store the seed, the seed will likely die during storage.

Scarification

Scarification is usually necessary for seeds that have a thick or waterproof seed coating. Water needs to be able to penetrate the outer layer of the seed before it can germinate. This condition is a form of exogenous dormancy—when conditions outside of the seed embryo prevent germination.

A simple test method is to soak a few in water for at least 24 hours and take a picture right before and after. If the seed doesn't absorb water (it doesn't appear to have increased in size after soaking), it will benefit from scarification.

There are a few ways you can go about scarifying a seed. The most common method is mechanical scarification, using a knife, file, or sandpaper to weaken or break the seed coating so water can penetrate and be absorbed more effectively. This method works best on large seeds, such as seeds from pumpkins, melons, and legumes, since trying to do this with smaller seeds can damage the seed, rendering it unable to germinate.

You can freeze smaller seeds for a few weeks before thawing them again. This step will weaken the seed coat enough or cause micro tears through which water can then penetrate better.

Stratification

Stratification has to do with the characteristics of the embryo itself, meaning that the embryo in the seed contains hormones or growth inhibitors that stay active until certain conditions are present. Sometimes, seeds that require stratification also have a hard seed coating.

Without going into too much of the science behind it, these hormones and growth inhibitors (and often accompanying hard seed coatings) aim to ensure a seed stays protected and doesn't germinate in the middle of winter because a seedling will never survive those conditions.

Summer crop seeds require heat stratification, meaning they germinate better when outdoor temperatures are warmer during summer's first few weeks. This type of stratification involves only sowing your seeds when the weather warms up (and remember to trap that heat using a greenhouse or transparent container).

To cold-stratify your seeds, pop them in the fridge or freezer. Remember that the time that seeds need to be stratified will depend on the species. Some plant seeds only need a week in the refrigerator, whereas others might require three months. It would help if you researched the specific seeds and variety to determine how long the seed needs stratification.

I can say that freezing and thawing seeds seem more effective for improving germination rates than keeping them at a constant fridge-like temperature. Stratifying seeds in the fridge raises the chances of mold growing on them (though the chance of mold in the refrigerator is still much less than in room temperature conditions). Check on your seeds regularly and ensure they're adequately dried.

An easier way to stratify your seeds is to sow them when the weather turns chilly enough and leave them be. This method works best with plants that are familiar with the local climate. However, doing it this way (even though it's less work) gives you less control over the process. It might lead to the seeds sprouting (and immediately dying from the cold) if you sow them too soon, and you also risk pests or rodents eating them.

Hand Pollination

There are a few reasons why you should consider manually pollinating your plants. The first is if your plants are in an area where pollinators can't quickly get to them (inside the house or if you live in an urban area). The second is if you have more than one variety of a particular plant that can cross-breed (for example, you grow chilies and bell peppers in the same gardening space).

Even self-fertile flowers have a chance of cross-pollinating, which can be an issue if you're planning on saving the seeds for next year's crops, if you want to donate them, or if you plan on swapping them out. When saving seeds, the motto is always "Better safe than sorry."

You don't need to hand-pollinate your crops if you're growing a single variety of all your crops. Still, if you have multiple crops in the same family that can cross-pollinate, you must isolate and hand-pollinate self-incompatible varieties. Or you'll at least have to separate, and hand pollinate a few flowers on each plant and save only the seeds from these specific fruits or flowers.

Hand pollination is the act of manually pollinating a flower. And it's easier than you imagine it to be. You only need a small, fluffy paintbrush, knowledge, and practice.

First, a little anatomy lesson: for a plant to be pollinated or fertilized, pollen from the stamen of a male flower needs to reach the pistil of a female flower. You'll need to look up what your specific crops' male and female plants look like so you know where to find the pollen and where to transfer it. Some species of plants can only be male (carrying pollen) or female (containing seeds), meaning you have to have both to get a yield.

The good news is that most crops are hermaphroditic, meaning every flower has both male and female reproductive parts, or every plant contains male and female flowers nearby. These are usually easy to hand pollinate since they require you to shake the entire plant so the pollen falls off the stamen and can float onto any nearby pistil. However, this isn't always the case, as some hermaphroditic flowers are also self-incompatible (like brassicas).

To hand pollinate female flowers, take your paintbrush and dab it on the stamen of a few male flowers before dabbing the loaded brush onto the center of a female flower.

You'll have to take pollen from a different plant for self-incompatible crops. Take broccoli, for instance, which is both a hermaphroditic and a self-incompatible crop (meaning it has male and female flowers but will reject pollen from the same plant). To hand-pollinate crops like broccoli, go around and load your brush with pollen from a different broccoli plant. An example of the strategy I find helpful and easy is as follows:

1. Collect only pollen from plant A.
2. Move to plant B and pollinate all the female flowers before collecting pollen from plant B.
3. Move to plant C and pollinate all the female flowers before collecting pollen from plant C.
4. When you get to the last plant, fertilize it with the previous plant's pollen before collecting pollen and going back to pollinate plant A.

Remember that you'll need to cover your flowers with blossom bags before the flowers even open to prevent cross-pollination. Only take the bag off the flower (or cluster of flowers) you're pollinating by hand and immediately put it back on afterward. Keep the bag on until the plant starts fruiting.

You must thoroughly clean the brush if you're using it on crops within the same family tree (when hand-pollinating broccoli right after you've done the cauliflower, for example). You can do this by wiping it on a clean cloth, but rinsing it under running water is the best option.

REMEMBER

It's important to sterilize your harvesting or gardening tools frequently, especially if you're using them on a plant that looks diseased, pest-ridden, or infected to prevent contaminating healthy plants. Also, to avoid future problems, don't save seeds from plants that look like they might have genetic diseases (or from plants that fail to thrive).

Harvesting seeds comes down to making sure the seeds mature, which is as easy as leaving the fruit or pod attached to the plant for as long as possible. Some seeds also require some extra steps during the harvesting process.

Sowing the Seeds of Knowledge to Save the Seeds of Life

"The best way to predict the future is to create it."

— PETER DRUCKER

Seed saving is an often overlooked area when it comes to gardening guides, but we only have to return to that shocking fact about lettuce varieties to see how important it is. From 500 types of lettuce to just 36 in 80 years! Unless we do something now, this is only going to continue.

As small-scale gardeners, it's hard to imagine that we'd have that much effect simply by saving seeds, but imagine the impact we could have if we all did it. All it takes is a mass commitment to preserving biodiversity, and we can make an incredible difference – and the sheer number of people moving toward sustainable gardening practices is enough to show that the motivation exists. Plus, the benefits to the individual gardener are immense – the money savings alone are enough to convince most people that saving their seeds is the way forward.

However, this is an area that is seldom targeted at gardeners who are new to the practice, and there's quite often an assumption that people know what to do. My goal with this book was to make the practice accessible to anyone, no matter how little they might know about seeds or saving and preserving them effectively. And now, just as a garden relies on its pollinators to spread its seeds, I'd like to ask you for your help in spreading this information – and the good news for you is that it will take you no more than a few minutes.

By leaving a review of this book on Amazon, you'll show new readers where they can find everything they need to know to make a success of seed saving – and you'll inspire them to try it too.

Reviews help readers find the guidance they're looking for, so it's a sure way to spread important information like this.

Thank you so much for your support. It makes a huge difference.

Scan the QR code below

5

SUSTAINABLE GARDENING
THROUGH SEED SAVING

You might not start seed saving with sustainability in mind, but you could take the credit for it anyway. Sustainable gardening and seed saving are more closely connected than expected.

I understand the thought process behind the question, "If everyone doesn't participate and get with the program, how much of a difference am I going to make in the grand scheme of things?" This thought process is also known as environmental apathy. People acknowledge climate change and the need to do things differently. Still, they can't find the motivation to do anything because they're unsure their actions will have any impact, so why bother doing anything?

While it's true that a handful of people living sustainably aren't going to reverse climate change or have a significant impact, this narrative of "I'll do it when everyone else does" isn't exactly helping—two words: double standard.

A decent percentage of the global population has environmental apathy. Imagine if everyone holding onto this mindset went ahead and lived more sustainably anyway. Yes, one person isn't going to make a difference, but what about 10% of 8.1 billion? And that's being liberal—way more people than that think they can't make a difference.

To clarify, I'm not saying all this to make you feel bad for not living sustainably or for doing anything that leaves a carbon footprint. I'm also not saying your goal should be to make your carbon footprint zero. The aim is improvement, making better choices, starting small, and doing your best.

One way you can do that is by looking into permaculture gardening techniques and principles and seeing where it takes you. I want you to remember that we don't have to force the world to live sustainably—we need to convince them it's possible and inspire them.

PERMACULTURE PRINCIPLES

The entire message and cause behind permaculture principles is about caring—not only about all other life forms on this earth but also about our impact on the future and what we leave behind. The only way to ensure the planet takes care of us for generations is for us to take care of it right now. We do that by living a sustainable lifestyle based on the 12 principles of permaculture, which are as follows:

Observe and Interact

Know your planting space inside and out. Know which areas get the most sun, shade, wind, and rain. You'll save so much time and effort if you're not trying to keep plants alive when they're growing in places where they have no business growing in the first place.

Catch and Store Energy

Store and use abundance by catching or redirecting rainwater, pickling or preserving fruits and vegetables so you can enjoy them during winter and even beyond, or investing in a solar system. There are so many ways to utilize naturally occurring energy creatively—all you need to do is think outside the box.

Obtain a Yield

The gardening goal is fresh produce, which means obtaining a good yield. Good planning from the start (and permaculture techniques) will pay off by reducing the maintenance needed in your garden and maximizing your yield's quality and size.

Apply Self-Regulation and Accept Feedback

When something isn't working, your garden will let you know. Your job is to observe and listen to what your garden tells you so you can get to and solve the problem's root cause. Let nature deal with nature; don't try to fight it because you will lose.

Use Renewable Resources and Services

Caring about the future means using resources that replenish themselves. This method ranges from planting perennial crops to composting to building your house so the sun's heat warms it up instead of relying on non-renewable energy sources.

Produce No Waste

Create closed-loop systems wherever you can. Only throw something away if it can't be repaired or reused in some other way. Examples of this strategy are feeding kitchen scraps to worms, using dried grass clippings or weeds for mulch, or repurposing plastic jars for propagating seeds or housing seedlings. Instead of throwing out a broken wooden chair, you can repair it, build an insect house, or make a side table or footstool. And if you can't avoid garnering plastic, use it for as long as possible. I've seen videos online of people making an outdoor area rug with single-use plastic bags. There's always a way!

Design From Patterns to Details

Only plant what your family enjoys eating to reduce waste. Plant your garden in zones based on what makes the most sense (herbs near the kitchen, hardy plants that need little attention further away, crops that prefer shade right next to a building). Map out routes around your garden and use every inch of space as nature would.

Integrate, Don't Segregate

This rule applies not only to your plants but also to your community. Share seeds, abundant produce, and tools amongst your neighbors to build community and encourage self-sufficiency.

Small, Slow Solutions

Permaculture has taught me that you can substitute everything or make yourself from scrap or affordable materials. Don't run to buy expensive or gimmicky tools if you're getting by just fine with what you have now (or if you can substitute or make it yourself).

Value Diversity

By now, you know how important diversity is in your garden. It comes down to placing only some of your eggs in one basket. You will have a more extensive variety of nutrient-dense food, and a diverse garden will be more resilient to pests.

Use Edges and Margins

Maximizing space means using all space you have: balconies, the edges of footpaths or driveways, or that corner of the yard where junk had accumulated for years. Get creative with it.

Respond to Change Creatively

One thing that's for sure in life is change, which can't be more true regarding gardening. The state of your garden can change overnight, even if you pull out all the stops to protect it from pests, wind, rain, hail, snow, and heat waves, so while you should come up with creative reasons to protect your garden, that also includes coming up with creative ways to solve problems.

Living a lifestyle as close to permaculture practices as possible seems extreme, and it can be. Living off the grid is only possible and plausible for some. Remember, even small changes are significant in the grand scheme of things. No matter how small of a step you take with it, it's still a step in the right direction and a good deed for the planet and our future.

THE CONNECTION

We previously discussed how seed saving benefits you and the environment: it makes you more self-reliant, preserves biodiversity and genetic material, saves money, and contributes to food security. And regardless of why you started gardening or saving seeds in the first place, much like a domino effect, it cultivates a sustainability mindset.

Think about it. More than likely, you went into starting a small garden in your backyard with little to no knowledge or experience. You wanted to know more as you've improved at keeping your garden alive. What's the best way to do this? What's the easiest way to do that? How can I keep this from happening again? How can I improve my yield and quality of produce?

You want all the information and to know what to do when challenges inevitably arise. But more than that, you've come to care about your garden and every plant in it. Your gardening journey has led to you appreciating nature more (like it did for me), so you want to do whatever you can to keep your garden alive, happy, and thriving.

Every tiny thing you do has the potential to create massive ripples and carry them to the person next to you. You contribute to more significance and change as you learn and share that knowledge with others.

Seed saving is connected to sustainability because it convinces you that you can make a difference in your life and future generations. It builds your confidence and leads you to conclude that it's easier than you thought. And with every step you take, your mind expands. You become comfortable learning and practicing new skills and ideas and gaining experience through trial and error.

It starts with planting a seed and ends with you doing everything possible to make better choices.

Your Carbon Footprint

Additionally, practicing seed saving reduces your carbon footprint by contributing to growing crops compatible with the local climate. Crops comfortable with the environment need less synthetic input from chemical fertilizers or pesticides.

Not buying seeds or seedlings from a store every year means less emissions and waste. Large-scale seed harvesting, drying, and packaging are possible with machines that produce harmful emissions and by-products. These machines also require maintenance, fuel, humans, etc. Distributing the seeds also involves long-distance transportation. Not only does this make the prices of seeds skyrocket, but it also poisons the environment.

Moreover, seed packaging material (often than not) contains plastic, packaging in flimsy plastic trays that typically break or rip when you're trying to get them out for transplanting (meaning you can't reuse them and end up needing to throw them away). By cutting out the middle man and saving your seeds, you save money and reduce your impact on the planet.

The Environment

Seed saving has a net positive influence on the environment. As mentioned earlier, it promotes biodiversity and resilience, which is incredibly important for us by strengthening our food security and for the future of gardening.

With every generation, your crops emerge stronger, meaning you are less likely to need to use chemical fertilizers and pesticides, and in doing so, you also preserve the health and quality of your soil. You also don't accidentally poison pollinators and predatory insects that visit your garden with nothing but good intentions and a positive impact.

An abundance of local plant foliage also attracts biodiversity in the form of insects and wildlife, which contributes massively to the overall health of your garden (and can act as a natural pest deterrent) and the local environment. A bustling garden is a happy garden.

SUSTAINABLE SEED SOURCES

There might come a time when you want to expand your garden, try a different variety of a specific crop, or build on your seed bank. Of course, getting seeds harvested locally is the best option, but if you need help finding someone to swap seeds with or there's a scarcity of local seed-saving communities in your area, you can still source seeds sustainably.

Source your seeds from reputable, certified organic, non-GMO seed suppliers. Additionally, you can find out if these companies have taken the Safe Seed Pledge or refer to trusted online growing guides for recommendations on the best varieties of crops for your climate or region.

Look up regional seed suppliers. It's better to buy seeds harvested a few towns over than from the store that could've gotten them from the other side of the world. Here's a short list of recommended companies to source your seeds from that all undertake organic and sustainable principles:

- Seed Savers Exchange
- High Mowing Organic Seeds

- Johnny's Selected Seeds
- Peaceful Valley/Grow Organic

SEED SAVING FOR YOU

While we're on sustainability, I want to mention one crucial consideration: your current gardening routine or schedule. If saving your seeds will interfere with your lifestyle, it won't be sustainable because you're likely going to stop doing it.

You need to seamlessly integrate seed saving into your current gardening routine for it to be worth doing. To do this work, you'll need to consider when to harvest the seeds for every crop and when you'll have some extra time to process, preserve, and store all the seeds.

That's why I recommend starting with only a few crops with seeds that are easy to harvest and require little additional effort. For example, if you're already setting aside an entire day for cutting up harvested fruits and vegetables every other week (to preserve, pickle, or freeze), you might rinse the seeds and put them aside to dry. If you're harvesting on a more regular basis, such as every day (so you have fresh produce for dinner), put the seeds aside and return to them when you have a few minutes (maybe while the sauce is simmering) so you can rinse them off and let them dry.

Keep in mind this suggestion is only an example. The best way to stick to something new is to adapt it to your current routine and lifestyle (not the other way around), or at the very least, make small and gradual changes so the process is manageable and sustainable.

By following this strategy, you make seed-saving work and don't need to dip into your minimal free time to keep up with it. Of course, you might have to rearrange your approach if you have a more extensive garden or save many seeds. Please find a way to make it work within your lifestyle and schedule, and play around with routines and time-saving tips until you find the most efficient method.

LEGAL CONSIDERATIONS

A patent grants individuals or organizations property rights to materials, processes, machinery, or improvements to any of the formerly mentioned. This distinction means that companies or individuals can legally prevent (and pursue) anyone who isn't them from making, using, selling, or distributing the product or manufacturing processes that they invented or created.

So, not just seeds that can be patented but also the processing method. There are some restrictions on what can and can't be patented. The methods or materials must be unique or nonobvious, recognizable, and described in clear and definite terms.

Legally, you can't save seeds from patented crop varieties without explicit, documented permission from the patent holder. Nor can you sell or distribute these seeds. Even collecting seeds from plants on public land requires a permit.

To ensure you do everything by the book and prevent potential legal troubles, always verify that an individual or business entity has yet to claim the seeds you buy, receive, and swap. You can do this in a few ways:

Check the Labels or Packaging

Seeds you buy from the store will disclose patent information regarding the specific seed variety. There will usually be something on the packaging like: "Patent [number]" or "Pat. [number]."

If you're looking to plant crops you can save the seeds from, avoid seeds with this information on the packaging.

Talk to Your Distributor

If you're swapping seeds or getting them from anyone who functions independently, ask where their "seed dealer" got them. However, don't just take their word for it. If you plant these seeds, before you harvest and save the seeds, make sure you identify the variety and do some research.

Ask the Internet

You can look up active or pending patents on websites like Patent Public Search, Global Dossier, Patent Application Information Retrieval (PAIR), or look up Patent and Trademark Resource Centres (PTRCs).

Shifting towards a more sustainable and eco-friendly way of living will not happen overnight. There are also a lot of mental obstacles you need to overcome, such as environmental apathy. The mere fact that you're considering saving seeds is a monumental leap in the right direction.

Refrain from overwhelming yourself with the burden of trying to do everything right or always making the right decisions. Start by mastering seed saving, then revisit this topic later; know that you're already coming ahead by saving seeds from your garden.

6

PEST AND DISEASE MANAGEMENT IN SEED SAVING

A happy and healthy garden starts with the seeds you choose to grow. You can prevent future genetic conditions or diseases by ensuring that the seeds aren't affected by them during the growing, harvesting, and preservation process.

PEST AND DISEASE IMPACT ON SEED QUALITY

Seeds growing mold or fungi in storage will significantly affect and, in most cases, destroy the viability of the seed for apparent reasons. But did you know that the plant's health can also affect the quality and resilience of the resulting seed? This outcome occurs because pests and other ailments caused by bacteria or fungi lower the protein content in seeds—and protein is like a building block of life.

It's simple: an unhealthy plant, caused by a genetic defect or external disease, is most likely to produce an ill seed, and a less-than-optimal seed won't grow into a productive plant. If you save seeds from sick plants or try to grow unhealthy seeds, you will start a cycle where every generation becomes weaker and more vulnerable. That reasoning is why you should only save seeds from your best and healthiest crops and get rid of any plants or seeds that look suspicious.

Moreover, a contaminated seed can infect other seeds around them. So, if you store a "bad" seed with other "good" seeds, you risk losing the entire batch. However, this outcome only occurs with external pathogens (like mold, fungi, bacteria, etc.) and not genetic diseases.

Certain fungi that grow on plants and seeds (most commonly grains and nuts) produce what's known as mycotoxins and can lead to adverse health effects like immune deficiency, kidney damage, and even cancer when ingested. Mycotoxins are heat resistant (unless you're heating your food to 500°F, they're still there) and can take years to break down entirely.

Beneficial fungi (mycorrhiza) grow alongside your plant's roots and enhance the plant's nutrient and water intake. Still, it will never rise above ground or negatively affect your plant. So, as a general rule of thumb, if there's any sign of fungi or mold growing on your plants, produce, or seeds, dispose of them immediately (do not compost or mulch with moldy grain and nuts since you run the risk of introducing mycotoxins into the soil and the rest of your garden).

You've probably seen what mold looks like on food (such as fruits and vegetables), but spotting a fungal infection on seeds can be trickier because they're much smaller. Signs of fungi are discoloration and a shriveled or "hairy" appearance.

Pests and Seedborne Diseases

Seedlings are susceptible to many pests, like beetles, worms, slugs, and snails. However, your seeds aren't safe from pests either and are typically the target of insects (like mites, ants, moths, and crickets), rodents, and birds. The important thing is getting to the seed before they do, and proper storage containers will prevent rodents and other pests from getting into the free buffet that is your seed bank.

Seedborne diseases, on the other hand, happen when a seed succumbs to a pathogen (fungi, virus, or bacteria), which carries over to the next generation of plants due to the seed's exposure.

You can prevent pathogens from infecting your seeds by maintaining proper garden hygiene. Keeping your plants healthy and pest-free is the first step to having and saving healthy seeds. To do so, follow basic gardening precautions like:

- You are choosing healthy seeds and plants to start your garden before even getting into seed saving.
- Grow patent-free, disease-resistant, locally adapted (or heirloom) plant varieties.
- Harvesting at the proper time to ensure the seeds are mature.
- Practicing crop rotation yearly and ensuring soil health and quality are up to par.
- Inspect your garden regularly for diseased plants, pest infestations, and weeds, and implement ways to reduce or prevent these issues naturally.
- Keep gardening tools clean and disinfect them between uses.
- You are introducing diversity into your garden concerning plant species and beneficial insects.

- You are only harvesting seeds from healthy plants. Additionally, you can isolate plants you plan on saving seeds from by growing them in pots where you have more control over their exposure.

Since moths, ants, and other garden pests like to feast on seeds, you should be looking for any indication that your fruits or flowers are being eaten alive. Holes in the fruit or hollowed-out seeds can be hard to spot, so inspect the seeds thoroughly.

Timing is another crucial element in harvesting seeds. As previously mentioned, you want to leave the fruit or flowers that carry the seeds attached to the plant for as long as possible. However, if your garden has a pest problem, harvest the fruit or flowers when they're ripe enough. You can add a note on the batch of seeds stating that harvesting was earlier than you would've liked or that pests were present.

Given enough time, anything is possible. If you know rodents or specific pest problems exist in your area, take extra precautions to protect your seeds in storage. Please familiarize yourself with common plant diseases and how to prevent or treat them (and don't save seeds from sick plants). This reasoning is also why you should save more seeds than you think you'll need—if one batch turns out to be infertile (for whatever reason), infected, or mutated, you have more.

Take care of your garden to prevent the common problems, and you'll figure out the rest with patience and experience.

7

COMMUNITY AND SEED SHARING

We had to barter before we used pieces of paper with numbers printed for payment. Even though gold and silver existed, people often traded goods and services with each other because they knew that sharing resources amongst the community was important. Many people didn't have much back then, but they had their skills and a generous, caring community.

If you've ever been part of a close-knit community, you'll know what I'm talking about. Sharing is the whole point. When you share knowledge, skills, and experience, you contribute to and invest in the future. When you share kindness, you're contributing to the strength of the community.

There's a reason why many people feel so fulfilled when they give back to others in the form of charity or kindness. As cliché as it might sound, when you share seeds, you share life.

WHY COMMUNITY IS IMPORTANT

The 2020 pandemic brought the whole world to a screeching, crashing halt. The first few weeks in quarantine were manageable; people were in denial, and the excitement of working from home (for those who could) made everything seem less scary. Of course, the number of lives lost during that time is and was horrific.

Nevertheless, people were coping with the uncertainty and dread. Sleeping in for an extra hour helped with the added stress and uncertainty. But as days of isolation turned into weeks of zero contact with friends and family, people started going a little stir-crazy. Introverts naturally managed to last a bit longer than the average person, but even they got to a point where the lack of socialization became mental torture.

We tried filling the void. Many people picked up old hobbies, started learning new skills, or worked on self-improvement (primarily by prioritizing their physical and mental health). The economic uncertainty that the pandemic brought on incentivized a decent portion of the population to start their home gardens (which was a big reason for the seed shortage during that time). All of that is fantastic!

But the thing is, communication and community are not desires—they're needs. It's a basic human need. It provides us with a sense of belonging and more significant purpose, serves as a source of connectedness and unity, and fosters understanding, support, and growth by exposing us to people who share similar or even alternative points of view.

Being part of a community broadens our horizons by giving us access to knowledge, experience, generosity, encouragement, and a more profound sense of fulfillment. It's there—all you need to do is reach for it.

START BY SHARING

You can join a seed-saving or gardening community before you've saved enough seeds. Join local social media groups or pages and watch for gatherings. Put yourself out there by attending farmer's markets and conversing with the other shoppers or the sellers.

However, once you have some extra seeds to share, why not? Think of it as an act of good faith. There are many simple yet practical ways to share seeds:

- Invite local gardeners to exchange seeds.
- Donate your seeds to local schools, community gardens, or seed libraries.
- Make cards (greeting cards, birthday cards, or other occasion cards) from recycled paper and embed seeds into them (this way, you can tear the card into pieces and plant them directly in the ground).
- Make DIY packets with seeds and some easy-to-follow instructions for beginner-friendly seeds and gift them to kids, friends, or family members to kickstart their gardening journey.

You establish rapport with community members by spreading and sharing the seeds (and love). You'll find that gardening communities are typically friendly, warm, and inviting.

Organizing a Seed Swap

Hosting a seed-swapping event is optional. You're welcome to attend existing events and get all your seed-swapping needs met that way. But if you are more daring and ambitious and have what it takes, hosting your seed swap can be a great way to make a name for yourself within your gardening community (or even beyond).

Whether you want to keep it small or make it elaborate, there are a few things to keep in mind beforehand:

Who's Your Audience?

Consider how many people there will be, how many seeds they might bring, and their experience. However, it's impossible to have a way to know this information with certainty in advance; it will largely depend on how and where you promote the event.

How Will They Know?

For people to know there's a seed swap happening, you need to spread the word. You can do this by making a couple of flyers and putting them up on notice boards at local garden centers, health-food stores, community bulletin boards, or local social media networking pages. If you have some friends who are into gardening, you can invite them to a small get-together and swap seeds amongst each other only.

Where Will You Host It?

You might need to acquire a venue depending on how many people will attend your seed swap event. You can partner with local gardening groups, schools, libraries, or community centers to find a suitable indoor or outdoor venue for free (or at a way more affordable price).

Do You Need Sponsors or Donors?

You can reach out to local nurseries, gardening clubs, restaurants, caterers, or seed banks to donate towards or sponsor the event (again, depending on how big the event will be). Businesses will be more likely to sponsor events or donate if there are a lot of opportunities for publicity or marketable audiences. If the event is small, you likely won't need sponsors or donations, but it certainly can't hurt to ask. If you don't ask, the answer is always "no."

Will You Need Volunteers?

Even at a small seed-swapping event, you'll need help with setup, clean-up, etc. You can approach friends and family members for help or go to outside sources like social media platforms or post flyers. Make sure there's some incentive for the volunteers.

How Will You Set Up the Venue?

Offer refreshments in the form of beverages and snacks. Sprinkle in a few educational displays between the seed exchange tables. Include demonstrations, talks, games ("identify the seed," for example), or raffles to keep people engaged and entertained.

What Will the Cost Be?

Decide whether the event will be free or people must pay a small fee. If you are charging people, the aim should be to cover the costs, not to make a profit. Remember, you want to join or bring the community together, so it should be a fun day that encourages everyone to participate and leave with a willingness to attend again.

Share Your Knowledge

Spreading information and education is no one's responsibility, but we wouldn't be where we are today if people didn't take on this vital task. You don't need to go out of your way to educate others or convert people to the seed-saving lifestyle, but taking on that responsibility does benefit us all and ensures the future of the plant species and seed-saving tradition. But don't be a nuisance, either. People who are interested and eager to know more already have one foot in the door.

You may not have all the knowledge and information yet, but you can collaborate with people who know more and share what you have learned (even if it's just a heart-warming story about your journey and experiences).

By organizing workshops, giving presentations at schools, volunteering at local seed banks or community gardens, and being hands-on wherever you can, you contribute to keeping this vital tradition alive!

SEED SWAPPING ONLINE

The internet can be a horrible place, but it has also made connecting with a larger community more accessible. Yes, being able to come together and physically swap seeds with the locals is excellent, but the internet is a close second if you don't have the option or opportunity.

Going online to swap seeds with strangers has its downsides. For example, you can never trust whether the person on the other end is who they say they are or will do what they say. And it would be best if you were always cautious about keeping your personal information private. But it makes getting a hold of specific varieties you want to grow in your garden easier.

You can share or trade seeds online through trustworthy online platforms:

- Seed Savers Exchange
- Southern Exposure Seed Exchange
- Dave's Garden
- GardenWeb's forums
- BASIL

You can also check out social media platforms for seed-saving groups:

- Great American Seed Swap (Facebook)
- "r/seedswap" (Reddit)
- Other blogs, forums, or websites that allow their members to make requests and offers for seeds

CREATING YOUR OWN SEED BANK

It would help if you started your seed bank for many reasons, regardless of your goals. You might have a smaller stash if you're planning on simply storing seeds for personal use, but you can also take it further if you have the means and want to share your seeds with the community.

What Is a Seed Bank?

Think of a seed bank as a personal insurance policy for your garden. You'll be able to plant the seeds and varieties you want to grow every year for free, and you're also sure of your future garden's production quality and vigor.

The proper definition of a seed bank is a facility (or designated space) for storing various types and varieties of seeds in a controlled environment. The purpose of a seed bank is to preserve genetic variation and to safeguard the supply and availability of all plant species.

Starting Small

Start a small-scale seed bank if you have limited space for storing the seeds or when you have a small garden. The key is to be creative: use envelopes or Ziploc bags instead of containers so that everything fits into a small cooler or insulated lunch bag.

If you have a small garden, you'll have a limited amount and variety of seeds. To grow your collection, consider swapping seeds with your local gardening community. By doing so, you can expand your seed collection quickly.

The point is that you have to start somewhere. Don't be discouraged because you only have 50 tomato seeds in your seed bank. Don't feel like you're not a legitimate seed saver because you're using an old shoebox for your seeds. Your collection will grow quicker than you think with some perseverance and determination.

Always ensure you're employing and implementing the proper methods for harvesting, cleaning, drying, and storing your seeds. And make sure that, if you are swapping seeds, the person you're exchanging with is also following the correct practices.

Going Big

Get involved with other seed savers in your community by joining local farming groups and contacting commercially or privately owned seed banks. Many seed banks offer memberships that are free or require a small donation.

Furthermore, you can volunteer in community gardening programs, attend seed swap events, or start a community or local seed bank if there isn't one already (and if you have the means to do so). Creating a large-scale seed bank is no easy feat and will require you to:

- Acquire a seed inventory through local donations, exchanges, swapping seeds, or purchasing them yourself.
- Find a facility with the proper storage requirements if you outgrow your home.
- Establish rules for memberships.
- Recruit a team to manage daily operations such as inventory management, quality control, maintaining proper storage principles, etc. However, this requirement only applies once the business grows to a degree where it needs ongoing daily support and you need help to keep up with everything.
- Abide by any applicable bylaws or legal requirements.

Starting a business in the seed industry might not be your goal, and that's okay, too. You can also keep it small by creating a Facebook page, getting as many gardening and seed-saving enthusiasts to join, and then holding monthly get-togethers or seed-swapping events. However, you may also be completely content joining an existing seed-saving community group in your area.

Being a part of (or creating) a community that shares similar goals and interests is one of the most fulfilling things you can do in life. Even if you're not social, I guarantee you will enjoy joining a like-minded community and building your seed bank simultaneously.

Starting your seed bank (even on a small scale) with the idea of swapping, donating, or exchanging them means implementing strict storage and organizational practices to ensure seed viability, health, and seeds are true to type (or open-pollinated).

There's much to consider regarding seed saving and your ultimate goal, so start with one thing at a time. Perfect the steps before you go off script.

You don't have to jump into the deep end with seed saving. Organizing your seed-swapping event or starting your seed bank might sound exciting, but it's not a requirement. You can attend a few events and get involved before you make that leap. Make a few connections in the community first and see where it takes you (and consider whether this is what you want).

8

SEED PRESERVATION FOR COMMON GARDEN CROPS

Now that we've covered the basics, we will put all that knowledge into practice. This final chapter is a step-by-step guide for harvesting and preserving the most common beginner-friendly garden crops (fruits, vegetables, herbs, and flowers). Some of these crops are already in your garden.

What better way to hone and perfect your seed-saving skills than to use what we've learned throughout this book in your backyard? Remember: Before you'll be good at it, you'll be bad at it—getting good is the journey.

FRUIT

Arguably, the easiest plants to save seeds from are fruits. Typically, the seeds are in the fruit itself. All you need to do is separate it; that process is always straightforward. There are exceptions to the rule, like how bananas have transformed so much that there's barely any trace of seeds left where they were supposed to be. But bananas are hardly a beginner-friendly crop, so that's beside the point.

Tomatoes

"Knowledge is knowing that a tomato is a fruit. Wisdom is knowing not to put it in a fruit salad"(O'Driscoll, 2015). That quote always cracks me up. Tomatoes are easily the most common garden crop. They're a staple in gardens of all sizes, and for good reason. My dog once stole a tomato from the kitchen, and a couple of months later, a tomato plant was growing in the chicken pen. The point is tomatoes are easy to grow and maintain, delicious, versatile, and easy to save seeds from. Here's how to harvest tomato seeds:

1. Please wait until the end of the season before saving seeds from tomatoes to ensure they're ripe and ready. Start by picking an open-pollinated tomato right before you want to process and harvest the seeds.
2. Cut open the tomato and squeeze the seeds out (or scoop them out with a spoon) onto a plate or other broad, shallow container (or a glass jar if you're fermenting). You can use the remnants of the seedless tomato like any other tomato, but making purees or sauces with them works best.
3. You have a few options: you can spread everything out and let the seeds and pulp dry down for two to three weeks before picking out the seeds, rinsing, drying them again, and storing them; you can rinse the pulp away using a strainer or sieve before drying and storing them; or you can ferment the seeds and pulp (in a glass jar with water) for five days. Fermenting the seeds results in a better quality seed and a higher germination rate. If you plan to

save the seeds for a long time (longer than a couple of years), use the fermentation method.

4. Please make sure the seeds are dry before storing them. Do the fingernail test to check (if the seed leaves an imprint or feels like it has some give, let it dry for a couple more days). Avoid direct or even bright indirect sunlight during the drying time.

If dried and stored correctly, tomato seeds can be viable for up to twelve years.

Strawberries

Not only are strawberries the only fruit that carries seeds on the outside, but they also have a juicy secret—strawberries are not berries at all! They're known as "false fruits" and contain numerous tiny fruits. Essentially, each seed is a separate fruit attached to a receptacle (everything surrounding the individual fruits, including what they're bound to in the middle).

I'm not here to slander strawberries. We should all forgive them for their deceit. After all, who doesn't like fresh strawberries and wouldn't want strawberry plants in their garden? They're the perfect beginner crop you can plant anywhere you have an open spot of soil (as a ground-cover crop to keep the weeds at bay). But be warned, they spread very quickly if you don't keep an eye on those runners!

To harvest seeds from strawberries, here's what you're going to do:

1. Leave the fruit on the bush for as long as possible. At this point, it's standard procedure. Choose the biggest, boldest fruit from the healthiest plants to harvest your strawberries from.

2. Again, you have a few options to choose from when separating the seed from the fruit: use a toothpick to meticulously dislodge every individual seed from the strawberry into a plate or container (the most labor-intensive approach); cut thin slices of skin (with the seeds still intact) off the strawberry and place them on a paper towel to dry out for a week, and once they're dry you can rub the seeds off onto a plate relatively easy and dry them some more before storing them; or press the fruit through a fine mesh or strainer—the seeds will remain, and you can proceed with rinsing and drying them.

3. Whatever method you choose, it's always a good idea to rinse your seeds before drying them to eliminate any pulp or residue that might result in mold or fungi growth.

4. Most strawberry varieties need to be cold stratified, meaning they need a simulated winter to break them out of "dormancy" and increase their germination rate. To do this, place your seeds in the fridge for at least a month (let them come to room temperature by taking them out of the refrigerator for 24 hours) before planting them.

I want to note that strawberry seeds might very well germinate without a cold stratification process, but they will take much longer to do so, and your germination rate will be much lower.

Strawberry seeds can be stored for two to three years or even longer when frozen (though the germination rate will naturally decline with time).

Blueberries

Famously known for containing the highest levels of antioxidants than any other fruit or vegetable, blueberries are praised and labeled as a superfood and relatively easy to grow. But one thing about these powerfully healthy berries is that their seeds are so tiny that straining them through even the finest sieve will leave you empty-handed. However, where there's a will, there's a way. Here's what you do:

1. Harvest blueberries from multiple healthy plants.
2. Macerate the blueberries by blending them in a food processor or mashing them in a bowl with water.
3. Give your blueberry puree a good mix. The pulp will float to the top, and the seeds will sink to the bottom. Scoop off the floating pulp. You might have to add water, remix everything, and skim off the pulp until all is gone.
4. Pour off as much water as you can and scoop the seeds onto a paper towel. Dry them and store them like you would any other seed.
5. Blueberry seeds benefit from scarification (nicking the seed coating), but because the seeds are so tiny, you risk damaging them if you try to do this (even rubbing them on sandpaper might cut too deep). So, a more accessible and safer way to do this is to place the seeds on a damp paper towel in a Ziploc bag and place the bag in the freezer for at least 90 days. Then, defrost them and allow them to come to room temperature before you plan on sowing them. Freezing the seed will soften the coat enough to let the embryo break through it more easily.

Remember that blueberries are not self-fertile, so you must ensure you have enough genetic variation by having five or more of the same variety but with different parent plants (and introducing genetic variation every other year or so).

You can effectively store blueberry seeds for two years.

Cucumbers

Like tomatoes, botanists consider cucumbers a fruit because they grow from a flower and have seeds on the inside. But regardless of how you use them in your dishes (or skincare routine), they are easy to grow from seeds. However, harvesting seeds from cucumbers requires a delicate hand because the seeds are soft and have that gel seed capsule, just like tomato seeds.

The process of harvesting cucumber seeds is very similar to harvesting tomato seeds:

1. Cut your ripe, freshly harvested, healthy cucumber in half and scrape out the middle parts (with the pulp) into a glass jar with some water. Allow it to ferment for three to five days, and remember to stir daily.
2. Scoop or pour off everything that floated to the top after three to five days of fermentation.
3. Remove the seeds left at the bottom of the jar and rinse them before spreading them out on a tray lined with parchment paper or paper towels.
4. Leave the seeds to dry completely before labeling and storing them.

You can store cucumber seeds for up to five years.

Capsicums

Regarding capsicums, you will likely have chilies or bell peppers (or both) in your garden. Capsicums are easy to grow and versatile, making them a popular and common crop for any kitchen garden. As it turns out, saving the seeds from these beauties is also very straightforward:

1. Leave a few fruits on the plants until they wrinkle. This process can take months. Mark these fruits with a ribbon so you don't accidentally harvest them.
2. When you harvest the peppers or chilies, the seeds will fully mature and dislodge with minimal effort. Cut the fruit open and firmly shake or tap it over a plate or tray until no more seeds are inside. You can use the fruit in conserves, sauces, or stews as usual, although the texture might differ slightly.
3. Inspect the seeds and discard any that appear damaged, discolored (seeds are typically off-white), or smaller than the rest.
4. Rinse the seeds with a strainer or sieve, spread them out on a tray lined with paper towels or parchment paper, and let dry away from direct sunlight for at least a week. If you have a fine mesh screen, you can use it to dry the seeds (this way, you don't have to turn them every other day to ensure proper airflow). Do the fingernail test to check if they're dry enough; if unsure, let them dry for a couple more days and check again.

Capsicum seeds can remain viable for an astonishing 25 years when stored properly. However, a more realistic time frame (and for best germination rates) is under five years.

Pumpkin or Squash

Another multi-purpose, beginner-friendly crop to grow is pumpkins (or their little cousins: squash). These vibrant fruits are a must-have, from soups to veggie bakes to Halloween decorations.

The best thing about saving seeds from pumpkins or squash is that you can also eat them. The seeds contain manganese, vitamin K, and many other nutrients. Here's how you can save pumpkin seeds:

1. Cut open your overripe pumpkin and scoop out the seeds and pulp. Just like with the tomato and cucumber seeds, if you plan to store them for longer than a couple of years, opt for fermenting the seeds for five days. Otherwise, rinse everything and manually pick out the seeds from the pulp. Whether or not you ferment the seeds, spread them out on a tray with paper towels, parchment paper, or a mesh screen.
2. Dry the seeds in a dark, well-ventilated room for about two weeks or until they pass the fingernail test. Make sure you stir or turn the seeds every couple of days to make sure they dry evenly (unless you're using a mesh screen).
3. Once all the seeds are dry, pick out the most significant seeds to save for planting. More giant pumpkin seeds have a better chance of germinating. You can keep smaller seeds for eating; alternatively, you can blend them into a powder and add them back into your garden bed.

You can store pumpkin seeds for up to five years.

VEGETABLES

Unlike fruits, vegetables don't carry their seeds on the inside but rather in a pod, capsule, or flower. Despite that distinction, harvesting seeds from vegetables is far from rocket science. I will walk you through saving seeds from the most common garden vegetable crops in a few easy steps.

Brassicas

This category includes leafy greens like spinach, lettuce, kale, cabbage, Swiss chard, Brussels sprouts, cauliflower, and broccoli. The entire Brassica family tree grows similarly, so the methods for harvesting the seeds from various crops are identical.

The way collard or leafy greens make seeds is by sending out a long stalk (usually from the center of the plant but can be on the side depending on the type of brassica you're growing) from where the flower, and eventually the seed pods, will grow from. This process is called bolting and is relatively easy to identify: look for a stalk instead of a leaf! And it usually happens closer to the end of the season. To save brassica seeds, follow the below steps:

1. Once seed pods start to form, pick one now and then to check on their maturity. The best time to harvest the seeds is when the seeds inside the pod start turning brown. Picking them when the pod is completely dry and brittle might result in a lot of seed loss (since they will break open at the slightest touch, spilling seeds everywhere).

2. Take seed pods from every plant you have (and grow as much variety as possible) to retain genetic diversity. Allow the seed pods to dry out completely after you've harvested them. You can break open the pods with little effort when they're brittle. Winnow the seeds to separate them from the trash and debris.

3. You need more than air-drying brassica seeds if you're planning on saving these seeds for years. You can use rice cooked in the oven for 45 minutes or silica gel packets. Fill a glass container halfway with the baked (and cooled) rice or silica gel. Put the seeds in an old pair of stockings or

mesh fabric and secure them with a rubber band. Place the seeds in the glass jar and screw the lid on tightly.

4. Leave the seeds in the air-tight glass jar with the rice or silica gel for at least two weeks. This process will cause the seeds to enter dormancy entirely and last for years.

5. After two weeks of drying, you can remove the seeds and store them in another labeled container or Ziploc bag with the rest of your seeds.

Remember, all brassicas can cross-pollinate, so if you're growing spinach and broccoli in the same garden, you'll need to be careful since most brassicas are also self-incompatible and require pollinators. The easiest way around this is to grow only one brassica variety (only spinach, broccoli, etc.) and rotate the array of brassica every year (grow spinach this year and broccoli next year, for example).

Under the proper conditions, you can keep most brassica seeds for five years.

Alliums

Alliums include all varieties of the onion family and garlic, chives, leeks, shallots, scallions, and spring onion. It is rare to find a hearty, savory dish that does not include some form of onion. Are they even more of a staple than potatoes? You're doing something wrong if you don't have "stinking lilies" in your garden. They're hardy, delicious, and easy to grow from saved seeds. Just as is the case with the brassica family tree, the method of harvesting seeds from alliums of any variety is pretty much the same across the board:

1. Alliums will flower in late spring. The bulbous flower stalks will tower over the foliage. The best time to harvest alliums is generally on the cusp of fall when the flower heads wither and turn brown.
2. Once the flowers start to brown, you can collect the seeds by cutting the flower stalks and shaking them into a bag or container. You may need to use your fingers to dislodge some of the seeds gently.
3. Dry your onion seeds like any other: Spread them thinly on a paper towel (or mesh screen) and let them dry for one to two weeks until they pass the fingernail test.
4. Remember to store and label them correctly.

Keep in mind that all species of alliums can cross-pollinate. Alliums are self-compatible (but they do require pollinators). This classification means that you can grow more than one species in your garden, given that you take the proper precautions to prevent cross-pollination. You'll have to pollinate them manually.

Allium seeds don't have a long shelf-life at all, with the germination rates declining by as much as 50% every year they're kept in storage. Don't plan on storing allium seeds for more than a year for best results.

Potatoes

Whether baked, fried, or mashed, there's a way to enjoy this starchy, blank canvas root vegetable for even the most picky of eaters. Potatoes flower and produce seeds in fruit that look like tiny tomatoes, but in many cases, potato flowers dry out and fall off before they have fruit with seeds (in colder climates, the potato "berries" are more likely to develop). The most popular way to grow potatoes is from "seed potatoes," which are just regular potatoes you plan to use as "seeds" next year.

Growing potatoes from seed requires a few steps:

1. Collect the berries and carefully mash them in a bowl to not damage the seeds. Add water and allow the concoction to ferment in a warm area for five days, stirring it at least once daily. Pulp will float to the top, and seeds will float to the bottom.
2. Pour off the floating pulp, strain the seeds, and rinse well. Spread the potato seeds onto a tray with parchment paper or paper towels.
3. Let the seeds dry for one to two weeks or until they pass the fingernail test—label and store in an air-tight container.

Alternatively, to grow potatoes from potatoes, follow the steps below.

Store-bought potatoes are covered in chemicals to prevent sprouting, so growing potatoes from them is not advisable. Instead, buy potato seeds from the start and save seed potatoes from the resulting yield. Here's how to grow potatoes from potatoes:

1. Choose potatoes to use as seed potatoes next year. Brush the soil and dirt off, but do not wash them; doing so may result in premature sprouting.
2. Storage conditions for seed potatoes are essential. Store them in a dark, cool area (below 50°F) and away from other vegetables and fruit. They will likely start to sprout within a few months regardless, but keeping the temperature and conditions consistent will prevent this from happening for as long as possible.

3. You can plant small potatoes whole, but you can cut larger potatoes into pieces as long as you ensure at least two or three "eyes" on each piece.

The downside to growing potatoes from seed potatoes is you can only store them briefly. It would be best if you planted them the following season; otherwise, the potatoes will rot. However, the seeds retain a high germination percentage for up to five years.

Carrots

Carrots are root vegetables and biennials, meaning they'll only produce flowers and seeds in the second year. To save seeds from carrots, you must sacrifice some of this year's yield and leave them in the ground until they flower and produce seeds next year. Luckily, waiting patiently for carrot seeds to form is, quite frankly, the hardest part of the entire process:

1. Leave the flower heads to ripen and mature on the plant until they dry out and turn brown.
2. Cut the flower heads off and place them in a paper bag until the seeds have darkened and the plant material is dry and brittle. This process might take a couple of weeks.
3. Transfer everything to a plastic container with a lid and shake vigorously to release the seeds.
4. Winnow the seeds using your method of choice before labeling and storing them in their final containers and resting place.

If it's any consolation, carrot flowers are beautiful and attract various pollinators and predatory insects to your garden, which aids in the yield size of other fruits and vegetables as well as pest control.

The shelf-life of carrot seeds is three years.

Beetroot

While beetroot is primarily grown for its sweet and vibrant root, its foliage is also edible and packed with vitamins and nutrients. You can add it to salads, smoothies, and sauces or prepare them just like other leafy greens (by itself, steamed, or boiled). Beetroot is also a biennial like carrots, meaning you'll have to wait two years after your first sowing before you can harvest seeds from them.

1. Once the beetroot starts flowering in its second year, wait for the foliage to turn brown before cutting four inches off the top of the plant.
2. Store the browned foliage you cut off in a cool, dry place for a month to allow the seeds to ripen.
3. You'll need to thresh and winnow the seeds since they're attached to the dried foliage. You can do this step with your hands (while wearing protective gear) or by putting everything in a bag and pounding it to release the seeds. Be careful not to crush the seeds.
4. Once you've separated the trash and debris from the seeds, they can be stored.

Beetroot seeds are attractive because most varieties contain multi-germ seeds. One beetroot seed will result in two or more seedlings. It's advisable to thin out your sprouts and keep the ones growing with vigor.

You can store beetroot seeds for up to four years.

Legumes

Growing beans is easy—plant them! Okay, okay, there's a bit more to it, but not much, in all honesty. Beans are one of the most popular garden crops, right underneath tomatoes. They have been elevating stews and soups for many generations. They're nutritious, easy to grow, and nitrogen-fixers (meaning they're great for soil health). Whether you're growing beans, peas, or lentils, the process of harvesting and saving seeds is the same:

1. Leave the pods on the plant or vine until brown. If you shake the pod, you should hear the seeds rattling inside. This process might take a few weeks.
2. Remove the pods from the plant and allow them to dry in the pod (in a cool, dry, dark room) for two to three weeks.
3. Carefully break open the seed pods and store them in airtight containers. It might be worth adding some silica gel packets to the containers for extra security. Beans sprout very quickly at the slightest hint of moisture.

There have been instances where legumes have been stored and successfully germinated a millennium later. However, aiming to keep them for at most ten years is advisable.

HERBS

Leveling up a dish with fresh herbs or brewing medicinal tea with leaves plucked from your garden is a special feeling for every aspiring (and experienced) gardener. Many home gardeners start their journey with a herb or "kitchen" garden before it blossoms into a miniature version of a fruit and vegetable forest. Either way, most herbs are easy to grow and even more straightforward to harvest seeds from. Not only that, but many herbs have exceptional pest control characteristics, which make them perfect for intercropping.

Parsley

Parsley is easily one of the most common herbs grown in a home garden. And even though it's a biennial, it's well worth the extra effort. It can be used as a garnish or condiment, adding flavor to virtually any dish.

To save parsley seeds, you'll have to wait until its second year when it starts flowering. Then, follow these simple steps:

1. Wait until the flowers dry out on the plant and the seed heads darken.
2. Cut the seed heads off with a sharp pair of scissors or pruning shears.
3. Gently roll or rub the seed heads over a plate between your fingers. The seeds should fall out with little effort. Some dried plant debris might fall with the seeds, so you might also have to winnow them.
4. Allow the seeds to dry for another week or until they pass the fingernail test before storing them.

You can store parsley seeds for up to two years.

Basil

Having such a distinctive and unique taste and aroma would cause the basil to be a finicky herb to work with, but it's pretty popular. Like most other herbs, it can be the perfect garnish or addition to many dishes, but you can also use it as one of the main ingredients in pesto sauce.

In cooler climates, it's typically grown annually; in warmer climates, it's a hardy perennial. In either case, it blossoms and produces seeds yearly at the end of its growing season. Here's how you save their seeds:

1. Once the flowers are dried and spent, it's time for harvesting. Carefully cut the flowers and place them in a paper bag, allowing them to dry for a few more days.
2. Vigorously shake the paper bag containing the flower heads to release the tiny seeds. You can also use a rolling pin or a similar tool to break the flower heads open, but be careful not to use too much force or pressure so you don't damage the seeds.
3. Pour all the contents into a bowl or shallow tray and winnow out the trash and debris by gently blowing (use eye protection) until only the seeds are left.
4. Store the seeds.

Basil plants keep flies, gnats, and mosquitoes at bay, so keep them close to your kitchen windows to reduce flies in your home during the summer months.

You can store basil seeds for up to five years.

Rosemary

Rosemary is not only an excellent herb for cooking, but the bright blue-purple flowers and full foliage give them an ornamental function. However, compared to all other crops listed in this chapter, rosemary is at the bottom of the list regarding how easy it is to grow.

The seeds are slow to germinate, and you'll have to grow them indoors (under fluorescent lighting) at the start of winter to be able to transplant them in the spring. But because rosemary is a perennial, you only need to sow them once (or again when you want more). Whether you take on the challenge of growing them from seed or you bought a couple of rosemary seedlings from a nursery, harvesting the seeds isn't complicated at all:

1. At the end of the season, allow the flowers to wither and dry on the rosemary plant before carefully picking or cutting them off. Place the flowers in a paper bag.
2. Let the flowers dry in the paper bag for two to three weeks. Shake the bag to allow the seeds to dislodge from the flower heads.
3. Pour everything into a bowl and ensure all the seeds separate from the flowers by rubbing the flower heads between your fingers or palms.
4. Winnow out the trash and dry debris using your method of choice before properly storing and labeling the seeds.

Rosemary seeds will stay viable under the proper conditions for up to six years.

Oregano

Oregano is a part of the mint family and a hardy perennial that can withstand even the harshest winters with only a thick layer of mulch for protection. Harvesting oregano seeds is easy:

1. After the growing season, oregano plants will flower. After a couple of months, the flowers will brown and become brittle. Pick them at this point.
2. Once you've harvested the flowers, hang them upside down to dry for a few days. Use wire and string and keep a plate underneath to catch falling seeds.

3. After a few days have passed, flick the seed heads to release the seeds into a plate or tray. Pick or blow out any plant debris and let them dry until the seeds pass the fingernail test.
4. Store and label them.

Oregano seeds (along with mint seeds) will remain good to go for up to three years.

Mint

Versatile herbs for you, your kitchen, and garden mint are at the top of that list. Eating or drinking it as tea has plenty of health benefits, including improved digestion, brain function, immune system, and oral health. In the garden, it is low maintenance, attracts pollinators, and repels pests.

Mint is a perennial but has a reputation for being a weed. If left unchecked, mint *will* take over your garden. You won't need to save mint seeds for your own sake because they spread like wild-fire. However, if you do want to keep the seeds for whatever reason, here's how you do it:

1. After the mint flowers wither, the seed pods will develop. Please wait for the seed pods to turn brown before picking them. You can keep them in a paper bag or spread them on a tray.
2. Let the seed pods dry for another two to three weeks before squeezing the seeds out of the pods.
3. After squeezing the seeds out, do a fingernail test to see whether they need more drying time. If they're not dry enough, let them dry for another week and repeat the test.
4. When the seeds are dry enough, label and store them.

Consider planting mints in containers instead of in the garden bed to keep mints in check. But even then, mint might still "jump the fence" and end up choking out your other plants, so be sure to keep an eye on them.

Chamomile

Chamomile is another herb with many benefits for your garden, cooking, and health. Most home permaculture gardeners grow chamomile for its natural pest-repelling properties and to brew their chamomile tea. Chamomile tea has many health benefits and is famously known for its calming properties. And when incorporated into baking (or infused with butter, milk, or oil), it adds a delicate floral taste.

However, if you want to harvest seeds, you'll have to leave some blossoms there when you gather the flowers for tea. Here's how you harvest chamomile seeds:

1. Keep an eye on the blossoms—the seeds will form in the flower's yellow center. The seeds are tiny, so be diligent.
2. Once the seeds start to separate from the flower easily, you can cut them and use your thumb to rub off the seeds gently into a container.
3. Spread the seeds on a tray with parchment paper or paper towels and dry them for at least a week or until they pass the fingernail test.
4. Label and store the seeds.

You can store chamomile seeds for four years.

FLOWERS

Unless you're only growing self-pollinating fruit and vegetable varieties (which is very restricting and dull), you need flowers in your garden. Flowers are essential for two reasons: they attract pollinators, which results in a more bountiful yield, and they attract predatory insects who feed on pests that invade and destroy your crops.

However, I also consider beauty a necessity if it's functional. I mean a non-invasive, non-competitive flower with a primary function that isn't just to look pretty. Flowers you should avoid are toxic or poisonous ones (such as belladonnas, castor beans, and daffodils) or ones that grow exceptionally fast—which also means they quickly deplete the water content and nutrients from the soil (like aloe, morning glory, and butterfly bush).

When growing flowers, you want the most "bang for your buck." You want something that is easy to grow and requires minimal maintenance. For that, perennials are your best bet. However, the annual flowers I included in this list are well-versed in re-sowing or self-sowing. If you let them do their thing and don't harvest all their seeds or cut every flower, I can guarantee they will drop some seeds and germinate again next year.

Even though you don't need to save seeds from perennial flowers for yourself (unless you're expanding your garden), they make perfect gifts to friends and family members. Alternatively, you can donate them.

Most annual flower seeds will retain high germination rates under proper storage conditions for three to four years, and perennial flower seeds are typically good for five to seven years.

Alyssum

Let's start with one of the annual flowers on this list. Unless you're in a warm climate, alyssums are annuals, meaning they need replanting yearly. And while that is an absolute pain, besides that, they require minimal effort to maintain, and they are a great addition to your garden. The pros outweigh the only con of having to replant them every year.

Alyssum is part of the mustard family and boasts white or purple (or light purple) flowers. The seeds look like flat disks that line the stem where the flowers are. To harvest the seeds, wait for the flowers to wither and follow these steps:

1. Keep a close eye on your alyssums. You might have to take a trip to your garden every day when trying to harvest enough of these seeds. Gently flick each stem (where a cluster of flowers used to be) over a bowl—the seeds that drop freely are mature enough to be harvested.
2. Make sure you separate each "session" of seed harvesting so they all dry thoroughly. For example, keep today's seeds on a paper plate (write the date on the plate) and use a fresh paper plate for tomorrow's collection. Following this step, you can ensure all the seeds dry thoroughly before storing them.
3. As each batch of seeds passes the fingernail test, pour them into a container. If you're putting all the seeds in one container, note the date range of when you collected the first batch of seeds to the last. For example, you might write "June 22 to July 30."

The seeds fall off easily and quickly, so the trick is to collect them before falling off themselves. The good news is that Alyssum self-sows very well, so they'll likely pop up again next year.

Lavender

Lavender is a must-have in your garden! It's low-maintenance and gorgeous. Besides looking great on the ground, you can also dry them and use them as decoration in your home or pick a fresh batch and place them in the bathroom when you shower (they're great in aromatherapy for headaches, anxiety, and chronic fatigue).

The seeds are pretty small, about half the size of sesame seeds, but they're black, which makes them much easier to spot (unless they're on the ground). Harvesting lavender seeds is super easy:

1. Please wait for the flowers to fade and the seed pods to form in their place. You'll also have to wait for these seed pods to dry out while attached to the plant. You know they're ready for harvest when the pods turn light brown or grey. The seeds are loose and may fly out when gently shaking the stem.
2. To collect the seeds, you can snip off the entire stem and tip them over into a bowl or tray, giving only a light shake to ensure any seeds that you may have trapped inside the pods are also released.
3. There might be minimal trash and debris amongst your seeds. If they bother you, you can winnow them by blowing into the tray or bowl until they're gone.
4. Dry the seeds the usual way (spread out in a tray on paper towels or parchment) until they pass the fingernail test and store them.

Lavender seeds need a few months of cold stratification, so move them to the fridge for two or three months before you grow them.

Coneflowers

There are many varieties of coneflowers, but the most popular coneflower to grow in your garden is Echinacea. Not only are they attractive to pollinators and drought-tolerant, but they're also great for your health. Echinacea tea can help alleviate cold and flu symptoms and boost your immune system so you recover quicker!

To make Echinacea tea at home, pick a few fresh flowers (dried flowers also work) and infuse them in hot water for about 10 minutes (add a few chamomile flowers or mint leaves for extra flavor). To harvest the seeds, follow these steps:

1. When the leaves dry out and fall off, you can cut the remaining part of the flower (the spiky center) and leave it to dry for a week or two on a tray or paper bag.
2. Once the flower heads are completely dry, the seeds should come off quickly when you rub your thumb over them. However, the seeds are pretty sharp and pointy, so wear gardening gloves during this part.
3. The seeds should be dry now, but you can do a fingernail test and leave them to dry for a few more days to be safe.

Borage

Another annual on this list is borage. It's an excellent bee attractor, making it a perfect companion for your open-pollinated crops. The flowers are either strikingly blue or white (depending on the variety) and edible, making them great for garnishing or decorating fruit salads, cakes, pies, and anything else.

You can plant borage with cucumbers, beans, squash, and toma-toes to enhance the flavor of these crops and enrich the soil with calcium and potassium. Borage is an annual, but just like Alyssum, it does a great job of self-sowing. But if you want to, harvesting the seeds is easy since they're large and unique (a small black or brown pod with grooves and a white "cap" on one end). To harvest borage seeds, perform the following steps:

1. At the end of the flowering season, the flower petals will fall off, and a seed head will form. If you were to open up one of the seed heads now, the seeds would be green, meaning they're not ready to be harvested yet. When you break open a seed head, harvest the seeds when they're black.
2. To harvest the seeds, you can hold the seed head over a container and knock the seeds out.
3. Dry the seeds for a few more days if they still need to pass the fingernail test before storing them.

Borage leaves and stems have fine, silver hair and contain silica, which can irritate one's skin. It's best to wear gardening gloves when handling borage or harvesting its seed.

Marigolds

Most marigold varieties are annuals, but you do get perennial marigolds, too, so if you want to go that route, you certainly can. However, it won't matter once you know how to save these seeds yourself. Marigold flowers and leaves are also edible and make great additions to salads.

The cheerful petals of a marigold flower close (forming the seed pod) and dry instead of falling off like other flowers. Aim to harvest the seed pods when the entire flower is dry and the base of the seed pod (closest to the stem) turns brown. Then, follow these steps:

1. Cut and collect as many seed pods as you would like.
2. Ready a tray lined with paper towels or parchment. You'll see little black and white spears. If the spears don't have a dark side, they're not mature enough yet, and you harvested them too soon. The achenes (or spears) are pointy, so watch out.
3. Discard as many dried seed pods and petals as possible and spread the spears on the lined tray. Let the seeds air dry for at least a week before storing them.

Yarrow

Yarrow is an attractive perennial that improves soil quality (by bringing nutrients to the surface) and structure (because of its robust root system). Yarrow attracts beneficial insects like wasps, ladybirds, and hoverflies that keep aphid populations in check. Many gardeners believe that the yarrow's scent is a pest repellent.

In addition, you can harvest yarrow leaves, stems, and flowers and steep them in water until the plant material breaks down. This process will cause the potassium, phosphorus, nitrogen, and other minerals to be released into the water, effectively making liquid fertilizer. However, you'll need to harvest plant material before they start to form seeds. Just leave enough flowers so you can harvest seeds from them as follows:

1. Wait until the flowers have withered and the seed heads start drying out. Then, cut the seed heads and store them

in a paper bag to finish drying (for at least two weeks or until the heads are completely dry and brittle).

2. Rub the seed heads between your fingers over a bowl to collect them. The seeds are black and tiny, so be careful not to spill them.

3. Winnow any debris by blowing gently into the container. Store the seeds in an airtight container.

Because yarrow seeds are so tiny, they can easily take over your garden bed, so you'll need to be more careful. An easy way to get around this possible problem is to use blossom bags after the petals fall off and the seed heads start to form to prevent as many seeds as possible from going rogue.

The Next Step

Seeds give us so much, and we have a duty to protect them. Take your seed-saving to the next level, and inspire a new reader to get started too!

Simply by sharing your honest opinion of this book and a little about what you've learned here, you'll show new readers the value of seed saving and point them in the direction of everything they need to get started.

Thank you so much for your support. When we work together, we can make a huge difference.

Scan the QR code below

CONCLUSION

Every crop type, species, and variety exists today because someone decided to store them and pass them on to the next generation. But the decline in diversity is due to our collective negligent, capitalistic, or perhaps ignorant mindset. Don't get me wrong, I'm not saying that you are personally responsible for the decline in plant diversity. However, you can be part of the solution.

Seed saving is rooted in sustainability and self-sufficiency, first and foremost. It's a more cost-efficient option than buying seeds year in and year out, and it gives you way more control over the type and quality of food you grow in your garden.

On top of that, with every generation, the quality and resilience of your crops improve because your plants adapt to the local environment and reserve beneficial traits as a result. They may even become pest and disease-resistant. This adaptation leads right into preserving plant species and genetics of certain varieties of crops, which we know is very important for the future of gardening (along with food security and the planet in general).

When you think about how evolution works, technically speaking, all crops are hybrid crops (even heirloom varieties). What I mean by this concept is that if you go back in time far enough, all animal and plant life on earth share a common ancestor, and through a mix of evolution, natural selection, and time, different "branches" started forming. But in the end, we all come from the same single-celled amoeba.

The difference is that heirloom varieties are tried and tested. They have become stable over an unfathomable amount of time and will produce the same results no matter how many times you save and replant the seeds. If you cross two different crop varieties, the seeds will not produce fruit or seeds that are "true to type" for many generations. This concept means that while any hybrid plant can become a stable heirloom variety, it will be challenging.

You don't have to own heirloom plants or seeds to be considered an avid seed saver, but they do have inherent value—more so to the environment and the preservation of genetic material than us. The point is that heirlooms are essential and valuable to the environment, and therefore, they should also be necessary to us.

When it comes down to it, the seed-saving process starts way before there are even seeds available for harvesting. A healthy garden means healthy seeds, so ensure you do what is necessary to keep your garden well cared for. Whether that process includes permaculture principles and techniques, managing diseases, pests, and all other gardening obstacles is essential.

The most important thing to ensure your seeds survive storage and retain as high of a germination rate as possible is the drying of the seeds and the storage conditions. It is nearly impossible to dry a seed too much, but not drying it enough can have devastating consequences like mold growth or premature sprouting (which can result in the loss of an entire batch of seeds).

Additionally, you can sum up the conditions in which you store the seeds in three words: cool, dark, and dry. However, the consistency of the conditions is critical. Severe fluctuations in temperature and humidity can lower germination rates rather rapidly or result in bacteria and mold growth and cause them to sprout in their containers. Sunlight can damage the seed, so you shouldn't dry seeds in direct sunlight.

For these reasons, you should continuously monitor and intermittently inspect your seeds' storage conditions. This process is especially so if you store your seeds in a fridge or freezer since losing electricity (for whatever reason) can affect the consistency of the storage conditions. You never know when a refrigerator or freezer runs out of gas, there's an issue with the wiring, or it just stops working.

Running a germination test at least once a year for seeds you plan to keep in storage for more than two years will provide you with valuable data. For example, it will tell you how quickly your seeds are declining. If last year's test was 80% and it dropped to 40% this year, it may indicate that your storage conditions aren't optimal or consistent (and need closer monitoring or an alternative approach).

As with all other things in life, seed saving will include a lot of trial and error—so try not to be discouraged when you fail immediately. You'll eventually know all the ins and outs and how to troubleshoot (or even prevent) seed-saving obstacles or issues.

If you keep this energy going and save seeds from your garden crops every year, before you know it, you'll have more seeds than you know what to do with. When that happens, you have a few options, such as donating them, swapping them, gifting them to friends and family members, or starting your seed bank. And with a little commitment and time, eventually, you'll have a collection of precious heirloom plants (which are so unique they have an entire chapter dedicated to them) in a resilient and thriving garden.

You'll never have to settle for store-bought seeds again because you now have the essential information on seed saving, which you can go back and reference at any point. Please put it to good use, gain first-hand experience, and get involved with the seed-saving community.

Seeds are tiny vessels of life, a symbol and architect of abundance and continuity. Let us protect and nurture their legacies and pay tribute to their profound connection to the past, present, and future. So here's to them! May there come a day when everyone appreciates and respects the continued promise of a bountiful yield that seeds deliver us with every season!

REFERENCES

20 Insightful and Inspiring Quotes About Sustainability. Jersey Girl Organics. Last modified March 29, 2022. https://www.jerseygirlorganics.co.nz/post/20-insightful-and-inspiring-quotes-about-sustainability

Adams, J. (2022, April 9). *How to harvest and save allium seeds*. Seed Saving Hub. https://howtosaveseeds.com/learn/save-allium-seeds/

All That Grows. (2023, August 21). *What are heirloom seeds?* https://www.allthatgrows.in/blogs/posts/what-are-heirloom-seeds

Allaby, R. G., Stevens, C., Lucas, L., Maeda, O., & Fuller, D. Q. (2017). Geographic mosaics and changing rates of cereal domestication. *Philosophical Transactions of the Royal Society B: Biological Sciences, 372*(1735), 20160429. https://doi.org/10.1098/rstb.2016.0429

Andrychowicz, A. (2018, August 22). *How to collect lavender seeds from your garden*. Get Busy Gardening. https://getbusygardening.com/collect-lavender-seeds-garden/

ASerna. (2022, August 15). *Ways to garden sustainably and reduce your carbon footprint*. Vizcaya. https://vizcaya.org/posts/ways-to-garden-sustainably-and-reduce-your-carbon-footprint/

Balltech on Demand, & PanAmerican Seed. (n.d.). *Best practices for storing and handling seeds*. https://www.ballseed.com/documents/Seed-Storage-Best-Practices-BallSeed-TechOnDemand-PanAmericanSeed.pdf

Braun, M. (2023, April 25). *Gardening 101: Collecting yarrow seeds for A thriving garden*. Shuncy. https://shuncy.com/article/how-to-collect-yarrow-seeds

Castaldo, N. (2018, May 29). *How (and why) to be a seed savior*. NRDC. https://www.nrdc.org/stories/how-and-why-be-seed-savior

Charbonneau, J. (2017, December 20). *The importance of heirloom seeds*. Southern Exposure Seed Exchange. https://blog.southernexposure.com/2017/12/the-importance-of-heirloom-seeds/

Charbonneau, J. (2020, May 6). *10 Reasons to save seed*. Southern Exposure Seed Exchange. https://blog.southernexposure.com/2020/05/10-reasons-to-save-seed/

Charbonneau, J. (2023a, March 31). *Saving seed: Ancient beginnings*. Southern Exposure Seed Exchange. https://blog.southernexposure.com/2023/03/saving-seed-ancient-beginnings/

Charbonneau, J. (2023b, May 2). *Top 10 tips for growing heirloom vegetables.* Southern Exposure Seed Exchange. https://blog.southernexposure.com/2023/05/top-10-tips-for-growing-heirloom-vegetables/

Charland, D. (2014, September 16). *Seed preservation methods for home or community garden.* Connecting Communities to the Land. https://seewhatgrows.org/seed-preservation-methods-home-community-garden/

Chatterjee, R. (2013, May 13). *Why humans took up farming: They like to own stuff.* NPR. https://www.npr.org/sections/thesalt/2013/05/13/183710778/why-humans-took-up-farming-they-like-to-own-stuff

Chelsea Green Publishing. (2023, February 27). *8 Seed-saving myths.* https://www.chelseagreen.com/2023/eight-seed-saving-myths/

Cohen, B. (2021, June 8). *Why seed saving is important, for the plants and ourselves.* Grit. https://www.grit.com/farm-and-garden/do-it-yourself/saving-our-seeds-saving-ourselves-zm0z21jazbut/

Courtney. (2021, August 3). *How to save parsley seed.* The Kitchen Garten. https://thekitchengarten.com/how-to-save-parsley-seed/

Crossley, H. (2023, August 10). *How to harvest coneflower seeds – for more fabulous flowers next year.* Homes And Gardens. https://www.homesandgardens.com/gardens/how-to-harvest-coneflower-seeds

David, L. (2023, August 18). *Why heirloom seeds matter.* Food Print. https://foodprint.org/blog/heirloom-seeds/

Dian. (2022, December 22). *Rosemary: Everything you need to know.* Learning to Grow Our Own Food. https://dianfarmer.com/rosemary-how-to-propagate/

DLF. (n.d.). *Seed storage.* DLF Pick Seed. https://www.dlfpickseed.com/ag/technical-information/seed-storage

Dowell, T. (2015, February 4). *Seed saving law: What farmers need to know.* Texas Agriculture Law. https://agrilife.org/texasaglaw/2015/02/04/seed-saving-law-what-farmers-need-to-know/

Espace Pour La Vie. (n.d.). *Tips for harvesting self-fertile vegetable seeds.* https://espacepourlavie.ca/en/tips-harvesting-self-fertile-vegetable-seeds#:

Farmer Jer. (2023, May 30). *How to harvest and store oregano seeds ~ farmer jer's gardening.* Farmer Jer. https://farmerjer.com/how-to-harvest-and-store-oregano-seeds/

Fast Company. (2012, May 11). *In 80 years, we lost 93% of variety in our food seeds.* Fast Company. https://www.fastcompany.com/1669753/infographic-in-80-years-we-lost-93-of-variety-in-our-food-seeds

Genova, A. (2020, December 28). Seed saving movement calls for seeds to be publicly owned. *The Guardian.* https://www.theguardian.com/uk-news/2020/dec/28/seed-saving-movement-calls-for-seeds-to-be-publicly-owned

Grant, A. (n.d.-a). *Bean seed storage - learn how to save bean seeds.* Gardening Know How. https://www.gardeningknowhow.com/edible/vegetables/beans/harvesting-bean-seeds.htm

Grant, A. (n.d.-b). *Borage harvesting: How and when to harvest borage plants.* Gardening Know How. https://www.gardeningknowhow.com/edible/herbs/borage/harvesting-borage-plants.htm

Grant, A. (n.d.-c). *Cucumber seed saving - how to harvest cucumber seeds.* Gardening Know How. https://www.gardeningknowhow.com/edible/vegetables/cucumber/cucumber-seed-harvesting.htm

Grant, A. (n.d.-d). *What is true potato seed: Learn about potato seed growing.* Gardening Know How. https://www.gardeningknowhow.com/edible/vegetables/potato/true-potato-seed-growing.htm

Grant, A. (2018, April 4). *Blueberry seed planting: Tips for growing blueberry seed.* Gardening Know How. https://www.gardeningknowhow.com/edible/fruits/blueberries/blueberry-seed-planting.htm

Grant, A. (2021, April 26). *Heirloom vegetables - tips for growing heirloom plants.* Gardening Know How. https://www.gardeningknowhow.com/edible/vegetables/vgen/heirloom-vegetables.htm

Grant, A. (2022a, January 26). *Can I save seed potatoes for next year: How to save your own seed potatoes.* Gardening Know How. https://www.gardeningknowhow.com/edible/vegetables/potato/saving-seed-potatoes.htm

Grant, A. (2022b, April 18). *Pepper seed viability and storage - how to harvest pepper seeds.* Gardening Know How. https://www.gardeningknowhow.com/edible/vegetables/pepper/harvesting-pepper-seeds.htm#:

Grant, A. (2023, March 27). *Can I harvest strawberry seeds - how to save strawberry seeds for planting.* Gardening Know How. https://www.gardeningknowhow.com/edible/fruits/strawberry/strawberry-seed-growing.htm

Grant, B. L. (n.d.-a). *Saving basil seed - how to harvest basil seeds from plants.* Gardening Know How. https://www.gardeningknowhow.com/edible/herbs/basil/harvesting-basil-seeds.htm

Grant, B. L. (n.d.-b). *Saving tomato seeds – how to collect tomato seeds.* Gardening Know How. https://www.gardeningknowhow.com/edible/vegetables/tomato/saving-tomato-seeds.htm

Hassani, N. J. M. (2018, July 2). *Seed storage - its importance and storage methods.* Forestrypedia. https://forestrypedia.com/seed-storage-its-importance-and-storage-methods/

Houzz. (n.d.). *Alyssum.* https://www.houzz.com/discussions/2150753/alyssum

Huffstetler, E. (2022, August 24). *How to harvest and save marigold seeds.* The Spruce. https://www.thespruce.com/how-to-save-marigold-seeds-1388591

Hughes, M. (2023, September 12). *Here's how to save seeds from your garden to plant next year.* Better Homes & Gardens. https://www.bhg.com/gardening/yard/garden-care/garden-seed-tips/

Jabbour, N. (2020, October 5). *Heirloom seeds: The ultimate guide to heirloom garden seeds.* Savvy Gardening. https://savvygardening.com/heirloom-seeds/

Jamie. (2023, January 25). *Wet vs. dry seed saving - complete guide for both methods.* Rennie Orchards. https://rennieorchards.com/wet-vs-dry-seed-saving/

Judd, A. (2022, January 14). *Seed storage & organization tips.* Growing in the Garden. https://growinginthegarden.com/seed-storage-organization-tips/

Learn Seed Saving. (2021, October 12). *Labeling, organizing, and inventorying.* https://www.learnseedsaving.com/labeling-organizing-inventorying/

Lee, M. (2015, May 11). *The value and significance of saving seeds and how it benefits you.* The Permaculture Research Institute. https://www.permaculturenews.org/2015/05/11/the-value-and-significance-of-saving-seeds-and-how-it-benefits-you/

Manner, L. (2020, September 11). *How the 12 principles of permaculture can transform your garden (and our world).* Green Connect. https://green-connect.com.au/heres-your-guide-to-the-12-principles-of-permaculture/#:

MasterClass. (2021, June 7). *Types of seeds: Heirloom, hybrid, and open-pollinated seeds.* https://www.masterclass.com/articles/types-of-seeds-heirloom-hybrid-and-open-pollinated-seeds

Mathews, T. (n.d.). *Easy small scale grain threshing.* Permies. https://permies.com/t/28254/Easy-small-scale-grain-threshing

Meserole, C. (2022, September 3). *3 Mistakes beginners make saving seeds.* Grow Your Own Vegetables. https://growyourownvegetables.org/3-mistakes-beginners-make-seeds/

123Helpme. (n.d.). *Importance of seed storage.* https://www.123helpme.com/essay/Importance-Of-Seed-Storage-PC6869V826

Pavlis, R. (2018, December 25). *Germination test: How to test seeds for viability.* Garden Myths. https://www.gardenmyths.com/germination-test-seed-viability/

Pavlis, R. (2021, February 20). *Floating seeds in water - is this a good seed viability test?* Garden Myths. https://www.gardenmyths.com/floating-seeds-in-water/

Plastic What You Preach. (2019, October 11). *How to harvest borage seeds DIY.* Hometalk. https://www.hometalk.com/diy/grow/flowers/harvesting-borage-seeds-43861125

Rai, S., Kumar, A., Singh, I., & Singh, A. (2020). Seedborne diseases and its management. *Springer EBooks,* 611–626. https://doi.org/10.1007/978-981-15-4198-8_31

Real Seeds. (n.d.). *Saving brassica vegetable seed.* https://www.realseeds.co.uk/brassicaseedprocessing.html#:

Rhoades, H. (n.d.). *Saving pumpkin seeds: How to store pumpkin seed for planting.* Gardening Know How. https://www.gardeningknowhow.com/edible/vegetables/pumpkin/saving-pumpkin-seeds-how-to-store-pumpkin-seed-for-planting.htm

Rhoades, J. (2021, July 4). *How to save seeds from carrots.* Gardening Know How. https://www.gardeningknowhow.com/edible/vegetables/carrot/saving-carrot-seeds.htm#:

Sakawsky, A. (2020, February 12). *How to grow an heirloom vegetable garden.* The House and Homestead. https://thehouseandhomestead.com/heirloom-vegetable-garden/

Samuel. (2022, February 27). *How do you collect mint seeds.* Gardens Of Mine. https://gardensofmine.com/how-do-you-collect-mint-seeds/

Seed Savers. (n.d.). *Learn to save seeds: It's a winner!* https://seedsavers.net/why-save-seeds/benefits-of-seed-saving/

Seed Savers. (2014, September 30). *Tools of the trade: Our top 10 seed saving supplies.* Seed Savers Exchange Blog. https://blog.seedsavers.org/blog/top-10-seed-saving-supplies

Seed Savers Exchange. (n.d.). *Seed saving.* https://seedsavers.org/learn/seed-saving/

Seed Sheet. (n.d.). *How to hand pollinate - A beginner's guide.* Seedsheets. https://seedsheets.com/blogs/tips-and-tutorials/how-to-hand-pollinate

SIPA. (n.d.). *Is your seed protected?* Seed Innovation and Protection Alliance. https://www.seedipalliance.com/seed-innovation/is-your-seed-protected/

Smith, B. L. (2023, September 6). *Seed saving: The opportunities and challenges.* Edible Communities. https://www.ediblecommunities.com/edible-stories/seed-saving-the-opportunities-and-challenges/

Sow True Seed. (n.d.). *Planting guide and seed saving notes for beets.* https://sowtrueseed.com/pages/planting-guide-and-seed-saving-notes-for-beets#:

The Credible Hulk. (2015, July 8). *Genetically engineered crops and seed saving myths.* https://www.crediblehulk.org/index.php/2015/07/08/genetically-engineered-crops-and-seed-saving-myths/

Thorn, S. (n.d.). *Easiest and hardest seeds to save.* Permies. https://permies.com/t/134652/Easiest-Hardest-Seeds-Save

Van Druff, K. (2022, May 6). *How to harvest chamomile: Harvesting chamomile for tea & seeds.* Bunny's Garden. https://www.bunnysgarden.com/how-to-harvest-chamomile/

Van Eendenburg, H. (n.d.). *Seed saving at the front lines of the climate crisis.* Green America. https://greenamerica.org/story/seed-saving-front-lines-climate-crisis

Wikipedia. (2021, October 9). *Seed saving.* https://en.wikipedia.org/wiki/Seed_saving

Wikipedia. (2023, October 11). *Heirloom plant.* https://en.wikipedia.org/wiki/Heirloom_plant

Wildfong, B. (2016). *How to dry your seeds to perfection.* Seeds.ca. https://seeds.ca/d/?t=09c1012100003118#:

Winger, J. (2018, January 23). *Where to buy heirloom seeds.* The Prairie Homestead. https://www.theprairiehomestead.com/2018/01/buy-heirloom-seeds.html

World Health Organization. (2018, May 9). *Mycotoxins.* https://www.who.int/news-room/fact-sheets/detail/mycotoxins

THE COMPANION PLANTING PLAYBOOK FOR BEGINNERS

A SIMPLE 7-STEP GUIDE TO THRIVING GARDENS, NATURAL PEST CONTROL, AND BOUNTIFUL CROPS

INTRODUCTION

There's this running joke amongst home gardeners that the plants in your garden die if you look at them funny. Meanwhile, dandelions grow out of the cracks in a sidewalk. I'm pretty sure I speak for everyone when I say we've all committed accidental mass "floracide" before (get it? "flora" as in plant life and "homicide" as in... Never mind.)

But what if I told you that it's possible to turn your garden space into a self-sustaining ecosystem, no matter how much space you have to work with? Oh yes! Imagine having a garden that—with a little bit of initial effort—is easier to maintain and keep alive in the long term. It sounds too good to be true, except it isn't. Companion planting builds on the foundation of permaculture gardening. And it's revolutionary.

There is such an overwhelming amount of information on gardening that it's no wonder many beginner gardeners put off getting started. You can only get started if you know where to begin in the first place.

By implementing the permaculture gardening technique of companion planting, you can manage and prevent all major gardening qualms, such as poor soil quality, ineffective pest control, weed management, and underperforming crops. Another thing many novice gardeners worry about is space. In today's economy, you're lucky to have a balcony, not to mention a small backyard.

While you need space to grow a garden, I've seen people grow enough strawberry plants in PVC pipes mounted against a wooden fence to feed a small army. Even in that aspect, permaculture has got you covered! And yes, you also need quality soil for a thriving garden, so even if you inherited a chunk of land from your grandma, it will only help if the soil's good. But once again, there's a way to fix it.

You may have grown a few tomatoes ages ago, but the aphids were so rampant they destroyed the whole yield before you could taste your hard work. I get it. It's exceptionally demotivating to put in months (sometimes even years) of hard work to have it disappear almost overnight. This problem is really where companion planting thrives: natural and organic pest control, resilience, and self-sufficiency.

Another common reason why many people are discouraged from taking the leap and starting (or expanding) their home gardens is time. You and every other adult in your household likely have a full-time job on top of other personal and familial responsibilities. You barely have time to juggle everything else, let alone a needy garden. But that's just the thing: when you leave nature up to nature (as is the case with companion planting), most of the gardening work that's usually considered laborious and time-consuming is taken care of *for* you.

With companion planting, you drastically minimize your time in your garden while reaping bountiful harvests. In addition, you significantly reduce your need for fertilizer or harmful pesticides or herbicides. You'll be saving money, time, and space.

The seven steps to companion planting outlined throughout this book focus on the "GROWER" method. It's an acronym that encompasses and includes all the necessary information you need to know, all condensed into one source. The acronym stands for:

- **G**et to know companion planting (chapter 1).

Regardless of your situation, you'll discover what it is and why it's the best option.

- **R**esearch the science (chapter 2).

We'll discuss why companion planting works so well by exploring science-based evidence.

- **O**ptimize the benefits (chapter 3).

You'll learn how to plan your garden to maximize all the fantastic benefits of companion planting.

- **W**ise pairings (chapters 4-7).

Discover an in-depth guide to tested and proven guilds and companions for vegetables, fruits, herbs, and flowers.

- Environment-specific strategies (chapters 8-10).

How to maximize planting in limited spaces, improve soil health, manage pests, and consider different climates.

- Resolve and refine (chapter 11).

Discover things to keep in mind, troubleshooting, and additional tips and tricks for companion planting.

If you've read any of my other books, you know that I grew up on a farm where my parents implemented some permaculture approaches. I was exposed to it growing up but only really put a little thought into it. We had a compost pile, mulched our crops, and saved rainwater, but nothing major. But as I grew up, I started seeing the benefits and impact of what a little bit could do, so I had to know more. Permaculture has leveled up my gardening skills. Our farm requires less work than ever, and our harvests are abundant.

Whether you want to turn a piece of land into a food forest or enjoy a few fresh herbs for everyday use, companion planting will ensure you get there with less effort and time spent in the grand scheme of things.

So many aspiring gardeners give up on trying after failing so many times or think that because they don't have a patch of grass, all hope is out the window. I'm here to tell you that if gardening is your passion (that you're not planning on giving up on any time soon), this is the only guide you need to bring your vision of a low-maintenance garden to life—no matter your circumstances.

You won't just be growing a garden but cultivating a healthier, more sustainable, and uniquely fulfilling lifestyle.

1

COMPANION PLANTING BASICS

P lants "talk" to each other. That sounds like some new-aged, sci-fi mumbo-jumbo, but it's true. Of course, it's not a language you and I can understand or even hear; instead, they mainly communicate chemically and via underground mycorrhizal (a type of fungi) networks. Through this type of communication, plants often alter their behavior or even share nutrients and resources in response to environmental changes or cues.

However, a recent study found that plants also emit ultrasonic "clicking" sounds that might be audible to insects and certain mammals (Khait et al., 2023). It still needs to be determined whether these sounds are intentional (used for communication, to attract pollinators, or to distract predators) or are just a result of microscopic, physiological processes within the plant itself.

Researchers can say that the frequency of the clicking sounds sounded different when a plant was healthy versus when it was distressed (dehydrated or cut). Remember that this doesn't necessarily prove that the sounds are because of pain or distress; it's simply a response. Either way, this discovery is both profoundly fascinating and unsettling at the same time.

However, there are several reasons why some plants might not "get along" with certain other plants. Welcome to your garden's social media network!

WHAT IS COMPANION PLANTING?

When you think of a garden, you envision traditional monocultural farming practices. Everything you plant is separated; there's an allocated spot or garden bed for your beans, far away from your tomatoes, and so on. However, monocultures are destructive for many reasons: they strip the soil, damage biodiversity, lead to pest infestations, and result in having to use large amounts of chemical fertilizers and pesticides for a satisfactory harvest.

Companion planting is an alternative approach to monocultures. It involves planting different crops close to each other so they benefit each other by providing ground cover, weed management, natural pest control, and so much more. But companion planting also helps the soil, attracts pollinators, saves space, and increases yields and better-quality produce.

This gardening method falls under permaculture practices and has been practiced worldwide for thousands of years. We are still determining exactly when companion planting started, most likely because it dates back to the nomadic hunter-gatherer era, where barely anything was well-documented.

The "three sisters" method, discovered by Native Americans, is a notable example of companion planting still in use today. The "three sisters" refers to planting beans, corn, and squash together in a guild. The corn is stable support for the climbing beans; the beans replace the nitrogen in the soil (keeping it fertile), and the squash covers the ground, preventing the soil from drying out (the leaves are also used as mulch once the season is over).

Companion planting forms a network of protection and mutual benefit for every plant. Every plant has a function and contributes to a self-sustaining ecosystem in your backyard (even if that function only provides you with food). By observing nature and working with it, you make your own life more manageable.

Does It Work?

Many skeptics say no scientific evidence supports the idea that companion planting is better than the average gardener or farmer's practices. Putting aside the fact that it makes your garden subjectively easier to maintain, there *is* solid, irrefutable proof that companion planting is highly beneficial on more than one front:

- Companion planting improves soil quality (Zhang et al., 2018) (Chen et al., 2020) (Xiao et al., 2013).
- Companion planting inhibits harmful bacteria growth that can affect the health of your plants and their root systems (van Elsas et al., 2012) (Xu et al., 2014) (Fu et al., 2016).
- Companion planting is effective for pest resistance (Riesselman, n.d.) (Saldanha et al., 2019) (Ben-Issa et al., 2017).
- Companion planting improves yield size and produce quality (Griffiths-Lee et al., 2020) (Montoya et al., 2020).

Whether you believe it works or not, companion planting is a natural observation. Nature always finds the easiest, most efficient way to do things because it has had tens of millions of years to figure it out. To go against that is to create endless work and, more often than not, perpetual disappointment for yourself.

Why It Works

Imagine you want to start a town from scratch for a second. What does a city need for it to thrive and be productive? Besides the physical infrastructure (buildings, roads, etc.), police officers, teachers, doctors, firefighters, builders, plumbers, electricians, business owners, cashiers, cleaners, sanitation workers, etc.

A garden is like a plant version of a town, with many essential roles to fill. Can a city occupied solely by police officers, for example, be productive? It would probably be the safest town, but what happens when a fire breaks out, a sewage pipe clogs, or a flu outbreak?

That's precisely the issue with monocultural agriculture. As much as we need to create a multifaceted community to fulfill everyone's needs, we need to foster diversity in every aspect. All the plants have separate functions and goals with companion planting, but they ultimately work together as a unit. Some plants strip the soil to provide food, while the plants beside it ward off pests and replenish the soil.

Certain types of crops will benefit your garden in different ways, but here are some things you stand to gain regardless of the types of plants you decide to grow in your garden:

- Maintaining Soil Health.

Crop plants always extract water, minerals, and nutrients from the soil to grow and reproduce through seeds. As you likely know, nitrogen, phosphorus, and potassium are the three most essential nutrients for the soil to stay fertile and support plant growth.

Companion planting will reduce your need to continuously fertilize your garden because some plants (like legumes and clover) are "nitrogen-fixers," meaning they put the nitrogen from the air back into the soil. Root vegetables prevent soil from becoming compacted. The remaining plant matter is left in the ground at the end of the season or used as mulch to replace phosphorus. The diversity that companion planting offers also helps maintain and establish helpful microorganism populations that live in the soil beneath your garden (which also contributes to healthy roots and plants).

- Pest Control.

Certain plants have natural pest-deterring capabilities, whether it be through emitting strong smells that ward off pests in general or camouflaging attractive smells (from fruits or vegetables), releasing certain chemicals into the ground or air, or simply attracting predatory insects that feed on harmful ones.

- Weed Management.

That's right! You can minimize or even prevent weeds from growing in your garden. There are two ways this can happen. The first is that some plants release chemicals that slow the growth of weeds, effectively keeping them in check. The second is planting ground cover crops in all the bare spaces in your garden (like clover, alfalfa, or creeping thyme) to suppress weeds from taking over in the first place.

- Maximizing Space.

Companion planting lets you plan your garden bed to fit more plants in a smaller space. By considering the different growth rates and root systems of the different types of plants, you can maximize your available garden space. You can plant a crop with a shallow root system way closer to a crop that has a taproot system because they won't compete for space underground.

The key is to be strategic about your crop placements and timing. Radishes, for example, grow so fast that they'll need to be harvested way before your carrots need that extra space. So, even though carrots and radishes are both root vegetables, you can plant your radishes in between your carrots with no issues!

- Increased Yields.

This result is more due to a combination of all the other benefits of companion planting. Fewer pests mean less loss of plant foliage and fruit, more biodiversity means more pollinators and better soil quality means healthier plants (and therefore more and better-quality produce).

PERMACULTURE PRINCIPLES

You don't need to adopt or implement permaculture principles in every aspect of your gardening regime; however, companion planting focuses on these principles. It would only be fitting to explore these principles briefly.

Permaculture is a portmanteau of "permanent" and "agriculture." The essence of this practice is to design any garden or farm space based on systems that are naturally present to work with Mother Nature rather than against it. Sustainability (for you and your garden) and self-sufficiency are at the core of permaculture practices.

Garden Ecosystems

Companion planting is integral to permaculture because it creates a self-sufficient, resilient, thriving garden. And again, even if you don't commit to all permaculture gardening principles, implementing companion planting involves creating an entire interconnected ecosystem in your backyard.

A garden ecosystem includes the following:

- Biodiversity.

All living organisms, including plants, insects, pests, fungi, and bacteria, contribute to the health of your garden. A diverse garden will attract life in all forms; that's a given. The aim is to create a natural balance between predator and prey—a circle of life. Your tomato plants attract aphids, ladybugs eat the aphids, and ladybugs attract birds, frogs, spiders, and dragonflies to your garden, which is good for pollination and keeping other types of pests under control.

Despite how you feel about spiders or other creepy crawlies, having them visit your garden is good. This biodiversity contributes to natural pest control, pollination, decomposition, increased yields, and a happy garden.

- Soil Microbiology.

At the beginning of this chapter, we talked about how plants communicate with each other through underground fungal networks. But there's more going on in the ground underneath your cabbage patch. Fungi, bacteria, and even worms all play an essential role in nutrient cycling and soil formation.

Many permaculture gardeners have worm farms and collect worm castings and something called "worm tea" (the liquid that seeps out of the worm farm, and yes, it's as disgusting as it sounds) to use as fertilizer in their garden beds. That's how valuable these slimy little creatures are!

The same principles that count above ground also apply to the underground population. You want to maintain a balance where the beneficial bacteria and microorganisms are thriving so the harmful ones don't take over and lead to the death of your garden.

That is why biodiversity in your garden is so crucial. A healthy and diverse ecosystem will keep your garden thriving indefinitely without you having to drench the Earth in chemicals or give up more of your valuable time trying to fight nature (to no avail).

CONCERNS ABOUT COMPANION PLANTING

Whether you're still on the fence or all in, I'm sure you have some concerns. It will require a lot of additional research (even after you read this book) and even some trial and error to achieve your gardening goals. Companion planting will help you get there regardless of your ambitions.

We will now be addressing the most common concerns relating to companion planting to set your mind at ease:

- Time Investment.

With an already busy schedule, the last thing you want to hear is that it will take longer. And the honest answer is that companion planting will require you to invest more time initially. The research, planning, and preparation will be the most challenging and time-consuming.

So yes, initially, it will be more time-consuming. However, in the long run, it will pay off. Imagine a garden with little to no weeds, minimum need for fertilization, no significant pest problems, and no need for chemical treatments. Now imagine, on top of that, the best yield your garden can manage to offer. That initial time investment will lead to your only general garden maintenance: stroll through it once a week to ensure everything is running smoothly and harvesting once the time comes.

- Space Requirements.

Again, while gardening requires some outdoor space (or at least a sunny windowsill or balcony), only gardening techniques like companion planting will maximize the available space. We will discuss this topic in more detail later, but you can grow more food in a smaller space than you think is possible.

Besides the fact that companion planting utilizes every inch of available space you have, other methods further help this, like vertical gardens, container planting, or making a raised garden bed on top of solid concrete. With a little bit of strategic planning, you can go far.

- Effectiveness.

The big question: Is it worth it? It depends on your gardening goals; I need help answering this question. When you look at the benefits of companion planting and the evidence that backs it up objectively, the answer is yes. You need to evaluate your goals and what you want your garden to be and decide whether companion planting will aid your approach or strategy to achieve the desired results. The answer is usually yes.

Now that you know the basics of companion planting and what to expect going forward, deciding whether you want to turn the page is up to you. Please put on your lab coat because next, we'll dive into the science of companion planting and why certain plants work so well together. Don't worry, it's pretty interesting.

2

THE SCIENCE BEHIND COMPANION PLANTING

I t's not magic; it's just science. Certain plants are helpful to certain other species of plants and vice versa, helping each other thrive by keeping the soil healthy, fending off pests, protecting each other from diseases or other environmental factors, or, in some cases, contributing to taste. But usually, it's a combination of all the above mentioned.

In this chapter, you'll learn about plant chemistry and the communication happening in the soil. And as dull as that may sound, it will answer most (if not all) of your questions about companion planting. You'll understand why it's an effective pest management strategy and how it contributes to soil health. We'll also be debunking some common myths about companion planting.

UNDERSTANDING PLANT CHEMISTRY

Just like our brains release endorphins and other chemical messages that keep us alive and determine how we react to our environment, plants have a similar process called allelopathy. Allelopathy is how a plant grows and defends itself from diseases or pests. But these chemicals also affect the health of the soil and all living organisms surrounding it (other plants, weeds, microorganisms, and insects). It also affects how plants talk and respond to each other.

The effects of these allelochemicals can be either directly or indirectly beneficial or harmful. Allelopathy is how a plant recognizes it's in danger. Based on the kind of danger (pests, pathogens, or competition in the form of overcrowding or weeds), it will release certain chemicals into the soil or even into the air that can inhibit the growth of competitor plants and weeds, ward off pests, and kill pathogens (bacteria, viruses, fungi, etc.) Allelopathy is so effective that researchers use it to create more effective organic pesticides.

These chemicals are known as volatile organic compounds (or VOCs) and include substances from a plant's secondary metabolic or decomposition systems, for example, water-soluble organic acids, straight-chain alcohols, ketones, amino acids, phenols, and long-chain fatty acids to name but a few.

When I first heard the phrase VOCs, my brain immediately thought of the word "biohazard." The word "volatile" is both accurate and not accurate when referring to plant chemistry. Volatility in plants is an entirely natural process; snake poison and cyanide, considered biohazards, are both naturally occurring compound chemicals. But I digress.

While VOCs are crucial to survival, producing allelochemicals can lead to autotoxicity (when a plant accidentally kills itself) and soil sickness (the chemicals released by the plant make the soil uninhabitable). Managing plant allelopathy is crucial for crop growth. Crop rotation, intercropping, and companion planting can help. When plants are happy and not fighting over resources, they work together.

Specific compounds are released depending on the threat or situation at hand. So, the type of VOC released when there's a drought is different from when there's a bacterial disease present in the soil, and so on. But VOCs are also responsible for attracting pollinators and other beneficial organisms and repelling certain pests. These chemical reactions within the roots are also how plants "communicate" with microorganisms in the soil and form a mutually beneficial relationship.

For example, plant roots release sugars and other organic acids (including nitrogen) into the soil. Then microorganisms (bacteria and mycorrhizae) will "eat" and break these compounds down, making them more accessible (or usable) to the plant. Soil microorganisms also form a protection barrier around the plant's roots, making the environment hostile to pathogens that seek to harm the plant.

THE MECHANISMS BEHIND NATURAL PEST CONTROL

Arguably, the most sought-after benefit of companion planting is the element of natural pest control. You're not spraying harmful chemicals on your plants that can seep into the soil. You're letting nature take its course by creating an environment where pest populations are kept in line (not eradicated, but managed); you're encouraging a circle of life and using it to your advantage. In addition, you can use structural strategies to control and minimize pest populations further.

Ideally, you want to integrate natural pest management protocols into your garden when designing it according to permaculture principles. However, there is always time to introduce natural pest management, regardless of where you may be in your gardening journey.

We'll cover the most common and effective mechanisms and techniques behind integrated pest management. Depending on the type and severity of the pests in your garden, you'll have to decide which method (or combination of them) will work best for your specific situation. You may have to tailor your approach to get the best results. Nevertheless, here are the most common ways to naturally manage pests:

- Predator Attraction.

Inviting predatory insects to your garden helps control the pest populations in a few ways. Certain adult insects themselves will feast on the pests, or their larvae will. You can encourage predatory insects to stick around by providing for their basic needs: food, water, and shelter.

Pollen and nectar from your crops (and even the presence of pests) provide them with food. Lots of foliage shelters them (you can also build insect homes by drilling holes in blocks of untreated wood and placing them around your garden). Dew droplets on leaves provide them with water, but you can take it a step further by putting out water in shallow bowls filled with pebbles (the pebbles prevent small insects from accidentally drowning and give them something to crawl onto if they do fall in the water).

- Pest Repellent Crops.

Some crops (typically herbs) are strong-scented and will deter certain types of pests because they don't like the smell. A few common examples of pest-repellent aromatic herbs are mint, garlic, coriander, chives, and thyme.

Plant aromatic, pest-repellent herbs and flowers along the perimeter or edges of your garden and between your crops (interplanting).

- Trap Cropping.

Trap cropping involves sacrificing one or two plants to lure pests away from the rest of your garden. Different pests prefer different crops; slugs favor lettuce, budworms, and aphids go after tomatoes, beetles and weevils feed mainly on legume leaves, and so on. However, they will make do with whatever your garden has to offer if need be.

The idea is to provide the pests in your garden with an all-you-can-eat buffet of their favorite fruit or vegetable. This tactic will prevent them from infiltrating your entire yield. So, if you find slugs on your tomatoes, for example, grow a single lettuce plant nearby. The slugs will choose the lettuce over the tomatoes any day of the week. Yes, you will likely destroy the lettuce plant, and you won't be able to harvest from it, but your tomatoes will remain untouched.

Furthermore, you can inspect your sacrificial crops now and then and manually remove any pests or eggs you come across. Remove the entire plant and replace it with another to eliminate tiny pests like aphids that have overrun the trap crop. Removing pests isn't ideal, but it can help keep the population from growing out of control.

In some cases, planting trap crops around the border or edge of your garden bed works well; other times, you might have to interplant the trap crops. However, this will depend on the type of pest, their population, and determination.

- Create Confusion.

Interplanting strong-scented herbs and rotating your crops can contribute to confusion. Aromas from herbs carry through the wind and can mask the smell of your fruits and vegetables to a degree. This confusion means pests will be less likely to stumble across your garden or follow the sweet smell of dinner. Moreover, rotating your crops adds to the confusion and positively affects soil health (two birds, one stone).

- Structural Strategies.

If nothing works to minimize or prevent pest infestations, turn to physical barriers. You can do this through mesh-covered frames or tunnels (over a plant or garden bed) or a greenhouse. However, this will require you to lift (or open) the structure for a few hours daily (preferably in the morning) so pollinators can still get in and out. If you have a full schedule, this strategy can be challenging, so it's more of a temporary solution and a last resort.

Remember that pests only appear at a specific time of year, typically when the weather is warm and humid. Have a plan before an infestation occurs rather than trying to treat it when it's already in full swing. Besides that, you'll have to experiment and see what methods are effective and maintainable (given your resources and capabilities) and which need to be improved.

SOIL HEALTH AND MICROBES

We've all done that experiment in elementary school where you scoop up some soil and mix it with water. If you haven't (or you can't remember it), after mixing the dirt and sand and leaving it to settle for a week, there's a clear separation between the different types of soil: sand, silt, and clay. Sand will be the first layer at the bottom of the container, followed by a layer of silt, then clay, and any plant debris will float. But soil has much more going on than simply the different layers it likes to settle into.

Soil, together with water, sunlight, and air, creates the basis of plant life. Soil characteristics include physical, chemical, and biological interactions that all contribute to the decomposition of organic material, the cycle of nutrients, and carbon storage.

The physical elements of soil are the non-living components (the granules of sand, silt, and clay, along with decomposed plant and animal material and enzymes) that make up the structure of the soil. Meanwhile, the living components are microbes that spend most or all their lives underground (including fungi, bacteria, protozoa, and microbial enzymes).

The amount of living components in the soil controls the rate at which carbon is taken and released back into the soil (also known as the respiration rate). Soil with diverse biomass (living microorganisms) is more resilient to stressors like environmental change and disturbances. They can quickly return to the original, balanced state and activity after such stressors have occurred.

Underground life forms (microbial or otherwise) and their populations play a crucial role in the decomposition of organic matter. This participation means that microorganisms recycle nutrients through eating, digesting, and excreting dead plant and animal material so other plants can use them again. Less microbial activity means decomposition and respiration rates (and therefore nutrient cycling) occur slower and less efficiently, which can lead to a buildup of toxins and harmful bacteria.

The bottom line is that the living components in the soil contribute to the health of your garden. Microbial activity controls everything from the arrangements of the physical components (sand, silt, and clay) to the pH levels of your soil.

Soil Food Web

Soil biota refers to all the living components in soil, whether single-celled, microscopic, or visible to the naked eye. The underground community is diverse, and every member has a different (but necessary) role to keep the soil healthy. Fostering diversity in your soil and garden involves balancing predator and prey, establishing mutually beneficial relationships, and balance.

An imbalance of soil biota or lack of diversity can cause garden issues that require additional maintenance. This imbalance means that if your soil is unhealthy, your garden will only flourish once you do something about it on a foundational level.

The soil food web refers to exactly what you think it is: the circle of life in the soil. The following is a breakdown of all the life forms that reside on the Earth below your feet and the roles they play:

- Bacteria.

Bacteria come in many forms. It's more like an entire species with multiple branches of different kinds of bacteria. Some are good, and some are bad. But all of them are necessary for balance within the soil food web.

Bacteria fulfill many roles to ensure the soil stays healthy. Some bacteria produce and release enzymes that break down dead organic material into usable nutrients for plants. Others form mutually beneficial relationships with plant roots; they eat sugars that the roots release, and in exchange, the bacteria provide the plant with nitrogen. In soil with minimal exposure to oxygen and sunlight (deep underground or below bodies of water), a specific group of bacteria feeds on nitrogen, sulfur, hydrogen, and iron to ensure enough nutrients in the soil for the surrounding flora.

Then there's the group of harmful bacteria or pathogens. These little fellas cause your plants and their roots to fall ill (root rot, wilt, powdery mildew, dampening off, etc.) However, most beneficial or good bacteria will prey on or eat harmful bacteria. So, keeping the good bacteria populations high should be a top priority of any companion gardener.

Actinobacteria is another type of bacteria, but what sets them apart from regular bacteria is that they grow hyphae or root-like networks (much like fungi). You know that earthy smell when it rains or when you till the garden bed? You can thank actinobacteria for that!

- Fungi.

When most people hear "fungi," they immediately envision mushrooms. And that's true; fungi are mushrooms. Mushrooms are equivalent to fruits or flowers, and the spores are the seeds. But there's way more to it than just that. For starters, fungi can be single-celled or multicellular, and they grow hyphae, a mesh-like structure that can be so small they grow in between the cells of plant roots.

Often, the hyphae network of a mushroom is vast underneath the soil, and they grow around and into the roots of other plants. The main functions of fungi are decomposing organic material, controlling or regulating pests and diseases, and nutrient cycling. The hyphae can grow deep into the soil and transport minerals, nutrients, and water closer to the surface for plant roots to absorb.

Of course, some fungi do more harm than good and can infect your plants with diseases. But again, balance is the key.

- Protozoa.

Protozoa are single-celled, microscopic organisms that mainly serve as decomposers. They eat decaying matter and turn it into nitrogen, one of the main ingredients in fertilizer and compost (necessary for healthy soil and thriving crops).

- Nematodes.

These are tiny, roundworms. Most nematodes are microscopically small, but the largest nematode ever discovered and recorded was just over 26 feet long and living in the reproductive system of a sperm whale. However, you won't have to worry about coming across a nematode in your garden that is more significant than 2 to 5 mm.

Nematodes prey on all soil biota, such as bacteria and fungi (remember, even the good guys need a natural predator to keep the numbers balanced), but nematodes aren't the bad guys since they release nutrients into the soil. However, nematodes (much like all forms of life) can also be carriers of diseases.

- Earthworms.

By burrowing in the soil, earthworms manage to do something fundamental that microorganisms can't: they create space or air pockets. This function is essential because it's tough for roots to penetrate compacted soil. Compacted roots will result in stunted growth, disease, decreased plant vigor, and underperforming yields. Earthworms are like tilling machines but are less destructive and traumatic to the soil biota.

But besides allowing oxygen to reach the routes via the space they create, these slimy creatures travel deep into the Earth, eating as they go. On their way up, they expel their nutrient-rich "castings" closer to the top layer of soil, effectively mining precious food and nutrients for your plants to use up.

- Arthropods.

Millipedes, centipedes, springtails, and mites can invade your garden and wreak havoc on your crops. But they can also help break down organic matter and increase underground activity. Controlling populations of these pests can be advantageous. Like earthworms, they help aerate and mix the soil, which improves water retention while keeping the soil well-draining (well-draining soil doesn't mean zero water retention). They even feed on other types of potential soil pests, like nematodes.

The bottom line is that all living creatures on Earth (and within it) form part of the food web. And whenever the food chain is broken or unbalanced, bad things happen. The underground food web is no different. When specific populations grow out of control (even when the organisms are highly beneficial), the whole system falls apart, and the soil becomes infertile or uninhabitable.

That's why diversity is so important, especially in soil biota. Ironically, one way to foster a diverse underground food web is to diversify your crops. Crop rotation, intercropping, cover cropping, mulching, no-till systems, not using chemicals, and inoculating soil with mycorrhizal fungi can also encourage a balanced, healthy soil biota.

COMPANION PLANTING MYTHS AND MISCONCEPTIONS

Companion planting is a sought-after home or kitchen garden approach because it has many benefits. And as wonderful as it can be when done right, myths and misconceptions can't be managed once they've taken root (pun intended).

Here, we'll be debunking some common myths and misconceptions about companion planting so you have a better idea of what to expect and what it might be like in reality:

- The "Rules" Are Universal.

While it might be well-documented that certain plants benefit each other, there might still be a chance that that's not the case in your experience. You may plant marigolds with your tomatoes because they are said to ward off hornworms (a common tomato pest), only to be disappointed that it's not working in your garden.

Plants adapt to their environment over time. This adaptation might mean that specific genes or characteristics change and aren't universally applicable or consistent. While there are guidelines for companion planting, it always comes down to being willing to learn from your experiences and adapt your approach accordingly, even if it means going off-book.

- It Eliminates the Need for Pest Management.

Unless you're growing your garden in a sterile environment (in which case your crops won't thrive anyway), pests will always be present. The goal of companion planting has never been eliminating pests but managing their populations and, therefore, minimizing and maintaining their levels of destruction.

- It Prevents Plant Diseases.

A diverse garden can build the resilience and health of your garden and the soil in which they grow, but this doesn't mean diseases can't still break out. Companion planting and proper gardening hygiene practices can significantly lower the chances of your plants contracting a disease or illness—but the chances are never zero.

- It Is Always Successful.

Look, companion planting is better for your garden and the environment and can improve the quality of your yields and soil. You may fail on your initial attempt, and that's okay. Many things influence gardening, and the soil and climate conditions must be acceptable regardless of whether you're practicing companion planting.

Before planting anything, addressing issues such as soil health is essential. And even if the conditions are favorable, nature can be unpredictable. Companion planting is great for building a healthy and resilient garden, but that doesn't mean it will always withstand a harsh heatwave, raging storm, pest infestations, disease, or a significant temperature drop.

The science behind plant life and companion planting is astounding. So much is happening, and this chapter barely scratches the surface. Luckily, you don't need to know everything there is to learn to maintain a happy garden. The basics of plant chemistry will suffice.

3

PLANNING YOUR COMPANION GARDEN

Here it is, the moment you've been eagerly anticipating. Now, we're getting to the fun part: planning and designing your garden. In this chapter, we'll be going over how to approach planning your companion guilds to maximize the benefits and advantages of companion planting while also using all the available space.

One thing you should keep in mind is to prioritize function over beauty. You may want the marigolds in the front of your yard where everyone can see them, but if your front yard isn't getting enough sun, you need to use that space for shade-tolerant crops and flowers instead. A functional and thriving garden *looks* beautiful right from the planning stage.

YOUR GOALS

Your gardening goals will influence what crops you grow or what you do before you plant anything. Take a few minutes to think about what you want to accomplish with your garden. Maybe you want fresh herbs for cooking or brewing tea. You may only want to grow your favorite fruits and vegetables to lower your grocery bill. You may want a flower garden that attracts hummingbirds for you to look at.

While planning your garden has a lot to do with your style and preference, here are a few more things to consider:

- Soil Quality.

You can buy DIY kits to test soil quality at most garden stores or send a sample to a lab for more accurate and detailed results. Either way, knowing the current state of your soil is always a good starting point. A top priority goal should be to improve the health of your soil in perpetuity, meaning that you're replacing nutrients (following permaculture gardening practices) as much as you can and not just stripping the soil. In a later chapter, we'll discuss how to improve the health and fertility of your soil.

- Harvest.

Please list all the herbs, fruits, and vegetables you want to grow for harvesting and consumption. Only add crops to this list that you will use wisely and estimate how much you'll need to cultivate based on how frequently you eat it. If you only eat tomatoes once a month, you don't need five tomato plants. If you don't like onions, don't grow them (unless you're growing them for pest management). If you want to pickle or conserve some of your crops and have them fresh, you'll need to produce more.

It would help if you also considered the specific climate you're in. You can only grow pineapples in Canada with special precautions like building a greenhouse and purchasing UV lamps. To make things easier, choose your crops from a trusted online source that lists what grows best in your state, region, or country.

- Pest Control.

Research the types of crops and flowers you want to grow in your garden (as per the previous point) and know what pests are most common for those specifically. Doing so will provide you with a list of potential future pests. You can narrow this list by looking into which pests occur more frequently or abundantly in your climate or area.

You now (hopefully) have a shortened list of pests to worry about. Use this list and look up herbs or crops that repel these pests and add them to your list of crops you want to plant. This second list is non-negotiable. Even if you don't wish to have fennel in your garden or don't like the taste of it, it's a small sacrifice you need to make to keep aphids at bay. Dry it and give it to your grand-mother, or use it as mulch at the end of the season. There's always a way to get as much use out of what you have, even if you didn't want it in the first place.

Your goals might be simple: Improve soil quality, grow food, eat food, repeat. Or you might have more elaborate plans like growing a community food forest (if you have the space for it) or saving the seeds. Nevertheless, you need to know what those goals are and break down the steps you need to take to accomplish them.

GUILD PLANNING

A guild is a small community of plants (in a small or medium garden bed or container) that work well together. By this, I mean every type of crop supports the growth and well-being of the other crops in the guild. You must fulfill three prominent roles in a guild that contribute to the overall success of the harvest: attract, repel, and cover.

To elaborate: In every guild, you need a crop that attracts pollinators for bigger harvests. Repels pests by either attracting predatory insects or exuding a powerful scent. It covers the ground, suppressing weeds and improving soil quality and structure.

Furthermore, a guild usually has one primary crop. This crop is either the biggest or has the most prominent fruits or the crop you use the most. An apple tree, for instance, is the center of the guild, and you can plant many things underneath it (but the tree is the main crop). Tomatoes are another excellent example; they only do a little for the guild itself and don't take up much space, but they're a staple in many kitchens.

Nutrient cycling aids or fertilizing plants are another aspect to consider. Most annual crops are heavy feeders and take much out of the soil, so you need nitrogen fixers to keep the soil healthy and fertile (legumes are excellent nitrogen fixers). However, legumes are only good companions for some of your other crops. You need an alternative if legumes aren't good companions for a specific crop type. The fix could be adding a plant to the guild that brings nutrients to the surface (a taproot) or topping the soil with compost more often.

Planning a guild can be complicated and requires significant creative problem-solving skills and intense research. Remember how much space all your crops will take up at maturity, both above and below ground (remember, the roots also need space). You need to consider sun, water, and soil requirements, which affect the layout of your garden. Even plants that are tried and tested companions may have slightly different needs, but it's usually not enough to interfere with the growth or production of each other, so it still works.

Some plants are the opposite of companions. Either they will die or kill each other if you plant them nearby (due to those VOCs we talked about), or their requirements are so different that you can't possibly accommodate both of them in the same space. Hence, more often than not, you'll need to plan multiple guilds to grow everything you want to grow.

For example, if you want to grow blueberries and cauliflower, they must be developed in separate guilds because they have different soil pH requirements. Blueberries like acidic soil, but cauliflower prefers alkaline soil; neither of these crops will thrive if you disregard entirely their pH needs.

Popular Guild Combinations

If you're still getting your feet wet with the companion planting thing, researching and putting together all the information to develop your guild can be overwhelming. It's better to start with one or two beginner guilds until you

become familiar with the process. I assembled a list of typical guilds that are highly likely to succeed since they've been well-documented and replicated by many home gardeners. You'll still need to research when you should propagate them, sun requirements, water needs, soil preference, etc. But for the most part, here are some beginner guilds that will likely do well:

- Tomatoes, basil, garlic, and marigold.
- Green beans, radish, celery, and nasturtium.
- Carrots, onions, rosemary, and leeks.
- Lettuce, mint, beets, and marigold.
- Squash, peas, dill, and marigold.
- Sweet corn, cucumber, beans, and borage.
- Potatoes, horseradish, cabbage, and marigold.

- Strawberries, spinach, chives, and alyssum.
- Blueberries, lemon balm, borage, and azaleas.
- Melon (of any kind), broccoli, garlic, and lavender.
- Capsicums (bell peppers, chilies, etc.), pumpkin, lettuce, and echinacea.
- Eggplant, potato, parsley, and marigold.

If you're not keen on mulching your garden bed every so often, try living mulch. Living mulch is low-growing (or ground-covering) crops you grow wherever the soil is exposed or between crops. Some good choices for living mulch are borage, creeping thyme, clover (a nitrogen fixer), dandelion, and yarrow. But you can also use other low-growing crops as living mulch, for example, chives, chamomile, chickweed, mustard, parsley, and even strawberries. Ensure your ground cover crops are compatible with all the other crops in that guild.

Incompatible Crops

There are many reasons why certain crops are incompatible with each other. The three main reasons why some plants don't get along are: a crop releases a chemical that kills or, at the very least, stunts the growth of another plant. They compete for the same nutrients. Or they attract the same pests (which could lead to an infestation).

As a general rule, you should avoid planting too many crops of the same family together in one guild (choose either garlic or chives, but not both, for example). But to make things easier for you, here is a list of common crops and what you should avoid putting with them in the same guild:

- Asparagus: Avoid planting with alliums (onion family), potatoes, and fennel.
- Beans (or legumes): Avoid planting with brassicas and alliums.
- Beets: Avoid planting with legumes or mustard.
- Brassicas: Avoid planting with legumes, tomatoes, lettuce, and strawberries.
- Carrots: Avoid planting with dill, fennel, or parsnips.
- Corn: Avoid planting with tomatoes.
- Cucumber: Avoid planting with melons (of any kind), potatoes, and sage.
- Fennel: Plant in pots or containers away from your crops since this herb can be very picky and incompatible with many crops. It's just easier to plant it completely separately (if you want it) instead of trying to include it somewhere.
- Lettuce: Avoid planting with brassicas.
- Peas: Avoid planting with alliums.
- Peppers: Avoid planting with brassicas and fennel.
- Potatoes: Avoid planting with brassicas, tomatoes, carrots, cucumbers, gourds, fennel, and asparagus.
- Pumpkins: Avoid planting with root crops (beets, onions, potatoes, carrots, radishes, etc.)
- Strawberries: Avoid planting with brassicas and fennel.
- Tomatoes: Avoid planting with brassicas, corn, dill, fennel, and other nightshades (peppers, eggplant, potatoes).

Always double-check from several sources whether all the crops in your guilds are compatible during the planning stage. Yes, it's a lot of research, but I promise it's necessary and worth it.

DESIGN AND LAYOUT

There's a lot to consider when planning not only your guilds but the actual layout of those guilds within your available space. The two most critical factors in designing a layout in your garden are space and light requirements. Most garden fruiting crops require full sun (6-8 hours per day), while some may benefit from afternoon shade (or will grow just fine in partial sun).

You need to know the sun requirements of all your selected plants and how much space they will take up once they mature. If you have minimal space available for a garden, you need to grow your guilds in containers or pots. If you have a large shade area, you must factor this in when choosing crops and designing layouts for your guilds.

Spend some time in your gardening space and map out where the sunny and shady spots are throughout the day. In addition, you should measure your space to accurately determine how big your guilds should be and make a garden blueprint to scale. Another thing to consider when designing your garden is water accessibility, though this is usually only a problem with larger gardening spaces.

There are a few approaches you can choose from when planning your guilds and their layouts in your space, for example:

- Blocks.

Divide your space into four squares and assign each square a guild. This approach doesn't mean the whole square should be a garden bed; it just means space is specifically for a particular guild.

This method ensures that you will receive four guilds without fail. An example of using this approach is: You plan out and divide your entire space into four squares. Square one is for guild one: Tomatoes, basil, garlic, and marigolds, for example. If square one is too big to make into a singular garden bed, you can further divide square one into multiple garden beds (with dividing footpaths in between for easy access from all sides). So now you have numerous smaller garden beds within an allocated square, and each garden bed within this space contains a guild consisting of a tomato, basil, and marigold plant, with a few garlic bulbs.

Repeat this for each of the four squares (or more if you have the space) with a different guild. Remember, the size of the crops will dictate how big your garden beds should be. But you should be able to reach all sides of the garden bed comfortably (by making it narrow enough if it's against a wall or has a path around it while still accessing the center).

The advantage of this approach is that you're way less likely to lose your entire guild and harvest to pest infestations, diseases, and so on. However, it could be more space-efficient.

- Rectangles.

With this method, you can use the classic gardening layout of planting rows (essentially slim rectangular garden beds). However, in nature, you never see crops growing in perfect rows, but whether or not there's a good, scientific reason for that (other than it being random) is still up for debate. If you plan on using rows for your guilds, make sure taller crops aren't casting shadows over the low-growing ones.

Alternatively, you can make as many large-ish rectangular garden beds (raised or otherwise) as you can fit into your space and assign a different guild to each one. This way (using the previous example), one rectangle has multiple tomato, basil, onion, and marigold plants—so you have one large guild instead of separating them like in the square approach (previous bullet point).

Remember to include footpaths between the rectangular garden beds and ensure you can reach every inch without slipping a disk in your back. This method's main "selling point" is that it makes good use of all available space, especially if space is limited. But the downside of having an entire guild in one garden bed is that pests and diseases might get to all of them before you can intervene.

- Square Foot.

For this method, you will make as many one-square-foot garden beds comfortably fit into your space (with narrow footpaths in between). From here, you can plant one to three plants in each bed (depending on how much space the crop needs). You can make each bed a tiny guild if they will all fit or plant the companion crops in neighboring beds.

This method is also a great space saver. Suppose you can only plant your crops directly. In that case, you can also grow your garden in a series of large containers (approximately one square foot in size or diameter), put the crops in the same guild, and separate them from the others.

- Vertical.

Vertical gardening takes home first prize when maximizing space in scenarios where you don't have space to spare, live in an apartment with only a tiny balcony for outside space, or barely have any yard to play with. This approach includes vertical planters, but you can also grow quite a lot in hanging baskets, metal shelves, or against trellises.

The only downside to vertical gardens (or any gardens not grown in the ground directly, such as container gardens or raised garden beds on concrete) is that they need watering more often.

SOIL PREPARATION

You have thoroughly researched every crop and flower you plan to cultivate in your garden. You know the specific requirements of each plant, where to place them, and how to layout your garden to maximize their growth. You've researched every crop and flower in every plant guild you plan to cultivate into oblivion. You know what makes them tick, what they need, where you will put them, and how you'll lay them out in your garden. What's next?

Your garden is only as good as your soil. Soil serves as both a literal and figurative foundation for your garden. There's no way around it; you need to know what's happening with your soil and whether there's anything to fix or be worried about. Luckily, you can learn quite a lot about the health and well-being of your soil with a few easy DIY tests.

But before we get into that, you can test your soil by sending a sample to your local county extension office, which is usually inexpensive or completely free. Professional tests are much more comprehensive since they test pH levels, soil texture, type, and amounts of available nutrients. They will also give you specific advice on what to do to correct any potential problems.

However, there are many ways you can test your soil without having to collect a sample, send it off, and then patiently wait for the results to come back. These home tests are way less accurate, but they will give you something to work with if professional tests are only an option after some time.

Testing Soil pH Levels

Most garden crops prefer neutral soil (between six and seven). Of course, some crops prefer either extreme (more acidic or alkaline soil), but that's the exception and not the rule. A neutral soil pH level likely means your soil is relatively healthy, and you won't need to do much concerning preparation for planting other than ensuring the soil stays healthy and fertile.

The problem with an unbalanced soil pH level (lower than six or higher than seven) is that there might be enough nutrients in the soil, but the plants can't absorb them properly. This results in the crops dying from a nutrient deficiency even though there's plenty of it to go around.

You can buy home test kits for testing soil pH levels (try your local gardening center or store). With the help of technology, we now have handy-dandy gadgets like pH meters that can test your soil's pH by simply pushing some prongs into the ground and getting immediate results—these devices are reusable, too!

I advise regularly testing your soil's pH levels every two years. The best time to test the pH levels is in the fall after the crops have died down; this will also give you some time to rectify any issues so your soil is ready to go when spring arrives.

Neutralizing Soil pH Levels

You'll be pleased to hear that solving a pH problem does not require a Ph.D. It's pretty simple. If your soil's pH level is below six, add garden lime, wood ash, or mushroom compost to your garden beds. If the pH level is higher than seven, you can add sulfur and compost.

Either way, you want to do this a few months before planting anything in the soil. It can take weeks for the pH levels to stabilize after corrective treatments. Test the pH levels every couple of weeks initially to ensure things are going in the right direction. Remember to mulch your garden beds after a neutralizing treatment and be patient.

Testing Soil Type

Generally, healthy soil contains around 40% silt, 40% sand, and 20% clay. Do you remember that test we discussed earlier that you performed in elementary school, where you mix soil with water and let it settle to see the layers? Determining your soil type at home is precisely that experiment, only more detailed and with additional steps.

You'll need a glass jar (a Mason or clear plastic jar will do) with a lid, a ruler, and a timer. Dig a hole about six inches deep into the soil of the area you want to use for gardening and fill the jar halfway with the dirt you just dug up; try to avoid collecting plant matter like grass, leaves, or weeds.

Fill your jar with dirt and add water until absorbed. Close the container and shake vigorously for three minutes. Place the jar down on a level surface and start the timer. After one minute, measure how much sediment has collected at the bottom with the ruler. This measurement is the amount of sand in your soil.

After four minutes, measure the sediment level again. The difference between the two measurements is the amount of silt in your soil. (If your first measurement was an inch, for example, and the second measurement was an inch and a half, the difference is half an inch.)

Now, go about your day and check back in with your mud jar in 24 hours. Measure the sediment again and calculate the difference between the second and third measurements. This figure is the amount of clay in your soil. (For example, Your second measurement was an inch and a half; after 24 hours, it's two inches. The difference is half an inch).

You can eyeball it; you don't have to whip out a calculator. The first two measurements should be equal. This equality means that the ratios line up nicely if you get an inch of sediment after a minute and there are about two inches after four minutes. The third measurement should be half of the first (half an inch based on our previous example).

Fixing the Ratios

Based on the test results, you can calculate whether you have loamy soil (40-40-20 ratio), sandy soil, or clay soil. Loamy soil is the golden ratio, in which case you don't have to do much of anything—sprinkle some compost, add a layer of mulch, and call it a day until you're ready to plant.

If you have more sandy soil, you can mix hummus, aged manure, peat moss, or sawdust into your garden bed (you can also try sourcing clay-type soil from somewhere and incorporating it into your garden bed). If you have soil with a lot of clay, add coarse sand, compost, and peat moss. And remember to mulch!

Testing General Soil Health

The easiest and most accurate way to determine whether your soil is healthy without lab tests is to check for life. Granted, you won't be able to see many of the life forms in your soil since they're microscopic. However, you can see earthworms and check if your soil has them.

Earthworms will only go anywhere near soil with enough organic matter or nutrients to sustain them. If there are enough earthworms in the soil you want to use for planting, there's a perfect chance your soil has everything it needs to support your crops.

You'll only need a shovel, a large piece of cardboard, and the right timing to perform the earthworm test. The best time to check for earthworms is in the middle of spring, and after it has rained, you can also hose down the area thoroughly and wait a day or so before performing the test.

Lay out your cardboard and dig precisely one cubic foot of soil out of your garden, throwing all the soil you dig up onto the cardboard. Look through the excavated dirt for earthworms and count how many there are (you can throw them back into the hole as you find them). Healthy, fertile soil will have at least ten earthworms per one cubic foot of soil.

Improving Soil Health

If you find less than ten earthworms or none in the soil sample, your soil needs organic matter. You can rectify this by gently mixing in compost, aged manure, or leaf mold into the top layer of soil. Adding a generous layer of mulch will also keep the soil moist and create an environment where microorganisms break down the compost and manure to release the nutrients quickly. The mulch will also break down over time, adding to the amount of organic matter available in the soil, which will also incentivize earthworms to come set up camp!

SEASONAL PLANNING

A decent portion of your crops will be annuals that you'll have to re-sow yearly. You need to know which plants stay long-term (perennials) and which ones are just visiting (annuals). As you know, there are different crops for every season. If you want to grow crops only some of the year, you should plant ground cover crops in the off seasons or at least cover your soil with a thick layer of mulch. This tactic will prevent soil erosion and keep the soil fertile.

This example brings us to two significant things you must remember when practicing companion planting and designing your guilds and layout: Crop rotation and succession planting.

Crop Rotation

Crop rotation refers to changing your garden layout so you're not indefinitely growing crops in the same garden bed. You should rotate your crops every other year for a typical home garden. But why?

There are three main reasons (or benefits if you want to look at it that way) as to why crop rotation is so important:

- To Replenish Nutrients.

Every type of crop requires a different ratio of nutrients. Crop rotation allows the soil to bring all the lost nutrients to equilibrium, so it never loses fertility. Of course, you'll need to aid in the general rejuvenation of nutrients by adding compost every so often.

- To Reduce Diseases.

Soil-borne diseases feed on specific plants and crops (like early blight and powdery mildew, for example). When you move the crops around from time to time, you essentially remove the host from the equation, meaning disease populations don't build up in the soil over time (which will blindsight you and destroy an entire guild or crop type).

- To Confuse Pests.

Crop rotation won't eradicate a pest problem or prevent it. Interrupting pest life cycles will slow population growth, making it easier to manage with natural pest control methods.

When implementing crop rotation correctly and successfully, the most important thing to remember is crop "families." When it's time to rotate crops, avoid planting anything related to the previous guild in the same area. For example, if you have been growing cucumbers (in the Cucurbit family) in one of your garden beds for the past two years, you shouldn't rotate with any other crops from the Cucurbit family (or guilds that have them as a member).

You should know which family your crops belong to and plan your guilds around it so it's easier to rotate them. So, here's a list of crop families based on what most home gardeners tend to grow in their backyards:

- Alliums: Onions (including green onions), shallots, scallions, garlic, chives, and leeks.
- Brassicas: Broccoli, cauliflower, cabbage, Brussels sprouts, kale, turnips, radishes (including horseradish), mustard greens, bok choy, and arugula.

- Cucurbits (gourds): Cucumbers, zucchini, all pumpkins and squash, and all melons.
- Legumes: All beans, peas (including cowpeas and chickpeas), lentils, soybeans, alfalfa, clovers, vicia, and peanuts.
- Nightshades: Eggplants, tomatoes, potatoes (including sweet potatoes), and capsicums (all peppers and chilies).
- Umbellifers: Carrots, celery, cumin, fennel, parsnips, parsley, dill, and cilantro.

It's important to note that you don't have to rotate your perennial crops since they take much less soil nutrients than quick-growing annuals.

Keeping track of which guilds to rotate and where to move them can be tricky. Color coding your guilds (and even individual plants) might help. Make each family a different color and try to keep relatives and cousins together (avoid placing a member of the allium family in more than one or two guilds, for example).

A simple way to keep track of which guilds you're growing where is to keep the sketch you make (when designing your garden space) until you need to rotate your crops and plan your rotation according to that.

In some cases, it might be impossible to rotate your crops, like if you have limited space. If this is your situation, you can get around it by supplementing the soil with compost and organic fertilizer more often than usual and letting the soil rest every winter (or for a whole year after three to five years of continuous planting). Remember the nitrogen-fixing cover crops; this is essential if you can't rotate.

Succession Planting

In agriculture, succession planting refers to timing your crop propagation or plantings to extend the harvesting period and reduce waste (due to abundance). It also allows you to maximize space in a miniature garden to get the most out of it.

Succession planting is not so much necessary for companion planting as it is a "pro tip." This gardening technique is typically employed only on crops that complete their life cycle within a year. But why should you do this? The main benefits of succession planting are that it utilizes space more efficiently, provides fresh produce for longer, and allows you to grow a more extensive variety of crops in a small space.

Let me explain: When you propagate or sow all your seeds at once, the fruit will all be ready for harvest within a short time frame. This method means you'll have fresh produce for a couple of weeks once they're ripe and nothing for an entire year.

Many home gardeners will preserve their produce by pickling, conserving, or freezing the abundance so they can consume it later and let nothing go to waste. Don't get me wrong, I love a good strawberry jam or pickled onion. But frozen fruits and vegetables and dried herbs just don't hit the spot like fresh ones, not to mention all the prep work that goes into preserving all the harvested produce.

Succession planting is relatively straightforward, but it is gratifying. All you must do is start propagating a few seeds indoors before the specific planting season arrives, waiting a few days or weeks and bearing a few more. The exact time frame for staggering your crops will differ based on how long a specific crop germinates or matures.

By starting your crops earlier and staggering their planting, their maturity rate will differ, which means you can have fresh produce very early in the season and up to the end or beyond.

To break it down even more, this is what you do:

Depending on how early you want to produce ready for harvest and how long it takes to mature and bear fruit, you can calculate how early you should start propagating your seeds indoors.

For example, tomatoes can take up to 16 weeks before the fruit matures. If you want tomatoes prepared for harvest earlier in the season, you should start propagating a plant or two (based on how many you want to have) every other week at least two months in advance. Start planting tomatoes (a summer crop) indoors in the middle of spring. By summer, they'll be ready to transplant with only a few more weeks before they start flowering and producing fruit.

Regarding how succession planting saves space, it's pretty simple: Annuals typically die after they've set fruit. This thinking means that when one plant has finished fruiting and starts to wither, you can immediately replace it with a younger plant instead of leaving the space barren.

Keep in mind the latest recommended sowing time. Propagating or sowing past this date won't benefit you much as the plant will likely die before the fruit is ready for harvest anyway. For quick-growing crops like radish (which you can harvest in as little as three weeks), propagate two weeks in advance and closer together every three days or so. But realistically, how much radish are you going to use? Be mindful when deciding how many plants you want to grow for each crop.

Planning a garden based on companions and guilds entails a lot of thought and research. Still, once you've figured it out, everything is much easier, from general maintenance to pest management, weed control, and soil health. Please take advantage of the planning because your garden will show its appreciation!

4

COMPANION PLANTING — VEGETABLES

"Double the yield, not the work." That's what I always say. And believe it or not, it's possible; I know because that's what I've been doing for many years. The subject of this chapter is fundamental pairings for vegetable guilds. Keyword: Pair. As in simple but effective guilds that only include two types of crops with a focus on veggies.

These simple, classic guilds are beginner-friendly and true space savers, perfect for those who want to try their hand at companion planting first and those who have limited space (but still want to grow *something*.)

CLASSIC VEGETABLE PLANT PAIRINGS

A guild doesn't have to be a collection of several different crop types; the "poly" in polyculture means more than one. So, even if you grow two types of crops that complement each other, you're not cultivating a monoculture anymore, which is a good thing!

I've selected these vegetable pairings because they work as is and don't require you to plant anything else. Everyone can grow them regardless of skill and experience. They can also work in multiple situations: Container gardening, raised garden beds, little space, or lots of space. You can quickly scale these guilds up; if you want a more significant yield, you can plant more than one of each crop type within the pairing (four pepper plants instead of one, for instance).

We'll also review each pairing's benefits, special planting and care instructions, pest and disease management, harvesting tips, and considerations so you know exactly how to take care of your guilds.

Basil and Tomato

Basil and tomatoes are soulmates. They taste phenomenal together in a hearty dish and can also be considered best friends in the soil. Although tomato plants require a lot of nutrients to grow plump and juicy fruit, basil is a light feeder. Which means they don't compete for nutrients in the soil. But that is just the tip of the iceberg regarding how these two crops benefit each other.

Benefits

Basil is the companion who pulls most of the weight in this pairing. Not only does basil repel common tomato pests (hornworms, whiteflies, aphids, and thrips), but it also deters any mosquitos and flies in the vicinity. This deterrence means your time spent around this companion pairing will be much more pleasant. Basil also aids in tomato plants' root growth, size, and general production.

Tomato brings one significant benefit: the leaves protect basil from the harsh sun while shading the soil so less moisture evaporates. Add a layer of mulch to the equation, and your basil and tomato guild will never go thirsty.

Many gardeners swear that basil also enhances the flavor profile of tomatoes. When used together in a dish, this is the case. However, there is no scientific proof to back up the claim that pairing basil with tomatoes in the garden enhances the flavor of the tomato by itself.

Care and Maintenance

Tomatoes grow best when the soil reaches a temperature of 60°F. If you're implementing succession planting, you must propagate your tomatoes indoors until the soil has warmed up enough at the start of summer.

Use well-draining soil; this is a general rule of thumb as 99% of crops need moist but not wet soil, or else, they can dampen off or develop root rot. As mentioned, tomatoes love lots of direct sun, so situate your guild in a spot that receives full sun (at least six hours a day). You'll also need to build or supply some trellis or support for your tomatoes; otherwise, the plant will not be able to support the weight of the fruit (tomatoes touching the ground will result in them getting squishy, rotten, or bursting open).

Basil germinates and matures very quickly. Once your tomatoes are ready to be transplanted, sow four or five basil seeds around your tomato plants (about 12 inches from the base of the tomato plant). As the basil starts sprouting, thin the seedlings (remove the smallest ones) until there are about two basil plants around every tomato plant if you're planting them in a garden bed. When planting them in containers, only one basil plant per tomato plant (depending on the container size or pot). The basil plants will start providing full-blown benefits within a few weeks.

If you are growing basil and tomatoes in separate pots or containers, you can still have them benefit each other by placing them right next to each other.

Harvesting

Tomatoes are ripe and ready for harvesting when they break away from the plant with a gentle twist. This time is usually when the tomatoes are completely red and have a slight give when squeezing them (as opposed to being extremely firm). However, tomatoes can be ripe and not entirely red, which could be because the tomato plant didn't receive enough sunlight. You *can* pick tomatoes with green spots, but store them indoors with the stem side down for a few days or until they turn red.

You can harvest basil at any time, but if you want the best flavor from your basil, pinch leaves off the top of a few stems in the morning right after the dew has evaporated.

Carrots and Onions

Root crops, in general, are great for your garden because they help aerate and essentially till the soil, preventing impaction and improving soil health. Even though carrots and onions are both root crops, they make for very effective pairings and can stand independently as a guild (though you will need to protect the soil with mulch). Since both carrots and beets are root vegetables, it is advisable to plant them at a distance from each other to avoid any potential competition for nutrients and space.

You can plant carrots with any onion; it doesn't have to be the classic white bulbous onion in the grocery store. For example, you can pair carrots with spring onions, shallots, red onions, chives, garlic, and radishes. You'll still get the full spectrum of benefits by growing carrots and any allium together.

Benefits

Speaking of which, the most notable benefit of a carrot and onion companion pair is pest management. Usually, only one plant supplies the remaining guild with pest-repellent properties. Like in the case of tomatoes and basil, the basil repels tomato pests, but the tomato does nothing to keep slugs from munching on basil leaves at night.

The imbalance is different here. The pungent alliums do an excellent job of repelling carrot flies, while carrots return the favor by keeping onion flies at bay. Besides preventing soil compaction, leaving a couple of onions and carrots in the soil to decompose after the season has passed can improve soil fertility. When root vegetables break down, they release nutrients, particularly phosphorus, into the soil. This process also leads to an increase in organic matter, which helps to boost the populations of beneficial microorganisms in the soil. Nutrient cycling ends up being more efficient as a result.

Care and Maintenance

For crops grown for their fruit, vegetables, or roots, it is advisable to use well-draining soil and ensure they receive full sun. In addition, you should water onions and carrots regularly when they're young (at least one inch every week) and avoid watering them overhead; instead, water them at the base.

Something to remember when planting onions and carrots together is that while they thrive as companions, they need their personal space. The spacing will vary depending on how big your onion and carrot varieties are (spring onions and chives will be fine if planted three or four inches from carrots, while the classic onion needs more space, so go with four to six inches instead).

You should leave enough space between carrots and onions to avoid accidentally pulling up neighboring carrots that still need to be harvested. Carrots don't do well when disrupted, so even if you replant a carrot, it will likely stop growing and start to decompose.

Remember to sow carrot seeds directly into the place you want them to mature since transplanting young carrots will disrupt them, and they will not fare well after the fact (that's if they survive at all). Carrots prefer cooler weather (they are winter crops, after all), which also makes them sweeter, which is why you should start sowing them in spring, about three weeks before the last frost is due (and again a couple weeks later if you're implementing succession planting).

Onions are pretty chill and don't need many precautions regarding care and maintenance. Cut off any flower "spikes" that appear so all the plant's attention is directed to growing the root (the part you want) instead of the flowers. Stop watering onions when the leaves start to sag.

Harvesting

Carrots and onions mature at the same rate (depending on the variety of carrots and onions you grow) and are typically ready to harvest three to four months after sowing. However, before you gather your entire yield of carrots, first harvest one and taste it; they should be sweet, crisp, and crunchy.

Bulb onions are ready to harvest once the stalks and leaves topple over (you'll see a noticeable bend close to the base of the onion plant) and start to turn brown. Grass-like onions (like spring onions and chives) are ready to use when they reach about eight inches in height.

Ensure you note the sowing dates when planting successively, so you only harvest these younger crops after they're ready.

Peppers and Marigold

Marigolds are always a safe bet if you need help deciding what to pair crops with because they get along with virtually every plant you can think of. When in doubt, marigold is the answer! They benefit your garden in many ways, and the flowers are also edible. Peppers include the entire capsicum family, from the flavorful bell peppers to the spicy jalapenos.

Benefits

This pairing is another tomato and basil situation where the peppers benefit more from the marigolds than vice versa. But since we love peppers so much, we let it slide. As mentioned, marigolds help your garden in many ways, including attracting pollinators, which means better yields. Along with bees, it also attracts predatory insects (like lacewings, ladybugs, hoverflies, and wasps), which feed on common garden pests that enjoy your peppers' spiciness.

Another unorthodox method of using marigolds for pest management is growing them into a sacrificial (or trap) crop. Weevils and beetles would much rather feast on marigolds than peppers.

Marigolds can also help control specific nematode populations, specifically those that cause root rot. And the strong scent of marigolds might help hide the smell of your peppers from pests, like a last resort. If all else fails, at least the pests will have a tough time figuring out where to go.

Care and Maintenance

Both marigolds and capsicums are sun lovers, so ensure they get six to eight hours of sun daily. Marigolds prefer it if the soil has time to dry between watering. Check the soil once a week by sticking your finger an inch or so into it; if the soil feels dry and very little is sticking to your finger, it's time to water it (otherwise, wait another day or so). Water them at the base; marigolds prefer to keep their leaves dry.

Marigolds are annuals but tend to reseed readily, so you'll find new ones pop up the following year. It sounds counterintuitive, but if you want your marigolds to flower for longer, frequently cut off dead or withering flowers, and new ones will grow in the same season! This process is called deadheading.

Capsicums like moist soil, so you must water your peppers more frequently than your marigolds. If your marigold and peppers are in the same garden bed or container, water around the base of the peppers twice a week and around the marigolds only once a week or so. Yes, there will be some water distribution, but if you space them correctly, this should be fine. It would help if you spaced marigolds and peppers at least twelve inches apart.

Aerate and fertilize the soil by mixing in mulching material and compost before sowing or transplanting, in addition to a layer of mulch on top. To feed your peppers (heavy feeders), sprinkle a generous layer of compost followed by more mulch at least once during the flowering period. This pair will benefit from crop rotation as well.

Harvesting

To harvest marigold flowers, cut them off to your desired stem length.

Harvesting capsicums are also relatively straightforward. You can harvest green bell peppers or chilies once they're big enough or wait to turn yellow or red. Fun fact: There are no color variations of peppers; they all start green and change to different colors (yellow or red) by being left on the plant for longer. Peppers might not come off the plant as efficiently as ripe tomatoes do, so to prevent damaging the plant, use gardening shears or pruners to cut them off their stems when harvesting.

Corn, Beans, and Squash (The Three Sisters)

The Three Sisters guild is an ancient, prevalent one that dates back to the 16th century. Native Americans made good use of this guild and have passed it down for generations. This trio is companion planting at its finest, and you'll see why.

Benefits

Corn, beans, and squash look after each other like family (hence the name "Three Sisters"). For starters, the corn serves as much-needed support for the climbing beans (a natural trellis, if you will). Beans, as we know, are nitrogen fixers that keep the soil fertile so the other two sisters can thrive. The leaves of the squash plant act as a natural covering for the soil, preventing weed growth and maintaining moisture and coolness. But squash leaves are also prickly, which helps keep more significant pests away (like raccoons and rabbits).

Care and Maintenance

Tending to your soil before planting anything is always advisable, but this is especially true when growing the Three Sisters. Besides primary soil care (adjusting pH levels, adding compost, and mulching), for the Three Sisters guild, you'll need to create mounds. Each mound should be at least a foot high and 3 feet in diameter and spaced 4 feet apart (if you're growing multiple Three Sister guilds). It would help if you flattened the mounds at the top to create a surface area of at least 2 feet in diameter.

Planting corn on the flattened part first and in the middle of the mound would be best. Sow four to six kernels (any more than this, and you risk overcrowding). You can make two or three one-inch-deep holes spaced apart evenly and place two corn kernels in each hole. If both kernels germinate in a single hole, you'll have to thin out the smallest since corn can't grow that close to each other.

Once the corn reaches around six inches in height, you can plant the pole beans (about four bean plants per mound, spaced evenly along the base of the corn). Wait another week before sowing six squash seeds around the mound's perimeter, again spaced evenly apart.

Planting small-leafed squash such as zucchini or Hubbard would be best since more significant squash variants will be too big and heavy for this guild. And the beans you choose should be climbers (not bush beans) but not vigorously so. However, you can use any variety of corn.

The squash leaves are only sometimes the best deterrent for more minor pests. If you want to add another layer of protection on the pest control front, plant a few marigolds between your squash or in front of them all around your mound (keep spacing in mind). It might be worth making some platforms for your squash to sit on (you can use grid wire to make a cube to lift it off the ground); if they're touching the ground, they might develop soft spots or go rotten.

Harvesting

You can tell that corn is ready for harvesting when the kernels are plump and release a creamy liquid when you press your fingernail into them unless you are growing a hard-kernelled variety like popcorn. Usually, this is around six weeks after the ear first appears on the stalk. To harvest, firmly hold the ear of corn, pull it downwards, and twist (you can leave the husk on until you're ready to cook it); it should break off relatively easily.

With pole beans (or any other climbing beans), the most crucial thing when harvesting is not waiting until the bean pods swell and the beans inside the pod reach maturity. Most beans are ready to be harvested about two months after sowing, but they will continue to produce more beans until winter is on your doorstep. Beans tend to snap off the plant with minimal effort.

Squash is ready to be harvested when it is firm, the rind is the correct color (based on the type of squash you're growing), and the stem is dry. This maturity typically takes two to four months from the time of sowing. Harvesting squash is simple; you can twist them off or use pruners to cut them off the vine if they're stubborn.

Spinach and Beets

These two vegetables bond over their love for cool weather. Spinach and beets complement each other beautifully. Spinach has shallow roots but will develop a taproot once it's mature, bringing nutrients from further down in the soil to the surface for the hungry, heavy-feeding beets to enjoy. And even though beets are a root vegetable, their roots are still shallow compared to a mature spinach's. This difference is perfect because these two crops won't compete for underground space either.

Benefits

Beets (just like any other root vegetable) are great for keeping soil aerated and preventing impaction. The leaves of beets are big and nutritious, which you can use as mulching materials to improve soil fertility or in a salad.

Similarly, spinach also serves as a living mulch, suppressing weeds and shading the ground to protect it from the harsh sun. However, you might have to supplement this guild pairing with a third party regarding pest management.

But while weeds or ground cover might not be an issue, spinach and beets attract various leaf-eating insects, aphids, spider mites, slugs, and snails. You can grow nasturtiums as a trap crop for aphids that love beetroot, zinnias repel certain spinach-dwelling pests, or opt for parsley to attract predatory insects.

Care and Maintenance

Spinach grows best in full sun but might benefit from partial or afternoon shade in warmer climates. Prepare the soil before sowing spinach by lightly spading in compost or aged manure into the top layer of soil. To prevent bolting (early flowering), under-production, or wilting of spinach leaves in hot weather, water lightly several times per week instead of watering heavily once per week (spinach is not drought-tolerant).

You can sow spinach seeds directly in the soil or germinate them indoors and transplant them later (especially useful if you're implementing succession planting). Nevertheless, spinach is a cool-weather crop you can cultivate from early spring to early winter (though some varieties enjoy warmer weather). It takes spinach six to ten weeks before the leaves are ready for harvest.

Beets require a moist environment to grow well. Hence, it is necessary to water them regularly. Beetroot prefers full sun but will tolerate partial shade in a warmer climate. It's widely believed that beetroot is mainly a winter or mild weather crop, but they are relatively hardy and will grow in cooler to warm conditions (not freezing, but not scorching either, right in the middle of two extremes). Because of this, you can sow beetroot at the same time as spinach, though it does take beets slightly longer to grow than spinach (between seven and twelve weeks).

Other than that, both spinach and beets are low-maintenance crops that won't require much more than an occasional checkup from you to make sure the soil is moist but not wet and to see if they're ready to be harvested.

Harvesting

The best thing about harvesting spinach is that if you do it right, you can harvest it again from the same plant in less than a week. That's right! Spinach will regrow its leaves and do so relatively quickly, too. Once your spinach looks lush and ready, only harvest the outer leaves off all your plants instead of pulling out the entire plant roots. You can repeat this until the plant starts flowering or dies off at the end of the season.

Unfortunately, the same can't be said for beets since the plant can't regrow or do much without the root itself. Nevertheless, you can harvest beets as early as seven weeks after sowing. At this point, they will be roughly the size of golf balls (baby beets), or at around twelve weeks, they'll be the size of tennis balls. Keep them in the ground for a short time, as they only get less desirable as time goes on, and they might crack and start to rot. Do not discard the leaves and stems of beet plants, as they contain a significant amount of nutrients. You can consume them, incorporate them into the soil, or use them as mulch or compost until the next planting season (ensure sufficient time to decompose).

If planning an entire guild sounds too overwhelming, start with two crops that do well together and scale up as you gain knowledge, experience, and confidence in your green thumbs. If you can't run, walk; if you can't walk, crawl. Please start somewhere, though. Once again, it all comes down to your short-term goals and using them as stepping stones to get you to where you want to be.

5

COMPANION PLANTING — HERBS

Herbs are the gift that keeps giving, from adding flavor or garnish to a dish to supplementing your medicine cabinet. And I'm not just talking about home remedies or teas here. The USDA reports that herbs, including essential prescription drugs, comprise roughly 40% of all medications sold in pharmacies. A lot of painkillers, anti-inflammatories, anesthetics, analgesics, sedatives, and even antidepressants are on the list of plant-derived medicines.

Granted, a lot of these chemicals are now synthetically made in labs (to make them more stabilized, concentrated, and mass-producible), but it doesn't change the fact that we got the ideas for most medicines we have today from plants that our ancestors used for thousands of years.

CLASSIC HERB PAIRINGS

Whether you're growing herbs for their health benefits or to spice up your cooking (or both), they also provide many advantages for your garden, namely pest management and disease prevention. You can interplant these herb pairings around your garden; make sure there are no conflicts of interest, so to speak (ensure the herbs are companions with the other fruits, vegetables, and flowers first).

Rosemary and Sage

If you've never cooked with rosemary, use it sparingly since you're a pinch away from turning a dish from elevated into overpowered. But beyond that, it also has beautiful foliage, and despite its strong scent, it goes well with many dishes.

Depending on how spiritual you are, you may or may not subscribe to the idea that sage can cleanse your home of evil spirits and even bring luck. Nevertheless, it adds much more than that to the table (or garden). These two herbs together result in a power couple specializing in keeping pests at arm's length.

Benefits

Due to the aromatic nature of rosemary and the fact that it's a flowering herb, it can ward off certain pests and attract pollinators. As a bonus, it leaves your garden smelling amazing. Rosemary is an easy herb to cultivate because it's drought-resistant and tolerates extreme hot and cold conditions very well.

Rosemary also has some exciting health benefits and is said to be anti-inflammatory, antimicrobial, and exhibit neuroprotective properties. This claim is evident from studies on the clinical effects of rosemary that show it can positively affect mood, learning, and memory, reduce pain and anxiety, and improve sleep (Rahbardar & Hosseinzadeh, 2020).

Sage also attracts pollinators, and they tend to flower for quite a while (can be evergreen in the right conditions), adding a layer of beautification to your landscape. Because it is excellent at accumulating nutrients (specifically potassium and calcium), you can compost it or even make "tea" out of it and add it back into your garden to nourish or replenish the soil for your fruiting crops.

Care and Maintenance

Rosemary, while being drought resistant, actually prefers the soil on the dryer side, just like sage. And both sage and rosemary do best in full sun. You can get away with watering this pairing once every two weeks or so. They will likely survive minimal watering but won't do well when overwatered.

But even though sage and rosemary have a lot in common regarding their sun and water requirements, they won't compete for the same nutrients—which makes them such great companions.

Sow rosemary seeds in late spring or when any threat of frost has passed (even though they're hardy, they're not indestructible; it's always better to be safe than sorry). It's important to note that, when sowing rosemary seeds, you should sprinkle a very light layer of soil over the seeds instead of burying them entirely because the seeds need to be exposed to sunlight to germinate. Rosemary is a light feeder, so planting them in soil with mixed compost will hold them over for quite some time; you only have to supplement with more compost once a year.

Sage seeds germinate slowly (can take up to a month), so it's best to propagate them indoors or buy seedlings from a nursery if you're impatient. Sage can be propagated from cuttings as well. You can also sow sage seeds directly into the soil at the same time as rosemary seeds, but remember they will take longer to pop up.

Both sage and rosemary are perennials, so they will be dormant (appear dead) in winter and reanimate in spring. To keep these hardy plants looking neat, trim them right before winter by cutting off dead leaves or flowers and about a third of the plant. Feel free to dry the healthy herb foliage you prune away and use them for tea or cooking.

Harvesting

A general rule of thumb for harvesting herbs is to snip off as much as you need but only take up to 20% of the plant at a time. This precaution ensures enough to retake it in a week or two while allowing new growth to catch up.

With rosemary, you always want to harvest the new growth. Avoid harvesting or cutting woody stems since this will alter the shape and spread of the rosemary bush but won't promptly encourage further growth. You'll be able to recognize new growth on your rosemary plant because the stems will still be tender and might be more saturated in color.

In the case of sage, you can take the same route: cut what you need. However, it can take a while before your sage plant is ready to be harvested. It is advisable to wait at least a year until the plant is fully grown and established before harvesting any leaves or giving it a trim.

Basil and Chamomile

Whether making your pesto sauce or trying to make a serving bowl full of jasmine rice look more sophisticated when hosting a family dinner, basil has got you covered. It's incredibly versatile and can be used fresh or dried.

Chamomile is best known for its calming properties, but it can also alleviate common cold symptoms, settle an upset stomach, and lower your risk for heart disease and cancer (Gupta, 2010). If that's not a reason to add it to your garden, what is?

Benefits

Did you know many home gardeners spray chamomile tea on their seedlings to prevent common crop ailments like "damping off," mildew, blight, and other fungal and bacterial infections? That's because chamomile has anti-bacterial and anti-fungal properties. The good news is that you can reap these benefits by planting chamomile in your garden.

Chamomile is also said to increase the amount of oil that basil produces, enhancing the taste and scent (also making basil more effective in pest management).

Care and Maintenance

Since we already covered the care and maintenance of basil in the previous chapter, we'll now focus on chamomile. Chamomile is a flowering herb that resembles dainty daisies that grow in clusters. They grow rather quickly, reaching maturity in as little as ten weeks. Chamomile is technically an annual herb, but it reseeds very well, and you might find it reappearing in your garden every year regardless.

Chamomile prefer full sun, but if you're growing them in a hotter climate, they might benefit from partial shade (preferably on scorching afternoons). Because they are annuals, chamomile will require rich, fertile soil for best results. Water the seedlings often until maturity, then reduce and allow the soil to dry slightly between watering them (timing may vary based on your climate).

Chamomile is quite a light feeder despite it being an annual and will thrive even in poor soil. However, you should still feed the soil with compost every few months for the basil's sake.

Harvesting

It's typically the chamomile flowers used for teas or cooking since leaves and stems tend to be bitter (though they are edible nonetheless). It's safe to assume that everyone knows how to pick flowers, but to get the best flavor from your chamomile and encourage the plant to grow new ones, there are a few things to consider.

You want to harvest the chamomile flowers when fully open and fresh (not wilted or withered). Chamomile flowers will be ready for harvest once the plant is mature (roughly ten weeks). When you harvest chamomile, be sure to only pick the flowers by holding on to the stem with one hand and picking the flower with the other; this will encourage the plant to grow more flowers immediately.

Thyme and Oregano

Like most herb pairings in this chapter, the synergy of thyme and oregano goes beyond what they offer you in the kitchen. Thyme is rich in vitamins A and C, which can help maintain healthy skin, mucus membranes, and vision. It can also strengthen your immune system, reduce inflammation, and protect against certain infectious diseases.

Both oregano and thyme are distant relatives in the mint family tree, so while they are beautiful when in bloom and fantastic to cook with, you should treat them the same way you would mint (as aggressively invasive if you give it a chance), which is why I would advise growing this companion pairing in containers or pots instead of directly in your garden.

You might be asking yourself: "If oregano and thyme are cousins, wouldn't that make them rivalries in the garden?" That's just the thing! They're both perennials and light feeders so they will be fine together in decently fertile soil (with yearly compost top-ups).

Benefits

Thyme and oregano offer your garden many benefits, especially if they're moveable (planted in pots). Relocating this pairing will allow you to place them where needed intermittently and move them indoors during the winter. These herbs are drought and frost-tolerant but don't like wet soil.

Thyme and oregano are flowering herbs that attract beneficial insects and pollinators while repelling garden pests with their scent.

Care and Maintenance

The most significant selling point of this pairing is its low maintenance needs. The hardest part is honestly keeping an eye on it to ensure it doesn't take over your garden (which is a problem easily fixable by simply planting them in pots or containers). Remember that nutrient-dense soil may be bad for both thyme and oregano; an initial compost or aged manure treatment to give the seedlings a good start to grow big and strong will suffice for a long time.

The mint family are the weeds of the herb world; they multiply and end up everywhere if you're not careful. For this reason, you'll need to check on them occasionally when cultivating them directly in your garden and remove any unwanted seedlings that might have popped up.

Thyme and oregano require full sun and weekly watering (make sure the soil has dried out somewhat in between watering). Mulch is always a good idea, but because thyme and oregano dislike overly moist soil, your best option is tree bark, a long-lasting mulch that you must only replace once a year. Besides that, you'll have to trim them back every so often to keep things neat and to encourage new growth.

Harvesting

Because thyme and oregano are such hardy plants, you can't go wrong with how or even how much you harvest (as long as you're not stripping them from all their leaves entirely or cutting them off at the base).

To harvest thyme or oregano, cut or pick off an inch of stem, with leaves attached from the tip of the various branches (which will be the newest growth available and taste the best). When dried, the flavor profile of thyme and oregano will change entirely to what they taste when fresh.

Cilantro and Dill

There's some debate about whether it's called cilantro or coriander. Most people believe it depends on where you live, and while there is some truth, there's a legitimate distinction between them. So, let's settle this once and for all: cilantro and coriander come from the same plant. When referring to the leaves and stems, it's cilantro. Coriander refers specifically to the seeds that cilantro plants produce.

While both come from the same plant, cilantro and coriander are technically not interchangeable terms because they refer to two separate things. Cilantro, as in the leaves and stems of the cilantro plant, has an entirely different taste and flavor than the seeds (coriander). You can't substitute cilantro for coriander in a recipe.

Cilantro, or coriander, is the oldest herb that we know of in the world. It dates back at least 5,000 years! It can also lower your cholesterol levels.

Dill doesn't have as much drama or controversy surrounding its name, but it does like to hang out with cilantro. Most people believe that dill flowers are edible and soothe the digestive system, just like most other flowering herbs.

Benefits

Planting cilantro and dill together really compounds their pest-repellent abilities. Dill is known to keep aphids and spider mites away, while cilantro chases flies, moths, and other fruit-boring pests. Mosquitoes are also not too fond of the smell of cilantro, which means fewer bites for you when working in the garden.

When planting this herb pair in pots, you can place them near your other guilds, specifically next to your leafy vegetables (spinach, lettuce, kale, etc.) and onions. Some say thyme improves the flavor of potatoes and onions, though, as we mentioned, this is purely opinion-based as of now and not scientifically verifiable.

If you're up for extra maintenance and want to cultivate this guild pairing directly in your garden bed, they will protect your soil from erosion and offer some ground cover with their foliage.

Care and Maintenance

Cilantro and dill seedlings will require regular watering, but they need substantially less water once they mature. However, if you wait too long between watering sessions, the plants may flower earlier, which could be an issue since it's always best to harvest herbs before they flower.

Both cilantro and dill are annual herbs, which means they grow quickly and only produce leaves for a handful of weeks before they start flowering. The good news is they are very efficient at reseeding themselves, meaning you might not even need to plant them again the following year; they'll appear.

The maintenance requirements of this pairing are minimal. Their root systems are shallow, and as long as you space them at least six inches apart, they will thrive together without trying to outcompete each other for nutrients. The soil should be well-draining and somewhat fertile. Whether you're growing them in pots or your garden bed, they prefer full sun but will tolerate partial shade.

Harvesting

Cilantro will be ready for its first harvest in 30 days, but if it's coriander you're after, you'll need to wait for it to flower and produce seeds (around three months after sowing or propagation). To harvest cilantro, go for the tender, new leaves at the very tip of the branches. To harvest coriander, wait for the flowers to wither and turn brown before snipping them off and breaking open the flower head. Separate the seeds from the plant debris and store them. You can use a pestle and mortar or put them in a pepper grinder to make your life easier when using them as seasoning.

To harvest dill (which you can do in approximately 70 days after sowing), you can snip off the top few inches of a branch or two to use. You can also harvest the edible flowers or seeds for cooking purposes, though you'll have to wait for the dill to flower or produce seeds first.

Parsley and Chives

Regarding the versatility and popularity of herbs, parsley will easily breach the top five in such a list (or it should, at least). Parsley and chives are widely used in or on a dish. Nothing says "I have my life together," like topping a dish you made from scratch with chives or parsley that you grew yourself.

Parsley has a distinct flavor profile, but it's more subtle and won't easily overpower a dish (like rosemary would, for instance). And that's why it's a staple in many homes and gardens. Not only is it easy to grow and beneficial for your garden, but it's also subtle yet noticeable. Iconic!

Chives are smaller, thinner, and more delicate versions of an onion. They're not onions, but they are related to one another. The mild onion flavor of chives can quickly go lost during even a short cooking period (plus, they wilt as soon as they hit the pan, which doesn't make for a very appealing sight), which is why they're predominantly a garnish. Nevertheless, they also have all the gardening benefits of onions.

Benefits

Is there anything parsley can't do? For starters, it's rich in vitamin C, aids in oral health (for you and your pets), it's a natural diuretic (which can help remove acid build-up, alleviating pain and other symptoms related to gout and arthritis), relieves indigestion, can be used in skincare, and can be used as a natural de-wormer for dogs and cats.

Furthermore, you'll be able to spot a nutrition imbalance or iron deficiency in your soil from the color of the parsley plant's leaves (if they turn yellow, you'll know it's time to add compost or aged manure to the soil). You can also use parsley as a trap crop for any vegetable or fruit guild since it attracts aphids and predatory insects (that might keep them in check, so they don't kill the parsley plant).

Besides making sour cream and chives dip for chips or baked potatoes, chives have much more to offer. You can use them as living mulch or ground cover crops, attract pollinators, and deter the same pests that other members of the allium family do. Chives can be "chopped and dropped" (used as fertilizer by simply picking the leaves and sprinkling them around the base of nearby crops right then and there).

Care and Maintenance

Parsley requires full sun (at least six hours) and fertile soil, so prepare your garden or pot soil with the appropriate nutrition. Parsley roots are on the shallow side but are considered tap roots, so make sure your soil can accompany an underground growing space of at least 12 inches deep (for a mature parsley plant).

Remember that parsley is a biennial, which means you'll be able to enjoy and harvest fresh parsley for two years. However, if you leave it to flower and drop seeds, parsley will reseed. Parsley is easy to maintain and care for, but it can be challenging to grow from seed. Buying parsley seedlings from a nursery might be easier if you're a beginner gardener.

Chives, on the other hand, are easy to grow from seeds. They're hardy perennials and will keep growing back yearly and throughout the growing season if you harvest them correctly. The only care and maintenance you need to dish out is dividing or breaking up (and replanting) dense patches every couple of years and ensuring the soil has plenty of nitrogen.

Sow or propagate your chive seeds a few weeks before expecting the last spring frost. Chive sprouts are delicate, so allow them to grow for at least eight weeks in a seedling tray, and be careful when transplanting if you go that route. Nevertheless, they are frost-tolerant and will regrow through the snow the following year.

Harvesting

It's always advisable to wait until a plant is mature before you harvest any leaves. A good rule of thumb for parsley is to wait until the plant has three leaf segments (or branches) before taking some. Harvest parsley from the outer edges of the plant first to give the very young and tender leaves in the middle time to mature a bit longer.

Chives grow in clusters of what looks like grass and are known to withstand heavy harvests. You can harvest every single chive, and as long as you leave the roots intact and about two to three inches from the base of the plant, it will regrow within a couple of weeks. The only reason I don't advise harvesting all your chives at once is so you can gather them again once you need them and not have to wait.

You can plant several guilds together in the same garden bed based on your gardening goals and planned guilds (or pairings). You'll need to ensure they get along, but this strategy will help you reap the most benefits from companion planting.

Herbs are the perfect place to start if you need to be more confident in your gardening skills. Most are hardy, easy to grow and maintain, and will bring life to your garden in preparation for more guilds or pairs!

Companion Planting for an Increase in New Gardens

"The garden is a love song, a duet between a human being and Mother Nature."

— JEFF COX

A study by OnePoll found that 55% of non-gardening respondents wished they knew how to garden, and a large proportion of them were worried about their lack of knowledge. There is a huge number of people who put off their dream of nurturing a thriving garden because they think it's too much work or they don't have the necessary skills – but as you're seeing now, it's possible to build a self-sustaining garden that's easy to maintain with no experience at all.

If I look at all the gardening information available out there, I can see why people give up before they've even gotten started. It's overwhelming, and for many people, it's impossible to see how to actually get their garden off the ground – or even think about applying any of the information they come across.

This guide is designed to do something different. By focusing on companion planting, a method in which the garden does a lot of the work for itself, I aim to make gardening more accessible and empower those who might otherwise be discouraged to pick up their trowels and give it a go. And this is where I'd like to ask for your help as a beginner gardener. You can show other people that it's not as difficult as they fear and point them in the direction of their launch pad.

By leaving a review of this book on Amazon, you'll show people looking for an easy and effective route into gardening exactly where they can find it – and you'll inspire them too.

Thank you so much for your support. A garden is a great source of joy, and I want everyone who dreams of building one to have the best chance of success. Together, we can help more gardens spring up everywhere.

Scan the QR code below to leave a review:

6

COMPANION PLANTING — FRUITS

L et's not kid ourselves; fresh produce has become ridiculously expensive. And who doesn't like a flavorful, seasonal fruit salad? You can kill two birds with one stone by growing and serving your fruit salad without entering a grocery store.

Besides epic bragging rights, you can also whip up fresh smoothies in the morning, make jams or conserves, or pluck a few snacks while tending the garden. Do you know what they say about an apple a day? It's the best thing since sliced bread. No, wait, that's not it.

CLASSIC FRUIT PAIRINGS

However, if you want to spin it, a garden filled with fruits will benefit you so much that it's hard to argue against having one. In this chapter, we'll review the best companion planting pairs suited for small gardens (but you can certainly scale up if you have the space to do so).

Strawberries and Borage

We know and love them; please give it up for Strawberries! Interestingly, strawberries aren't berries; they are technically not even considered fruit (since their seeds are on the outside instead of the inside). Tiny fruits embed each strawberry seed, resulting in the visible seeds on the outside. So, a strawberry is a collection of small fruits joined together. It's okay; we forgive you for lying to us, strawberries.

Strawberries are easily one of the easiest fruits to grow yourself, even from seed. However, they are prone to many pests that enjoy these juicy, sweet, non-berries, which is where borage comes in. Besides having one of the more unique flowers, borage comes in peace and will help your strawberries thrive.

Benefits

Borage is an excellent choice for pairing with your strawberries. The deep purple flowers of borage look phenomenal next to the bright red fruits. In addition to this, the mature foliage of borage is thick and hairy (snails, slugs, and worms don't like this). By planting borage around your strawberries, you can ward off pests, attract beneficial insects that feed on any remaining strawberry-loving pests, and bring pollinators to your midst so your strawberry bushes will produce a bigger and better yield.

Allegedly, borage also improves the taste of strawberries, though this is just an old gardener's tale, so you should take it with a grain of salt. This idea probably came from the fact that borage has a taproot that mines trace minerals and brings it closer to the soil surface for the strawberries to use, which (allegedly) makes the strawberries taste sweeter. But I'll let you be the judge of that.

Borage can protect your strawberries from (or improve their resistance to) diseases like fruit rot and wilt. But borage isn't just aesthetically pleasing; their flowers and young leaves are edible (they taste like slightly spicy cucumber) and a great addition to fruit salads.

What do strawberries do for the garden, you ask? Besides being delicious, they spread and cover the soil, suppressing weeds and keeping the soil aerated and moist on sunny days. You can plant strawberries in any open spot you have in the garden as living mulch or use trimmed foliage as actual mulch.

Care and Maintenance

Borage is an annual, which is a shame, but it also means they're easy to grow and maintain. The low maintenance makes up for the fact that you'll have to replant them yearly. Similar to strawberries, they're great gap fillers for any bare spots you may have. Borage can grow to be quite large, though, so make sure there's at least a diameter of 18 inches available for it.

You can sow borage seeds directly into your garden bed in mid-spring; they don't like to be transplanted. Borage will thrive in the soil even without compost preparation; if you ensure the soil is well-draining and has at least partial sun (4-6 hours), you can set it and forget it. Borage will reseed by itself if you let it. All you need to do is let a couple of flowers stay on the plant until it dies in winter. Just remember to thin out the herd in mid-spring so you don't end up with more than you need or more than your garden can handle.

Even though borage doesn't require fertile soil, strawberries very much do. So, staying on top of your strawberries' dietary requirements would be best by topping the soil with compost every month and every other week once they flower. Like most fruiting plants, strawberries need full sun (at least eight hours for strawberries) to produce fruits.

Strawberries are perennials, but they will send out what's called "runners" from time to time, from which an entirely new strawberry plant will grow. This process is essentially an asexual form of procreation. Having too many strawberry plants is not impossible, but you should keep an eye on this and occasionally thin out any new sprouts (or cut-off runners).

Harvesting

The harvesting process for both strawberries and borage is straightforward, almost self-explanatory. As mentioned, if you are harvesting borage for consumption, only harvest young, tender leaves that have yet to thicken or develop hairs. The thick, hairy borage leaves aren't harmful but have an unpleasant feel in the mouth and can be pretty tough. Harvesting the flowers before they seed and when they are open, vibrant, and healthy-looking would be best. If they're wilting or turning brown, they're no good. Pick the flowers or leaves you require and make a pretty salad.

Strawberries are ready for harvesting when they are entirely red. However, if you have a different variety of strawberries, the berries' time to ripen or mature will vary. In the case of the standard red strawberry, it will take about four to six weeks after the flowers open before you can start harvesting them. To do so, gently pick or snip the strawberry off the branch so you don't harm the plant.

The best strategy is to harvest strawberries every three days and only pick the ripest ones, entirely red and plump, while leaving some smaller or paler ones on the plant to continue ripening.

Strawberries don't store well (even in the fridge), so harvesting every few days will ensure you have only the freshest strawberries all season.

Apple Trees and Comfrey

Have you ever wondered how bonsai trees work? Are they genetically modified? Are they bred explicitly over thousands of years? And why am I bringing this up? Here's a fun fact about trees: The root ball's size determines the tree's size. The word "bonsai" means "planted in a container". And regardless of the size of the tree, it will still grow fruits and produce seeds. So yes, you can successfully grow an apple tree (or any other tree for that matter) in a large container, and it will grow to fit the size of the container perfectly and not an inch more (unless you size up the pot).

However, while trees planted in containers will be a smaller version of the regular-sized tree, the fruits will be regular-sized. If you have the space to grow a full-sized apple tree, do that. But if you're growing it in a large pot or container (I recommend the most significant container you can get your hands on), your best choice is self-fertile, dwarf apple tree varieties such as crab apples.

Comfrey is a member of the borage family and produces clusters of either purple, blue, yellow, or white flowers, depending on the variety you get. Together with apples, they benefit each other in many ways.

Benefits

Comfrey provides many of the same benefits as borage, like pest deterrence, attracting pollinators, weed management, and cycling nutrients. In addition, borage also acts as living mulch for your apple tree, protecting and shading the ground from erosion or excessive moisture loss. Comfrey also acts as a trap crop for apple maggot flies.

The benefits of having an apple tree are in its longevity. A single self-fertile apple tree will produce apples for many years to come. Established apple trees are hardy and resilient. You can use apple peels and cores to fertilize your garden by composting them or making fertilizer tea. Not to mention, they are easy to cultivate, care for, and maintain.

Care and Maintenance

Comfrey is a perennial crop found along riverbanks and grass-lands, so it's no surprise that it prefers soil that's always moist and at least partial shade (minimum of three hours a day). Like borage, mature comfrey leaves have a hairy texture. One of the major selling points is that it can be planted or grown at any time of the year if the soil is fresh.

Although comfrey has a history of being classed as edible, that's no longer the case since it contains pyrrolizidine alkaloids, which can cause liver damage in humans and pets when ingested. So, it might be best to stick to growing the flower for its beauty and other benefits rather than for consumption. You can, however, substitute comfrey for borage if you want a more functional crop.

Once established, comfrey requires yearly nitrogen top-ups in compost or aged manure sprinkled over the top layer of soil. It's also not partial on soil types and will grow in clay, sandy, or loamy soil. Given that you're pairing comfrey with an apple tree, you should opt for loamy, well-draining, fertile soil. If you give it what it needs while young, it will thank you by basically maintaining itself when it's mature.

Apple trees need full sun, well-draining and fertile soil, and regular irrigation (especially when fruiting) to yield the best. Choose a self-fertile variety if you only have space for one apple tree.

Prepare the garden bed or potting soil with a generous amount of compost. You can propagate seeds indoors or buy a young tree from a nursery and transplant it when ready. You can transplant a young apple tree at any time except when they're flowering or fruiting since this might negatively affect the yield, or you might lose the yield completely (winter is generally a safe bet when transplanting fruit trees of any kind).

Mulch your young apple tree and wait for it to become established enough (at least a year) before planting comfrey, borage, or anything else alongside it. Quick-growing crops might smother and kill a young fruit tree.

Your apple tree will need its first haircut when it's in its third year of growth and then as needed (inspect the tree at the beginning of every spring when it is still dormant; this makes it easier to see what needs attention). You can remove dead, damaged, or diseased leaves and branches at any time without risking the well-being of the tree in question; in fact, it will always benefit the tree if you do this. However, slightly pruning a tree differs from stripping dead branches and foliage.

Only prune your fruit tree when it's dormant (in winter or early spring). Only cut the central leader (the middle, main stem that goes into the soil and tapers towards the top of the tree) once the tree is fully mature or after its third year of growth. During the tree's first year of growth, you want to ensure that the branches grow evenly from the central leader. If two branches are too close together, cut one of them off.

In the second year, you want to remove competing leaders (scaffolding branches growing too vigorously and affecting the tree's shape). In the third year, trim the branches coming out of the central leader into a pyramid shape (so the bottom branches are long and get shorter as you reach the top of the tree).

You'll have to inspect your tree yearly and trim off any branches attempting to grow too low (underneath the canopy or near the base of the tree), branches that look like they're growing vertically upwards or downwards from a scaffolding branch, and any branches that look like they're emerging in clumps. If branches are rubbing against each other, remove the newest or thinnest one by cutting it close to whichever branch it's originating from.

You also want to reduce all scaffolding (or lateral) branches by a third of their length. This reduction will encourage the remaining branches to grow thicker so your tree can support more weight (resulting in a more significant yield).

Lastly, it would help if you netted your apples to protect them from birds. You can use bird (or pigeon) nets or pest netting as soon as baby apples form, but mosquito nets or any mesh fabric will also work. Secure the netting around the fruit with a ribbon or twine (most pest nets will have drawstrings) until they're ready for harvesting.

Harvesting

Your apples will be ready to harvest when they are the proper color (variety dependent) and come off the tree with a gentle twist and tug. You can have a taste right then and there to determine whether they're ready for harvesting. Standard apple trees will only start bearing fruits five to ten years after planting; if you're impatient, go for dwarf varieties that will bear fruit in two to three years.

Nevertheless, apples will generally be ready for harvesting at around 115 to 135 days after 90% of the flowers on the tree have opened (also known as full bloom).

Blueberries and Rhododendrons

Rhododendrons are azaleas because they are too closely related to class them as separate plant varieties (according to botanists). Someone else calls the shots because we call them two different things here. The flowers look slightly different, but both are beautiful, nonetheless.

Blueberries are notoriously difficult to form a companion guild with because they prefer acidic soil, whereas 99% of common garden crops don't. But rhododendrons share this love for soil with a pH of below six at the very least. In the spirit of diversity, we can't let our blueberry brethren stand alone!

Benefits

Blueberries are a sustainable crop because they are pest and disease-resistant (I'm guessing most insects and microorganisms also don't do too well in acidic soil). To be clear, this doesn't mean you won't ever have a pest problem in your blueberry bushes, so you should still monitor your crops and take some precautionary steps. You can use neem oil to make a solution to spray on the blueberry bush to protect against pests like aphids.

There are also a lot of blueberry varieties that are self-fertile if you don't have the space to grow more than one bush. Blueberries are a "superfood" because they have many health benefits, and it's hard to list them all without people thinking you're a sales rep.

Both blueberries and rhododendrons attract pollinators, so there's that. But, honestly, that's as far as their mutual relationship goes. They both have shallow roots and can be grown in smaller pots.

This pairing will be most beneficial if your garden has acidic soil that you want to use effectively. Growing something is better than nothing, and beggars can't be choosers. Of course, if you love blueberries and want to develop them, don't let anything stop you. They're easy to grow and maintain in proper conditions.

Care and Maintenance

The most important step to cultivating this guild is preparing your soil. Blueberries prefer soil with a pH level between four and five and should also be well-draining and fertile with lots of organic matter. Gardening stores sell acidic soil, but make sure it's organic. Alternatively, you can make the soil acidic by adding fertilizers that contain high levels of ammonium, nitrate, urea, phosphor, and sulfur.

However, you will need some way of testing the soil's pH levels. In this case, a reusable pH testing machine is a good investment. After you've amended the soil, give it a few months and test the soil again. Repeat the process until the soil reaches the preferred pH levels and test again every few months afterward. The soil pH levels will try to correct themselves and slowly move to a neutral state (especially if you're making previously neutral soil acidic). You must amend the soil again to maintain the preferred acidity levels. This maintenance is the bulk of the work when growing blueberries.

Blueberries grow well in full sun (but will tolerate minimal shade), like cold winters, and don't compete well with weeds, so make sure you mulch them generously. Mulching with pine needles and sawdust can help keep the soil acidic for longer. Blueberries should be watered deeply once a week, with the soil soaked for the first few inches. An irrigation system will save you some trouble, but it's not a requirement.

It would be best to space blueberry bushes at least 4 feet apart. If your blueberry bush's leaves start to yellow, it's a sign the pH is not low enough. To fix this, add garden sulfur or aluminum sulfur to the topsoil and water the soil to help it settle before mulching the area.

Harvesting

Blueberries are perennials, and while they can start producing berries in their second or third growing year, the quality and quantity of production will reach their full potential once the plant is at least six years old. Remember to pinch off any flower buds on the blueberry bush in their first and second year to encourage its general growth first; this will result in a bigger and better third-year harvest since the plant will be more established than it would have been if you didn't remove flower buds in the first two growing years.

How do you know when blueberries are ripe? The easiest and most reliable way is to pick a few and give them a taste. But as a general guideline, ripe blueberries are a deep blue-purple with a light gray dusting of what looks like powder and will be plump (but not firm) to the touch. A very firm blueberry with a hint of red (or that's still white or green) is not ready yet and will be tart and unpleasant to eat. Blueberries won't ripen further once picked like tomatoes or peppers, so only harvest them if you're confident they're ripe.

The trick to harvesting the sweetest blueberries is leaving them on the bush for at least a week *after* they've turned that deep blue-purple color completely. The berries will come off the branch effortlessly; hold a bucket or basket under a cluster of blueberries and pick them off with your free hand. You might have to pick out some stems and leaves afterward. Store them in the fridge unwashed (they'll stay fresh for up to a week refrigerated), and only wash them before eating or using them. The moisture might make them spoil sooner if you prewash them.

Your rhododendrons will unfortunately not bear fruit, but at least they're pretty to look at. Prune away dead, damaged, or diseased foliage or flowers as needed so it stays looking pretty and productive.

Grape and Lavender

Most bunching grape varieties are self-fertile, so you only need one grapevine to produce a yield, which is excellent news when you're short on space. Grapes can also start bearing fruit from as early as their second year. That's alright, considering they're perennials that will likely outlive you (most grapevine varieties can live to 100 years old!).

Then, of course, there's lavender, another distant relative of the flowering mint family. Its everyday use is for its calming properties in the form of essential oils, skincare or bath products, and even tea. Additionally, it can alleviate other health qualms and symptoms like migraines, anxiety, inflammation, allergies, and insomnia, to name just a few. Lavender is a big deal in the world of aromatherapy. Place a bouquet of freshly picked lavender in your bathroom and experience a relaxing bath.

However, lavender is also used in the kitchen and can be dried, finely chopped, and used (or infused) in rubs, marinades, sauces, desserts, syrups, sorbets, ice cream, and more. It can also be used whole, fresh, or dried as a decorative garnish. Nevertheless, lavender is an excellent addition to your garden and holds a lot of tricks up its purple sleeves.

Benefits

Homemade wine, anyone? I'm not here to judge what you do with the grapes once you've grown and harvested them. But growing lavender with your grapes is a good idea. While fruiting crops don't generally bring a lot to the table in companion planting— since we mainly grow them for the benefit of eating them—grapes are more beneficial for your garden than you might've expected.

Beneficial insects love grapes, which provide built-in pest management. They are also significant producers in the right conditions; on average, a single, established, healthy grapevine can produce between eight and ten pounds of grapes annually. That's more than enough for a small family.

Even when your grapevines are not producing fruit, they add charisma and interest to any garden in any season. Let them engulf a garden archway, belvedere, or pergola, and see your garden of dreams come to life (and it's super functional, too). Now pair that vision with some lush lavender, and you'll be the go-to person for hosting get-togethers with friends and family.

But lavender is also not one to sit back and look pretty. It is naturally pest-resistant and repellent and will also draw pollinators to your garden, benefiting all your crops. Lavender (a hardy perennial) thrives in most climates, is easy to grow, and can withstand drought.

Care and Maintenance

Lavender and grapevine guilds require little maintenance if you set them up for success. Both lavender and grapes have a low need for fertilizer. Too much nitrogen can increase the risk of grapes getting fungal diseases, and too much water will reduce the grapevine roots' ability to absorb enough nutrients (and can lead to root rot). And lavender prefers drier soil anyway.

Grapes are typically grown from cuttings rather than seeds. You can buy a grapevine plant from a nursery or purchase grapevine cuttings online (ensure the website is reputable). To grow a grapevine from a cutting, prepare a nursing tray or container with well-draining, fertile soil. Cut one end of the branch so it's slanted, like how you would cut a ribbon to keep it from fraying. Then, stick the cutting into the soil with the sloping end pointing up. Water the soil well so it stays moist but not soggy; proper hydration at this point is critical for the cuttings to grow good roots.

After about two months, the roots will be long enough to survive, and you can transplant them into their final spot in the garden. Yes, you can plant them in containers, but the containers need to be a minimum size of 15 gallons. Avoid dark-colored pots or containers since this might cause the roots to overheat. Wood is a good option. Wouldn't it be ironic if you grew grapes in an old wine barrel? If you ever need this information, an octave cask would be about 15 gallons.

Leave your grapevine be for an entire year to allow the roots and vines to become established. Then, in the winter of its second year, cut it down to right above the first two buds (little protrusions or "pimples" on the trunk). A drastic pruning indeed, but two thicker branches will grow from those two buds you left. This pruning, however extreme it may seem, will ensure your grapevine is as strong as it needs to be to carry a more significant yield. The year after this will mainly be spent "training" the vine by wrapping and tying it to your trellis or support structure.

Speaking of which, your grapevine will need a sturdy, long-lasting trellis or support for climbing. Remember, grapevines will live for many years and develop thick, solid, heavy vines and grapes; if it breaks, you can't replace the trellis or support without putting the vine in grave danger; if you can, go for a thicker steel structure of sorts from the very start.

After the second year, your grapevine will be all set up and ready to produce. The only maintenance you need from here on out is yearly pruning. You'll want to cut away any runners that grow beyond or away from the trellis and any dead or damaged branches.

Grapes and lavender need full sun and will benefit from a light layer of mulch. If you plant lavender with your grapes, ensure that the grapes aren't overshadowing the lavender. Lavender is slow to germinate (it can take up to a month) but grows steadily and will bloom for the first time in its second year of growth.

Sow lavender seeds over prepped soil, but don't cover or push them into the soil; they need exposure to sunlight to germinate. Pruning lavender is optional, requiring only yearly pruning to keep the garden neat. Funnily enough, you can also grow lavender from cuttings.

Harvesting

Like blueberries, the simplest way to tell whether your grapes are ready to be harvested is to taste a few straight from the vine. The flowers on the grapevine will stick around for a couple of weeks before they turn into small "berries." Typically, grapes will be ripe enough to harvest three months after their small berry-like first appearance (usually in late summer to early fall).

To harvest your grapes, pick entire bunches by cutting the stems. Don't pick the grapes individually; besides this method being wildly inefficient and labor intensive, your grapes will last longer if you leave them (and store them) attached to the stems.

Lavender doesn't lose its fragrance when dried; it's one of its many fine qualities. You can harvest lavender when the flower buds open to get the best flavor and fragrance. Cut the lavender flower at the base of the stem or as long or short as you need it to be. Did you know that lavender flowers are edible and can add color and taste to salads? You can also make tea out of it. But be careful; use it sparingly as it's very fragrant.

Peach and Garlic

Did you know that the fuzz on peaches is there to protect them from pests and other environmental factors? If only all crops came with this helpful feature pre-installed.

A peach is a "stone" fruit, which is a fancy way to say it has a thin skin and contains a seed within a hard pit (or stone) in the middle of the fruit. Apricots, cherries, plums, nectarines, and the like are all stone fruits. The point is that these decadent fruits contain large amounts of vitamin C and antioxidants, making them a great companion for garlic.

Garlic bread, garlic butter, crushed, minced, or confit are some of its uses. Garlic is another kitchen staple in most households. I can't remember the last time I made a dish without it! Some side effects of consuming garlic may include Mosquitoes (and occasionally, people) giving you a wide berth, improved digestive function, and a delicious meal. As long as you have garlic, do you even need anything else?

Benefits

Garlic is to your garden as a knight is to a king. Garlic, like all alliums, has strong pest-repellent properties and will keep aphids, peach tree borers, weevils, and fruit flies far away. It also adds potassium back into the soil and has natural anti-fungal attributes, which will keep the soil fertile and the roots of your peach tree healthy. You can also use garlic as living mulch to suppress weeds or chop and drop once it's time to harvest. Nothing goes to waste here!

This example is another guild pairing you can effortlessly grow in a large container or raised garden bed. Peach trees and garlic are hardy crops, and low maintenance is a benefit.

While peach trees don't do as much for the garden as garlic does, they benefit us with their longevity and abundant yields. And they provide shelter for beneficial insects and pollinators. It's not much, but it's honest work.

Care and Maintenance

Growing a peach tree from a seed is possible but will take some finesse. This requirement is because a hard coating or pit surrounds the seed; you'll need to first stratify the seed (with the pit intact) in the fridge for four months, then you'll need to gently crack open the seed without damaging the embryo on the inside (a nutcracker works well). After this, keep the pit in a paper towel or a seedling starting tray and consistently moist. Creating a greenhouse effect by placing the seed wrapped in a damp paper towel in a Ziploc bag or covering the seedling tray with a clear plastic container will prevent it from drying out and increase humidity levels (which aids in germination and early growth).

You can transplant your seedling into a bigger pot or its final place in the garden (in late winter after the ground has thawed) once it has its first set of true leaves. But if you want to avoid all this, purchase a young peach tree (about one year old) from a nursery to transplant. Prepare the soil with a complete fertilizer and top up twice yearly for the first three years of growth and water every other week (or every week in hot summers).

In either event, the young peach tree will need some attention eventually. Once the tree is about a year old, prune the shoots off the top by two or three buds. If you purchased a young tree, you can do this immediately or at the end of the following winter. This pruning keeps the tree from growing too tall and encourages it first to send all resources to the main branches to form a strong structure.

In the second year, you want to clean up those branches that matured in the first year. You do this by cutting back any scaffolding branches and leaving only the three thickest branches stemming from the leader (the stem). Also, remove any shoots forming below these three main branches.

After this, you want to leave the tree alone and only prune away the three D's (dead, damaged, or diseased matter) every year. Peach trees generally start bearing fruit in their fourth year. Peach trees need full sun and prefer colder winters to produce the best fruit.

Plant garlic in the fall before the first frost or in early spring in warmer climates because garlic also requires a short stratification period. It's very tricky to grow garlic from seed, so I advise you to grow garlic from the garlic itself. That's right! You can plant individual garlic cloves directly into the ground, and it will grow into an entire garlic plant.

Garlic likes full sun and moist, fertile, well-draining soil. To plant garlic, start by preparing the soil with fertilizer. Separate the cloves from each other, leaving the papery layer surrounding each one intact. Only use the biggest cloves for planting and use the rest for cooking.

Plant your garlic cloves two to three inches deep and at least four inches apart. You'll notice that each clove has a pointy and rounded end; plant the garlic's sharp end facing up. Cover the holes and add a thick layer of straw mulch (which will retain moisture and suppress weeds that will steal nutrients away from your garlic). In about two months, you'll be able to see leaves emerge from the mulch.

Water garlic weekly for the first month, reduce frequency after this, and account for rainy weather. Garlic should receive about an inch of water once a week; excess water will cause the garlic to rot. It takes about nine months for the garlic to mature and be ready for harvest.

You can try growing garlic from store-bought ones, but if you do this, ensure that the garlic is organic. They will often spray garlic with chemicals that discourage sprouting for a longer shelf-life; buying organic garlic reduces the chances of it having had this treatment. Alternatively, you can buy a few garlic plants from a nursery and save some from those for future sowing.

Harvesting

Peaches are ready to be harvested when no sign of green is present on the fruit. The color gradient of the peach may differ depending on your variety, but generally, the bottom of the peach should be yellow and the top red or deep orange. The good news is that even if you pick a peach before it's fully ripened, it will continue to ripen off the tree (place it in a paper bag, which you should keep in a dark cupboard).

As long as you pick it when there's no green left, you can let them ripen after harvesting. Peaches are a summer fruit and will generally be ready for harvest during this time. Use a light hand when harvesting peaches because they bruise easily. They should come off the tree with a gentle twist; if they don't, you can use some pruners to cut the stems (but bear in mind that these might not be fully ripe yet).

Garlic is ready to be harvested when most leaves or foliage have turned yellow or brown. You can dig one up to check for size. Avoid pulling the garlic up by the leaves since they are usually dry when the garlic is mature and will break off easily. Instead, use a garden fork to lift the garlic out of the soil from underneath the bulb.

Brush off any soil from the garlic bulbs and allow them to dry out or "cure" for about a month in a cool, well-ventilated room (or in a shaded area outside) before use.

Make sure you have enough space to start a guild. There is always a way to grow some fresh produce in small gardens or outdoor spaces. If you've been living under the impression that you can't have fruit trees because your garden is too small, now is the time to get rid of that idea and grow whatever you want!

7

COMPANION PLANTING — FLOWERS

You give them to your significant other on Valentine's Day or your anniversary. You bring them to your friend in the hospital to make them feel better. You use them as a pop of color on the dinner table when it's your turn to host family events.

Flowers do a lot of things outside of the soil as well as inside. Sure, they're pretty but also necessary for a functional and healthy garden. And quite a lot of them are edible, too.

CLASSIC FLOWER PAIRINGS

Do you want a garden that's both edible and beautiful? Companion planting allows you to enjoy the benefits of multiple plant species, enhancing your yields and creating a more diverse and healthy garden. While most fruits and vegetable crops do spawn their flowers for reproduction, having additional flowering plants to draw in some beneficial wildlife (and helping save the bees while you're at it) is in the best interest of your garden.

Marigolds and Almost Anything

Remember when I told you that you can never go wrong with marigolds? That's because beans and cabbage are the only known "bad" companions for marigolds. Because they attract the same pests, technically speaking, you can use marigolds as a trap crop to protect your beans and cabbage. The only time you shouldn't pair marigolds with another crop is when their requirements differ entirely.

For example, marigolds will fare poorly with blueberries because marigolds need a higher soil pH level. Marigolds will fare poorly with crops that prefer shaded areas or dry soil. But the margin of crops needing shade and dry soil is slim.

Since we already covered marigolds in a previous chapter, I'll summarize their benefits, care, and maintenance requirements.

Benefits:

- Easy to grow.
- Flowers are edible.
- Pest and nematode management.
- They attract pollinators and predatory insects (additional pest control).
- Serve as a trap crop.
- Use as mulch (chop and drop).

Care and Maintenance:

- They require full sun.
- Prepare the soil with fertilizer or compost and top up yearly (before flowering and not during winter).

- Allow soil to dry out somewhat between each watering (water once a week).
- Avoid overhead watering (water at the base).
- Cut off spent flowers to promote new flowers to grow immediately.

Sunflowers and Cucumbers

Did you know you can eat sunflowers? No, not the seeds; I mean everything. You can harvest sunflower heads when the seed coatings haven't formed yet (or haven't hardened), pluck off the petals, slather some oil, and cook it on a grill. I haven't tried it yet, and I'm skeptical. But people say it tastes like corn on the cob, and artichoke had a baby out of wedlock.

Nevertheless, sunflowers and cucumbers make for great companion plants. Note: Grilling and eating whole sunflowers is not a requirement. But feel free to harvest the seeds for a future snack!

Benefits

Pairing your cucumbers with sunflowers is a great idea. The sturdy sunflower stalks are a natural trellis for the climbing cucumber vines, which saves valuable space in your garden. Sunflowers also attract pollinators and predatory insects, which are known to improve crop yield and manage certain pests and their offspring.

Sunflowers are hyper-accumulators and will absorb any heavy metals and toxic chemicals in the soil, making it generally healthier. Besides a natural trellis, pest control, pollinators, and healthier soil, you are left with beautiful flowers in your garden that you can harvest for decorations and snacks. The bright yellow leaves of sunflowers also compliment the cucumbers' greenery perfectly.

You can use cucumbers to benefit your garden in a few different ways. One of which is making liquid fertilizer. Cucumbers (specifically the skin and leaves) are high in vitamins and minerals, such as potassium and phosphorus, that aid in the health and growth of all plants. Save any cucumber skin you may have from peeling them, and place them in a container that has a lid. Fill the container with cucumber skins (or leaves) and water, secure the lid, and leave it to soak for at least five days.

After this, scoop out the cucumber skins (or leaves) and let them dry on parchment paper. Once the skins are dry, you can chop them into smaller pieces and sprinkle them onto the soil around any crops you may have, or you can burn them and use the ash in the same way for a quicker release of nutrients. In the meantime, you can use the cucumber water to water any crops that look like they could use a "pick me up" or dilute it and water your entire garden evenly.

Care and Maintenance

Sunflowers are not picky or high-maintenance crops at all. Give them water, any soil type, and full sun, and they will accomplish their goal of growing big and strong no matter what nature throws at them. Wait until the last frost has passed in spring and sow your seeds regularly in a sunny spot in well-draining, fertile soil and water for the first few weeks. Once your sunflowers mature, reduce watering to once a week. Sunflowers are drought-resistant, but the flowers *will* droop if the plant doesn't receive enough water.

Add slow-release compost or fertilizer to the soil for best results before planting. This way, you will only need to amend the soil the following year (sunflowers are annual, so you'll need to sow them again yearly). To prevent diseases like powdery mildew, root rot, rust, and wilt, ensure your sunflowers get enough air circulation and space them at least six inches from each other when planting to avoid overcrowding.

Cucumbers also require full sun and well-draining, fertile soil. Cucumbers are vining plants, so if you're planting the companion pair in a container, you may only be able to fit one cucumber plant with a couple of sunflowers (cucumbers need at least three feet between them).

Cucumbers' most crucial care instruction is regular watering and mulch because they need lots of moisture to develop and grow a plump yield. Not watering enough will lead to small, wrinkled, and even bitter cucumbers. When watering, water at the base since overhead watering or irrigation via sprinklers may cause the foliage and fruits to rot quickly. Refrain from overfertilizing the plant; stick to an initial round of fertilizer (before planting) and top the soil with liquid fertilizer approximately one week after blooms start appearing.

Plant sunflowers first and allow them to grow to about 12 inches tall before you sow the cucumber seeds. By the time your cucumbers start vining or even blooming, your sunflowers will be prominent and robust enough to provide enough structural support for your incoming cucumbers. Your cucumbers may need some trellis "training" to do this; wrap the vines and tendrils around the sunflowers as they grow (you can also use twine to secure them if necessary).

Harvesting

It would be best to harvest cucumbers when they're the right size and color according to the variation you're growing. Most cucumbers start yellow or pale and develop into a dark green as they mature and ripen. A ripened cucumber should be firm, have no soft or squishy spots, and no yellowing.

Once your cucumbers bloom and start forming small berry-like fruit, they will grow fast. Check on your cucumbers regularly and harvest them as soon as they are uniform in color, firm, and crisp. For pickling varieties, the ideal size is generally two inches long, while slicing varieties should be between six to ten inches long.

Cucumbers are best when not entirely ripe as seeds are hard and taste bitter, so selecting based on size is optimal. Because you're harvesting cucumbers before they are fully grown, they won't come off the vine as effortlessly as a ripe fruit would. Use gardening scissors or pruners to cut the cucumbers when harvesting to prevent damaging the plant (and affecting the growth of other cucumbers that aren't quite ready to be harvested yet).

Sunflower heads are ready to be harvested once the back of the flower is yellow. This colorization is when the seeds are fully formed and ready to be eaten. Because cucumbers and sunflowers are annuals, they will die together once the harvesting period is over. You can leave the roots in the ground over winter to feed the soil and allow the dead plant matter to stay on the ground as mulch to keep weeds from popping up. Simply till the decomposed leaves into the soil before planting again the following year.

Nasturtiums and Roses

I know what you're thinking: "But didn't you say gardening has to be functional?" I did say that, and I stand by that statement. But this guild pairing is more functional than you might think. Yes, both plants are flowers, and their primary function is beauty. However, nasturtiums (flowers, leaves, stems, and seeds) are edible and can add a fantastic peppery flavor to soups, stews, and garden salads.

Plus, if you interplant this pairing between all your other guilds, they are a valuable addition to your garden, not only in aesthetics.

Benefits

As mentioned, nasturtiums and roses beautify your garden, but you can also use them as trap crops for pests like aphids. But don't worry because they also attract hoverflies, ladybirds, and lacewings, which eat aphids and other common pests. So not only will you keep aphids away from your other crops, but the predatory insects will keep the aphid population in check.

While nasturtiums are an excellent living ground cover and chop and drop mulch, roses are drought-tolerant and don't require much maintenance to look (and smell) as beautiful as they do. Of course, all flowers (including roses and nasturtium) will bring pollinators to the garden, which is always a plus.

Care and Maintenance

Roses and nasturtiums both need full sun and well-draining, fertile soil. However, nasturtiums thrive and flower best in soil that's not overly fertilized, while roses need regular fertilizing for impressive blooms. For this reason, you should amend the soil lightly with fertilizer or compost before planting the pair and only "spot-fertil-ize" roses around the base with liquid fertilizer (but you can also use regular fertilizer as long as you're only feeding the roses).

Sow nasturtiums once the soil has warmed up enough (mid-spring is best). They rarely succumb to dehydration, so water them when-ever you water the roses, which should be at least once a week (and water both at the base to avoid wetting the foliage). Nasturtiums only really need pruning if you want to neaten things up in the garden (in which case, be my guest).

Roses, on the other hand, will need minimal pruning. You should remove dead, damaged, and diseased matter throughout the year and as soon as you spot it. But other than that, cut back the previous year's growth to where the center of the branches (or canes) looks white. Remember: Major pruning should be done in late winter or early spring only, but you can remove brown branches, dead flowers, or leaves at any time.

Nasturtiums are annuals, but they tend to self-seed (meaning you probably won't need to replant them. Instead, you'll have to thin out the sprouts in spring), while roses are hardy perennials, which will become dormant in winter and come back to life in spring.

Harvesting

Nasturtium flowers and leaves taste peppery and can add color to a salad. Harvesting the flowers before they set seed would be best, so the best bet would be to pick them right as they open. The leaves taste best when young and crisp, so you should only harvest new growth.

To use nasturtium seeds as a caper substitute, pick them while they are still green and then pickle them in vinegar.

You'll likely harvest roses to display around the house, gift them to a friend, or sprinkle the leaves into your bubble bath. Regardless, for the best and longest-lasting result, harvest roses in mid-morning after the dew has dried, and only harvest roses that are still starting to open (cut the stem at a 45° angle). You can also dry the roses in salicylic acid for a longer-lasting, rustic display.

Petunias and Beans

There are so many crops you can pair up with beans, but if you want a better bean yield while adding a layer of pretty, beans and petunias are a good choice. This guild pair is especially great for beginner companion gardeners because it's so easy to take care of and can serve as that initial confidence boost you need to dive in even further!

Benefits

Petunias can act as a trap crop for bean beetles and aphids, but they also repel certain other pests and attract pollinators and predatory insects. This guild works in a very similar way to the previous guild pairing (nasturtiums and roses), but unlike nasturtiums, petunias aren't edible. But they are lovely and will have your garden buzzing with bees and butterflies!

Beans, being legumes, are perfect for soil health since they're nitrogen fixers. This characteristic means they increase nitrogen levels in the soil and make the nitrogen more accessible to nearby neighbors (in this case, your petunias). On top of this, beans are incredibly versatile in the kitchen and contain a lot of protein and fiber.

Care and Maintenance

Both beans and petunias have similar growing requirements: They need well-draining and fertile soil, regular watering (every couple of days when young and twice a week once established), and full sun. However, they will compete for nutrients if planted too close together. Sow beans and petunias at least a foot apart. For this reason, it might be wise to add a ground cover crop to the guild or mulch the garden bed (or container) well.

Petunias are biennials, meaning they complete their life cycle within two years before they die. But they are also known to self-seed quite effectively, and some might even make it through their third year, depending on which climate you're in. Most bean varieties are annual and will need planting again every year.

To cultivate climbing beans, you must offer support through a trellis. Remember to implement crop rotation unless you're planting in containers or raised garden beds (in which case you'll need a resting period every couple of years and amend the soil well between seasons).

Petunias and beans don't need pruning, but you might have to "train" your climbing beans so they utilize the support structure properly, and always remember to remove dead foliage.

As always, if you use certain plants as trap crops, you'll want to keep an eye on them to ensure pests are not overrunning them. Once a trap crop dies, nothing stops the still very much alive pests from looking elsewhere for sustenance and shelter. So, check on your petunias occasionally and cut off any stems or flowers with vast numbers of aphids or other pest babies (eggs) to help keep populations manageable.

Harvesting

You can harvest petunia flowers for display as you would any other flowers, but if you want them to reseed independently, leave a few flowers on the plant until they fall off by themselves so seeds can form, mature, and disperse via gravity.

Beans are a bit trickier. For starters, there are many different bean varieties, and the type of beans you grow will determine the best harvest time. But a general rule of thumb is to harvest bean pods before they harden and turn brown. Just for reference, bush beans will be ready for harvest about 50 days after flowering, and pole beans will be ready for harvest around 60 days after flowering.

The best advice I can give is to look up how your specific type of beans or pods should look and feel when they're ready to be harvested or how long it typically takes after flowering. Leaving them on the bean plant for too long will produce a tough and even inedible bean. Some beans will come in and be ready for harvest all at once, like bush beans, so you might need to stagger the planting for these types.

Zinnias and Cauliflower

If you're not a fan of cauliflower, you can swap it out for any other member of the Brassica family. Regardless, zinnias and cauliflower make an excellent companion pairing. Cauliflower does need quite a bit of space since you want to grow more than one for cross-pollination reasons and because one cauliflower head is only worth some of the work you put in for months in advance.

Therefore, I would not recommend you plant this guild in a container, but you can grow it in a raised garden bed. Zinnias fit perfectly between the gaps of your cauliflower and will provide the most benefits this way, too.

Benefits

Of course, where there's a flower, there are beneficial insects like bees and butterflies, which will help with pest control and pollination for your edible garden crops. Zinnias are edible, by the way. They are on the bitter side but can still work well as decorations for cakes you made yourself or in a vase on display (for long-stemmed varieties). Zinnias also make great trap crops for common cauliflower pests.

Cauliflower doesn't have many benefits in the garden, but you can use the leaves and any scraps you cut off when preparing a meal as mulch (or to make fertilizer tea). Another overlooked benefit of cauliflower and zinnias is that they don't require much maintenance.

Care and Maintenance

Zinnias and cauliflower have similar growing requirements. They both like full sun and fertile, well-draining soil. Zinnias are warm-season flowers, while cauliflower is a cool-weather crop planted in spring after the last frost or fall. In frost-free climates, cauliflower is primarily grown in the winter, but you can cultivate it successfully all year round with some protection against frost or extreme heat.

While zinnias are hardy annuals and will likely take anything you throw at them, they are not very fond of the cold, so it's best to plant them in late spring or start them inside and transplant them after the last frost. Deadheading is the only maintenance needed for zinnias during the growing season—cutting off spent or withered flowers to encourage the plant to produce more. You should amend the soil once or twice with liquid fertilizer (or fertilizer tea) during the flowering period.

The key to growing cauliflower is consistent cool temperatures in the 60°F range, so timing is essential. Amend the soil with a generous amount of compost or other organic material in advance. Plant cauliflower seeds about a month before the last frost date. Add a thick layer of mulch over the soil (at least three inches) and water deeply once a week.

You might have to cover the seedlings with tunnel hoops or greenhouse structures to protect them from extreme cold (you can make your own with sturdy wire and plastic sheets as a more affordable option). It would help if you planted cauliflowers at least 18 inches apart.

Once the cauliflower heads are the size of golf balls, gently wrap the most prominent and extended surrounding leaves over the head and secure them with twine. This process is called blanching, and its purpose is to keep the cauliflower heads white since exposure to the sun will turn them yellow. Blanching cauliflower heads will also offer some protection against larger pests.

Fertilize your cauliflower every two weeks throughout the growing season by adding compost or liquid fertilizer around the base of the plant. Cauliflower is, after all, an annual, which means it's a heavy feeder. A good layer of mulch will suppress weeds, but if some manage to squeeze through, pull them out as soon as you notice them.

Harvesting

You can harvest zinnias when they open or like any other flower. But if you're using zinnias as trap crops, I recommend against eating them or using them as garnish or decorations for food items.

Harvesting cauliflower when it's big enough to eat but still compact (ideally when they're no less than six inches in diameter) would be best. Typically, this is around one week after you tie the leaves up and around the head. You can untie the leaves to check on the cauliflower head before harvesting. If it's still small and compact, you can leave it be for a few more days before checking again. If a cauliflower head looks like it wants to open up (the individual florets separate from each other), harvest it immediately, no matter the size, because the quality, texture, and taste will only worsen once this starts to happen.

Use a serrated knife to cut the cauliflower heads at the base of the neck, right below the leaves. You can leave the roots in the ground to decompose and release nutrients back into the soil; this is also good for underground microorganism populations.

If you take away one thing from this entire book, let it be this: It is probably easier than you think, and you will only succeed if you're willing to try and fail. Yes, it will require troubleshooting and learning from mistakes, but isn't that just life?

8

GARDENING IN SMALL SPACES

One of the biggest reasons many home gardeners never get into gardening despite their keen interest is the need for more planting space. Cultivating crops requires soil, water, light, and seeds.

Will a limited space have obstacles? Yes. Will you need to compromise on the type of crops and the amount you grow? Absolutely. But if your green thumb is itching, there is always a way to scratch it. This chapter reviews maximizing your growing space, even with zero outdoor space!

AVAILABLE SPACE

From a small grass-covered lawn to an apartment without as much as a front porch, companion planting, and permaculture principles have got you covered no matter how much space you have. Allow yourself to get creative with what you have right now instead of waiting for the right time to become an avid gardener.

Having enough space to grow whatever you want and as much as you want would be ideal, but life doesn't always work out that way. Let's look at the different sizes of planting space available to you and think of a few ways you can make it work regardless.

Smaller Gardens

You fall into this category if you have some in-ground garden bed to work with. This space could be a small grass patch or backyard where you could utilize the space more efficiently.

Grass is the standard for yards, but it's a waste of space. If you have a front or back yard with grass, you can replace it with a gardening space. This tactic is a viable option even if you're renting since all that you'll need to do to restore the yard to its original state is remove all crops, till the top layer of soil, sprinkle some grass seeds, and water regularly a few months before your lease is up.

The easiest way to convert a small grass garden into a usable gardening space is to mulch the entire area until the grass is dead; you can mulch with leaves, straw, cardboard, or all the above combined, as long as you cover every inch of grass in a thick layer. Water everything well and weekly. After a few months, you can till the top layer of soil, add compost, and start gardening.

Just make sure you plan your new garden space so you can still get around to everything (walkways, dividing spaces, etc.) Additionally, you can include other solutions yet to be discussed in this chapter to give yourself even more space to work with.

You will likely be able to grow almost anything you want in a small garden, but not as much as you want. A pro tip is to go for dwarf varieties to save space. Grow cherry tomatoes instead of regular ones, grow shallots or green onions instead of regular onions, and so on.

Concrete Only

In some instances, you may have a decent amount of space but no in-ground soil. This option includes oversized balconies, court-yards, or simply a paved (with bricks or concrete) front or back yard. You need soil for gardening, but no one said the soil must be in the ground.

For this problem, you can use raised garden beds directly on the concrete or container gardening. You can build your raised garden bed with wood or steel frames and corrugated iron as the siding.

Gardening on top of concrete or bricks might stain the concrete or leave a mark, even after power washing the site, which is not good news for renters. In this case, you can use old oil drums (or any other reusable, sizable containers) cut in half either lengthwise or crosswise (each half is decently sized). If you slice lengthwise, you must stabilize the drum with rocks, wood, or other ways. Remember to wash the containers well, make drainage holes, and round off any sharp edges for metal containers (use a wooden or rubber mallet to make the edges blunt or bent so you don't get cut).

As discussed earlier, bigger containers like oil drums, barrels, or small water tanks will offer you enough space to grow small guilds or companion pairings. However, you can also use ceramic pots, buckets, planters, or any other sizable containers you can get your hands on and arrange them accordingly right on top of the concrete. This option will bring some life and greenery into an otherwise very industrial and flat-looking space, plus you get to have some fresh produce on occasion.

You can treat a raised garden bed or container garden like you would an in-ground garden bed. This tactic means you can grow anything in it if the containers are big and deep enough.

Remember that you'll need to water crops growing in raised or container gardens more frequently.

Minimum Space

If you live in an urban area where you don't have much outdoor space, like in an apartment with a tiny balcony, porch, or micro garden, you can still make the most of it by growing crops that vine or climb or using vertical planters. You can make your vertical garden with PVC piping or gutters that you mount onto a wall or other structure. Of course, you can also buy vertical planters or make them out of wood if you have the financial means.

Even something as simple as a steel shelf can become a vertical planter. You can place individually potted crops on it and put your vining crops next to it so it uses the side of the shelf as support. Just make sure you arrange everything in such a way that they all get enough sunlight.

If you have a covered porch, attach a wire fence across one of the sides (preferably the one that gets the most sun) with some planters in front of it. You'll be able to grow beans, cucumbers, tomatoes, summer squash, and even grapes like this. Another thing you can do in addition to this is utilize hanging baskets.

Use the walls or ceiling when you don't have floor space! Grow up instead of out. Crops you can plant in hanging baskets include cherry tomatoes, strawberries, collard or leafy greens, cucumbers, and herbs.

No Outdoor Space

This scenario is by far the hardest to work around. Having absolutely no outdoor space is a hurdle. The only viable solution here is to grow everything indoors, similar to houseplants. You can grow many herbs in windowsills as long as sunlight reaches it.

This option will also limit the size of the plants. Opt for shade-tolerant and shallow-rooted crops, and invest in growth lights to grow fruiting crops (fruit and vegetables).

But the most challenging thing about growing your crops indoors is the lack of pollinators. You can open a window to let in a few bees to help themselves to your windowsill garden if you are okay with them, but this is only effective if there's not a lot of movement (insects typically avoid humans). Since only a few people want bees, wasps, and other insects in their homes, you have two options. Only grow self-fertile crops or hand-pollinate them.

Crops that will thrive in pots, indoors, and with a bit of help from a growth lamp include microgreens, carrots, beets, radishes, onions, chives, garlic, thyme, mint, parsley, rosemary, peppers, and leafy greens.

MINIMALIST GARDENING

Earlier, we discussed how you should only grow crops you will use and eat. When you have minimum space, you don't have a choice in this regard. Every inch counts and must be used to its fullest potential.

A good starting point is to list all the fruits and vegetables you and your family eat regularly and cross out any incompatable for your garden space scenario or skill level. For example, you won't be able to grow a peach tree indoors. But you might be able to grow basil.

Don't tell anyone I said this, but ditch the flowers if necessary. They take up a lot of space, and besides a few outliers, the only real benefit most of them offer is aesthetics, attracting pollinators, and being used as trap crops, which is excellent if you have the space for it. Most fruit and vegetable crops have flowers anyway, which does an excellent job of attracting beneficial insects. You can use other crops and herbs to help keep pests at bay (and it's more functional and minimalistic).

Another thing to consider is quantity over price point. Growing potatoes takes up a lot of space and is very unpredictable. You might end up with marble-sized potatoes and months of wasted time and space. If you're not breaking your budget buying potatoes and onions at the store, buy them and grow something you like but can only sometimes buy because it's expensive (like strawberries).

FAST-PACED GARDENING

Time is a precious resource, and when you don't have much space to grow your produce, you need to raise as much as possible as quickly as possible. Instead of growing crops that need to grow and become established for a year before fruiting, go for quick-growing crops that will bear produce in a few months.

Succession planting and intercropping are non-negotiable when gardening space is limited. Growing something every season and planting companion crops together will ensure no space goes to waste. This approach and quick-producing crops will give you the best bang for your buck.

Here's a list of common vegetables and herbs that will mature and be ready for harvest within mere weeks or months of being sowed:

- Microgreens (two weeks).
- Beets (two months).
- Spinach (one month).
- Radishes (one month).
- Green beans (two months).
- Mustard greens (one month).
- Arugula and rocket (two months).
- Green onions (one month).
- Cucumbers (three months).
- Spring onions (three months).
- Mint (three months).
- Basil (two months).

We're gardeners. We do what we can with what we have. We're resilient, creative, and life-givers. Don't let a lack of outdoor space stop you from enjoying what you love or being surrounded by greenery and fresh produce.

9

COMPANION PLANTING AND PEST CONTROL

The second chapter discussed how certain plants (usually herbs and flowers) help with natural pest management. Some give off a strong scent that disguises crops or confuses pests; others attract predatory insects that eat the pests or their eggs and offspring. And in some cases, some plants are sacrificed as trap crops for the good of our food source.

The approach that will give you the best results is a comprehensive one that has aspects of all the above characteristics: either a single crop type for pest control that has a fragrant but undesirable scent and flowers for attracting predatory insects or a crop type for each of these (a strong-scented herb, a flowering plant, and a trap crop) in the same guild. This approach is sometimes possible, but some protection is better than none.

Managing pests with companion planting is possible, but it's not the only solution. You'll still have pests (you're putting food in their natural habitat; after all, we can't blame them for being hungry), but their populations won't be out of control to the point where all your crops will get ruined. In this chapter, we'll be going into more detail on which plants help keep common garden pests in check.

COMMON GARDEN PESTS AND WHAT TO PLANT

You will encounter a few common pests no matter where you set up your garden. You must know how to identify them and what to do about them. This section will review the most common garden pests, what crops they typically look for, and what you should plant to deter them.

Spider Mites

Spider mites are tiny, spider-like pests (almost microscopic at 1/50 of an inch when fully grown). Yes, they look like spiders (even fall under the arachnid species) and are most commonly red, orange, or brown. They suck the sap out of new foliage growth and live on the underside of leaves that are in direct sun. Spider mites leave behind webs on the bottom of the leaves they've inhabited (how they got their names), and despite being so small, they can deliver a lot of damage.

Planting cilantro, dill, and fennel will attract ladybugs, which will help keep spider mite populations in check, and strangely enough, thrips also snack on these tiny spiders (a pest feeding on a pest, how ironic). But if you're dealing with an infestation of spider mites, you can spray isopropyl alcohol on your leaves (be sure to get the bottoms especially), giving them a killer hangover; emphasis on the "killer."

Aphids

These creatures are about the size of a pinhead (once they reach adulthood) and pear-shaped, but some species of aphids can grow substantially larger (like the Giant Willow Aphid). But for the sake of naming common pests, we're only referencing the small, soft-bodied, and pear-shaped ones present in most gardens worldwide. Aphids can be any color, but most commonly, they are white, black, brown, green, or yellow with a waxy or hairy coating. They can also grow wings in adulthood.

Aphids like hanging out on the underside of leaves and will also be on the stems. Their primary source of sustenance is the sap, which they drink from the leaves and stems of young crops or new growth. In large quantities, aphids can have devastating consequences for your fruits, vegetables, and flowers.

When I say aphids don't discriminate against crops, they will camp on nearly every fruiting or flowering crop you have. You can manage aphid populations with scent and predatory insects (specifically ladybugs and their larvae, which actively feed on aphids).

Aphids aren't attracted to garlic, chives, catnip, cilantro, or marigolds, so planting these around the garden (especially near your fruiting crops) will help. In addition, the marigold and cilantro attract ladybugs and shelter them: two birds, one stone.

Thrips

Another tiny menace. Thrips grow to be about (1 mm.) in length, are long and slender, and have underdeveloped wings that allow them to fly for short distances. The color of thrips ranges between green, yellow, brown, and amber, and adults have an orange thorax (chest area). Similarly, they feed on a plant's sap, which you can find on the leaves' underside. They usually don't stay long; by the time you see the damage, they're usually gone (they move in large groups). However, they might leave behind "evidence" in the form of tiny black spots.

The damage they leave behind can be stunted growth, dying (or yellowing) leaves, reduced yield, fruit scarring, and can even lead to the death of some plants. They often attack seedlings, new plant growth, flowers (and blossoms), and fruits.

Basil, garlic, chives, and catnip seem to do a good job keeping thrips away; however, for maximum protection, you can also lure their natural predators into the garden (lacewings, ladybirds, and wasps) by growing goldenrod, yarrow, yellow coneflowers, and flowering herbs.

Whitefly

Whiteflies are a bit easier to spot since they are larger (1-2mm.) The bodies of whiteflies are yellowish, but their wings are white and covered in a powdery substance. If there are a lot of whiteflies on a plant, you may notice a swarm of them flying right above the area. They cause damage in the same way that aphids and thrips do by sucking the juices out of your crops' leaves and stems.

Plants under stress will be more susceptible to a whitefly infestation, but they will also attack all sorts of fruit, vegetables, shrubs, herbs, and flower crops. They cause what's known as "sooty mold," which may kill the plant. Whiteflies hate marigolds, and you can further manage them with predatory wasps and beetles. You can attract these insects by planting alyssum, dill, rosemary, or any plant in the carrot family around your precious crops.

Leaf Miners

This pest isn't necessarily a specific type of insect but rather the larvae of numerous insects such as moths, flies, and some beetles. In essence, leaf miners are just babies but can still damage crops. What happens is moths, flies, beetles, and the like will lay their eggs inside the leaves of your crops. When these eggs hatch, the larvae will bore their way out of the leaves, leaving behind white or yellow squiggly lines on the leaves.

If you see these white or yellow lines (it's pretty hard to miss), you know leaf miners were there. It's rare for leaf miners to cause severe damage to a plant; in most cases, the leaf will turn brown and fall off prematurely. However, severe infestations can leave the plant weak and susceptible to other pests and diseases, leading to the plant's death.

To minimize the chance of such an infestation, you can plant a variety of mint, lavender, marigold, thyme, cloves, and bay leaves around your garden, which will keep flies, moths, and other insects away.

Snails and Slugs

These slimy suckers are not picky when it comes to food and will eat anything in sight, including meat, waste, decaying matter, and even cardboard. They go crazy for leafy greens, so you'll usually find them amongst your lettuce patch, but they will not hesitate to invade berries and anything else you have growing. If it has leaves, they will make a meal out of it.

Snails and homeless snails (slugs) hate the smell and taste of mint and garlic (or even onions and chives, for that matter). To keep these pests away, plant either mint or garlic all around the border of your garden bed (raised or in-ground). Alternatively, you can dig a border around your in-ground garden bed and fill it with pebbles or sand (they don't like these textures), but this method could be more effective.

10

COMPANION PLANTING FOR DIFFERENT CLIMATES

I'm sure you know by now that different crops grow in different seasons, like cauliflower, a cool-season crop, whereas peppers are a warm-season crop. But your climate will also severely impact the type of crops you grow. Seasons look different depending on the environment.

CLIMATE ZONES

A climate combines a specific region's long-term average temperature, humidity, and precipitation (rainfall) levels. There are many different climates, but all of them can fit into five distinct categories of climate zones. In this section, we'll cover all these climates, their seasons, and which companion pairs thrive best in each one.

Tropical

Tropical climates are known for hot and humid weather. With an average minimum temperature of 64 °F (even in winter) and at least 60 inches of rainfall per year, tropical climates are perfect for almost any crop because there are no winters. Examples of tropical regions include Mexico, Central America, the Caribbean Islands, the top half of South America, and the Amazon rainforest.

Most famously, tropical climates are known for growing the best coconuts, pineapples, bananas, melons, gourds, grapefruit, mango, cashews, avocados, and guava, to name a few. You can grow these crops in other regions, but they tend to do best in tropical climates.

Some great companion pairs to grow in tropical climates include:

- Beets and broccoli.
- Bananas and sweet potatoes.
- Mango tree and nasturtiums.
- Eggplant and spinach.
- Avocado tree and garlic.
- Pumpkin (or squash) and chamomile.

Temperate

Regions or countries that fall under this climate have warm and humid summers with mild winters (typically without frost or snow). The average summer temperatures for temperate climates are above 50 °F, with the coldest months not falling below 37 °F. Due to the stable nature of this climate, you can easily overwinter your crops and get a more extended harvest period.

Some examples of countries that have temperate climates are the United Kingdom, Japan, North Africa, and most of Europe. Almost all crops can be grown in temperate regions. Because temperate climates are in the middle of the extremes when it comes to temperatures (it's never too cold or too hot), you can grow any companion guild or pair successfully.

Continental

This climate includes warm summers but frigid, snowy winters (as cold as -22 °F). Examples of continental climate regions include most of Russia, northern and northeastern China, central Canada, and some parts of the north of the United States.

You'll likely be able to grow a large variety of crops in a continental summer, fall, and spring. However, you will only be able to produce a little in winter unless you have a greenhouse (and even then, some crops that are sensitive to frost might suffer).

As mentioned, you can grow almost anything in continental climates. Still, I recommend starting your crops indoors or in a greenhouse as early as possible. Hence, your harvest period comes sooner since overwintering (letting crops continue to produce into early winter) is not an option.

Dry

This zone is self-explanatory, but dry climates are areas that receive less than 16 inches of rainfall per year and are known to be hot and dry (desert-like). Some examples include the Sahara Desert, Australia, and most of the southwestern United States.

Dry climates are the hardest to work with when it comes to gardening. It's not impossible to grow crops here, but there are limitations. You must put effort into your gardening setup and implement preventive methods to protect your crops from extreme heat and lack of rain. For example, raised garden beds or containers, shade netting, thick mulch, and more frequent irrigation are necessary in a dry climate.

Aloe and agave are succulents, work well in dry climates, and are great options for in-ground landscaping. However, there's little you can do with aloe and agave. Instead, your best defense will be to grow drought-tolerant crops and put measures (as mentioned above) in place to prevent your crops from dying. Here's a list of companion pairs that work well in dry climates:

- Rhubarb and cowpeas.
- Peppers and basil. (Basil is quite drought tolerant once established.)
- Lavender and alliums.
- Grapes and oregano.
- Zucchini and radish. (Once established, both these are pretty drought tolerant.)
- Swiss chard and chives.

Polar

The constant frozen state is a defining characteristic of polar climates. The average temperature in a polar environment is below freezing, and ice and snow always cover the landscape. They don't get direct sun heat for 50% of the year. Polar climates only occur around the northern and southern parts of the world (the North Pole and Antarctica).

Because of the extreme cold and icy conditions, growing anything outdoors in a polar climate is very hard. Even the hardiest crops and trees struggle to survive the freezing temperatures without artificial sunlight (growth lamps of UV light), heat, and complete shelter.

Besides a select few variants of mosses, lichens, and Arctic Poppies, nothing else grows naturally in polar climates. If you can manage to create the right conditions through greenhouses, growth lamps, heaters, and what have you, you'll likely be able to grow a variety of cold-tolerant crops, including:

- Spinach and peas.
- Carrots and onions.
- Cauliflower and cabbage.
- Garlic and turnips.

Knowing which climate you're in, like the back of your hand, will help you develop a better game plan when planning your guilds and pairings. Set yourself up for success by researching your climate, zone, and seasonal changes and planning your gardening schedule. It's so much easier to stay on top of everything when you know what plants thrive in your climate when to sow, and how long it will take before you can harvest.

11

TROUBLESHOOTING AND TIPS

No matter your skill level, years of experience, or research abilities, you will come across a gardening obstacle now and then. The good news is that by taking preventative action, you minimize this, and with the information in this chapter, you can overcome almost any problem that arises.

PREVENTATIVE MEASURES

Poor soil quality and inadequate planning are the most common gardening problems discouraging many novice gardeners. If you plant a seed, it will most likely sprout but only last for a while. To reach maturity (and produce a harvest), you must give it what it needs from the start.

You must take, implement, or consider preventative measures long before cultivating anything. These include:

- Amending the Soil.

Have your soil thoroughly tested, or use an at-home soil test kit. Based on the test results, add compost, fertilizer, mulch, sand, clay, ash, or anything else your soil might need. A healthy and productive garden starts with soil quality. You should amend the soil at least a few months before planting or sowing to give the soil some time to stabilize and grow beneficial microorganism populations.

- Considering the Climate You're In.

Growing crops unsuitable to your specific environment is possible, but such plants require much more rigorous maintenance and observation. You'll only make it much harder to keep your garden alive and end up with underperforming or inadequate harvests.

- Using Adjusted Seeds and Seedlings.

When buying seeds or seedlings, it's always better to buy those cultivated in and around your area because they will have specific resistance to your weather and climate conditions. For example, imported seeds will have a more challenging time adjusting and thriving than seeds or seedlings from a local lineage.

- Planning Your Guilds.

Certain plants get along well with each other, while others will result in catastrophe for your garden if planted together. Plan your guilds based on the best companions, their basic needs, the space they will take up, and other maintenance requirements.

AVOIDING COMMON GARDENING PROBLEMS

Pests, diseases, overcrowding, stripped soil. How do you avoid these gardening problems? And better yet, how do you fix the problem once you notice it? As I said, even if you do everything right, you still need the answers to these questions.

You should monitor your garden regularly to see signs of a potential problem rearing its head. To make this more efficient and effective, you can keep a garden journal where you record notes and observations on the general health of your plants. You can also write down any adjustments you should make to fertilization dates, planting schedules, etc. With gardening, there's almost always a lot to consider; you will only remember something if you write it down.

Nevertheless, here's a list of some common gardening issues and how to prevent or correct them:

- Pests and Diseases.

Never having pests or diseases is an unattainable goal when gardening. The goal is minimization and early intervention. Companion planting and intercropping will drastically reduce the chance of your garden spreading infection, disease, and suffering from pest infestations, but you should keep an eye on things.

If you notice more pests lurking around your garden than what is deemed "normal," you can step in and give your garden some external help by using things like netting, neem oil, traps or trap crops, and other non-chemical methods. In severe cases, unfortunately, you might have to discard the infested or infected plants entirely.

- Small Yields.

When a crop is underperforming, the resulting fruit might be smaller, or the plant may produce less than average. Factors such as disease, pests, genetic mutations, poor soil quality, lack of pollinators, or unmet basic needs and requirements could cause underperformance.

A comprehensive approach might be needed to determine what the problem is. Double-check that you meet the plant's essential water, sun, and soil requirements. Inspect the plant thoroughly for any signs of pests or disease. Then, amend the soil with liquid fertilizer and take action to invite pollinators to your garden (plant more flowering crops).

Another thing contributing to a poor yield is not letting the plant become established before allowing it to flower and fruit. Remember to pinch off the flower buds (for some perennial crops) in the first year so the plant can become more established —an adequately set plant will produce bigger and better quality fruit.

- Poor Soil Quality.

Your soil quality will depend on the crops you are planting and how often you feed the soil. You are likely stripping the soil if you mainly grow annuals (heavy feeders) but only add compost or fertilizer once a year. The soil quality will quickly deteriorate if you're not protecting the ground from the elements using mulch or living mulch. Not to mention, your soil will dry out quicker and leave your crops thirsty.

Not rotating crops (or not doing it correctly) will also result in the degradation of the quality of your soil.

- Overcrowding.

Always follow the general guidelines on how far apart you should plant crops from each other. These guidelines are there for a reason. Overcrowding can result in many problems, including poor yields, stunted growth, diseases, pests, and increased competition for nutrients. Find other ways to maximize space instead of overcrowding your garden.

If your garden is overcrowded, start by thinning out the most miniature, least productive plants and filling in the gaps with mulch or ground cover crops.

- Overwatering.

I am trying to remember where I read this rule, but I've been living by it for as long as I can remember: It's not about the quantity of water, but the frequency. If you have well-draining soil, it's almost impossible to give a plant too much water at once; the soil will absorb as much as it can, and the rest will drain away.

Don't get me wrong, overwatering a plant might cause some issues, like diluting or washing away essential nutrients and microorganisms, so you should water them sparingly. But the key is in how frequently you water your crops. It would help if you always allowed the soil to dry out a little before you water again, which is why most established plants only require you to water them once a week. Aim to saturate the top two or three inches thoroughly.

Overwatering can result in degrading the quality of the soil and root rot and might even suffocate your roots. Signs you might be overwatering include loss of old and new foliage, wilting leaves, or gray, slimy roots. To correct this, remove and repot the plant in a large enough container with very loose and well-draining soil (add pebbles or vermiculite to aid drainage and air pockets). Wait to water the plant until the top layer of soil is completely dry.

- Bolting.

Bolting refers to premature seeding (the plant switches from fruiting to seed production before it's supposed to). Especially when temperatures are too high, the plant can experience early seeding due to not meeting its basic needs.

Try amending the soil with fertilizer and moving the plant (or guild) to an area that receives partial shade. Alternatively, you can create a structure to shade the plant from the harsh afternoon sun.

As time goes on, you'll learn all the tricks and trades of gardening. You can only learn some things through experience and time. I only ask that you stay committed and not let a few hiccups stop you from doing what you love.

Inspire a Fellow Gardener!

You picked up this book because you love gardens and you wanted to build your own… so I know you're on board with helping more gardens flourish. This is your chance to inspire another new gardener.

Simply by sharing your honest opinion of this book and a little about your own gardening journey, you'll show new readers where they can find a clear route to gardening success.

Thank you so much for your support. I wish you many years of happiness in your garden.

Scan the QR code below to leave a review:

CONCLUSION

The answer to the question, "Why should I implement companion planting?" is simple but lengthy. Everyone will have a different reason for starting and following this permaculture principle. But companion planting is like a one-stop shop to cultivate a thriving, eco-friendly, diverse garden.

Nature has always found a way to persevere. Savvy gardeners know trying and going against Mother Nature's will is pointless. It's the responsibility of all humans to look after what we have. We share the planet with many other creatures, many of which were here long before we came along.

Whether people believe companion planting works is irrelevant, not only because many studies have proven it is effective and beneficial, but because it's simply the way things are. Despite not having any maintenance or human intervention, forests, grasslands, valleys, and open fields survive. No, they thrive!

We're simply conforming to the natural laws. When you let nature do its thing, it benefits every living thing around it. You might have to deal with bugs, pests, weeds, and diseases, but they all play a valuable role in the grand scheme. Using pesticides, insecticides, and chemical fertilizers does more harm than good. Not only does it eliminate the weeds and pests, but it also negatively impacts every other creature that comes into contact with these harmful toxins.

I'm certainly not one to preach about only buying organic produce or going entirely off the grid. But if you do want fresh, organic, and non-GMO produce that genuinely leaves the environment better off, the best way to ensure that's what you're getting is to grow it yourself.

If you're starting with companion planting (or gardening in general), you'll likely need some help. Every mistake or failure is an opportunity to become better at something, to learn, to experiment. Losing a plant you've worked hard to keep alive can be demotivating; having an entire batch of seedlings succumb to "dampening off" is devastating, and dealing with pest infestations is frustrating beyond belief. But don't think of it as time wasted; think of it as experience gained.

Planning the perfect guild according to your needs, situation, and climate takes time, creativity, and more research than you'll ever do in your entire life. But when you get it right, few things in life beat that kind of satisfaction, confidence, and pride.

And that's what inspired me to write this book. I wanted to give you a head start and make it more attainable. To put you in the thick of it, getting hands-on experience without all the potential things that can go wrong when you plan your guild.

So, whether you have a decently sized backyard or nothing but a windowsill, I hope you find it in you to at least try to make it work. Even if all you get out of it are fresh chives to put on instant noodles. It's the action that inspires motivation, not the other way around.

With the knowledge you have gained from this book, transform your space into a self-sustaining ecosystem with its circle of life. Keep pests, weeds, and diseases under control, and reap the benefits of an all-natural, minimal-maintenance garden. And remember to be patient with yourself and your crops.

REFERENCES

Adamant, A. (2018, August 23). *How to grow chives.* Practical Self Reliance. https://practicalselfreliance.com/growing-chives/

Albert, S. (2022, June 8). *How to plant, grow, and harvest cilantro.* Harvest to Table. https://harvesttotable.com/how_to_grow_coriander_and_cila/

Amendolare, N. (2023, November 21). *Climate zones: Definitions, types, and examples.* Study.com. https://study.com/learn/lesson/climate-zones-geography-types.html

Amy. (2015, July 20). *5 Reasons to grow chives.* Tenth Acre Farm. https://www.tenthacrefarm.com/5-reasons-to-grow-chives/

Amy. (2017, May 18). *12 Steps to preventing garden pests naturally.* Tenth Acre Farm. https://www.tenthacrefarm.com/preventing-garden-pests/

Anderson, T. (2020, September 25). *The easiest way to test soil pH and amend it.* Lovely Greens. https://lovelygreens.com/easiest-way-test-soil-ph/

Arcuri, L. (2021, September 23). *Everything you need to know about growing garlic.* The Spruce. https://www.thespruce.com/grow-great-garlic-3016629

Baessler, L. (2015, September 29). *Container grown grapes: Tips for planting grapevines in pots.* Gardening Know How. https://www.gardeningknowhow.com/edible/fruits/grapes/container-grown-grapes.htm#:

Balogh, A. (2019). *Caring for roses: A beginner's rose growing guide.* Garden Design. https://www.gardendesign.com/roses/care.html

Ben Issa, R., Gautier, H., & Gomez, L. (2016). Influence of neighbouring companion plants on the performance of aphid populations on sweet pepper plants under greenhouse conditions. *Agricultural and Forest Entomology, 19*(2), 181–191. https://doi.org/10.1111/afe.12199

Ben-Issa, R., Gomez, L., & Gautier, H. (2017). Companion plants for aphid pest management. *Insects, 8*(4), 112. https://doi.org/10.3390/insects8040112

Blooming Backyard. (2021, November 11). *10 Rosemary companion plants (& 5 plants to keep far away).* https://www.bloomingbackyard.com/rosemary-companion-plants/

Boeckmann, C. (2019, June 11). *Cucumbers.* Old Farmer's Almanac. https://www.almanac.com/plant/cucumbers

Bonnie Plants. (n.d.). *How to grow cauliflower in your garden.* Bonnie Plants. https://bonnieplants.com/blogs/how-to-grow/growing-cauliflower#:

Brillon, K. (2023, August 1). *17 Companion plants to grow with beets*. Epic Gardening. https://www.epicgardening.com/beet-companion-plants/

Cason, K. (2022, April 20). *The benefits of marigolds in your vegetable garden*. Senior Living Magazine. https://seniorlivingmag.co.za/2022/04/20/the-benefits-of-marigolds-in-your-vegetable-garden/#:

Chen, L., Li, D., Shao, Y., Adni, J., Wang, H., Liu, Y., & Zhang, Y. (2020). Comparative analysis of soil microbiome profiles in the companion planting of white clover and orchard grass using 16S rRNA gene sequencing data. *Frontiers in Plant Science, 11*, 538311. https://doi.org/10.3389/fpls.2020.538311

Cheng, F., & Cheng, Z. (2015). Research progress on the use of plant allelopathy in agriculture and the physiological and ecological mechanisms of allelopathy. *Frontiers, 6*. https://www.frontiersin.org/articles/10.3389/fpls.2015.01020/full

Dore, J. (2010, June 4). *Trap cropping to control pests*. GrowVeg. https://www.growveg.com/guides/trap-cropping-to-control-pests/

Durant, J. (2023, March 16). *How to grow parsley: A comprehensive guide*. Natural Seed-Bank. https://www.seed-bank.ca/how-to-grow-parsley-companion-planting/

Dylan. (2023, May 24). *The 11 best companion plants for oregano*. Make It Seasonal. https://makeitseasonal.com/oregano-companion-plants/

Ellis, M. E. (2022, March 22). *History of companion planting – how did companion planting start*. Gardening Know How. https://blog.gardeningknowhow.com/tbt/history-of-companion-planting/

Engels, J. (2016, August 22). *Guilds for the small scale home garden*. The Permaculture Research Institute. https://www.permaculturenews.org/2016/08/22/guilds-small-scale-home-garden/

Fu, X., Li, C., Zhou, X., Liu, S., & Wu, F. (2016). Physiological response and sulfur metabolism of the V. dahliae-infected tomato plants in tomato/potato onion companion cropping. *Scientific Reports, 6*(1). https://doi.org/10.1038/srep36445

Fuss, C. (2021, August 30). *Pepper companion plants: Produce pals*. Epic Gardening. https://www.epicgardening.com/pepper-companion-plants/#:

Gao, J., & Zhang, F. (2023). Influence of companion planting on microbial compositions and their symbiotic network in pepper continuous cropping soil. *Journal of Microbiology and Biotechnology, 33*(6), 760–770. https://doi.org/10.4014/jmb.2211.11032

Gardeners' World. (n.d.). *How to grow borage*. https://www.gardenersworld.com/how-to/grow-plants/how-to-grow-borage/

Gardeners' World. (2019, February 26). *How to grow zinnias*. BBC Gardeners World Magazine. https://www.gardenersworld.com/how-to/grow-plants/how-to-grow-zinnias/

Georgina. (n.d.). *Planting, growing and harvesting green beans.* https://www.georgina. ca/sites/default/files/page_assets/planting_growing_harvesting_green_bean s.pdf

Gibson, A. (2017, September 6). *5 Reasons to grow sunflowers.* The Micro Gardener. https://themicrogardener.com/5-benefits-reasons-to-grow-sunflowers/#:

Grant, A. (2023, September 3). *Best companion plants for thyme in the garden.* Gardening Know How. https://www.gardeningknowhow.com/edible/herbs/ thyme/thyme-companions.htm

Griffiths-Lee, J., Nicholls, E., & Goulson, D. (2020). Companion planting to attract pollinators increases the yield and quality of strawberry fruit in gardens and allotments. *Ecological Entomology, 45*(5), 1025–1034. https://doi.org/10.1111/ een.12880

Grow Forage Cook Ferment. (2020, May 25). *10 Reasons to grow oregano: A highly beneficial herb.* Grow Forage Cook Ferment. https://www.growforagecookfer ment.com/benefits-of-oregano/#:

Gupta, S. (2010). Chamomile: A herbal medicine of the past with a bright future (review). *Molecular Medicine Reports, 3*(6). https://doi.org/10.3892/mmr. 2010.377

Habas, C. (2012, April 6). *How to plant onions next to other vegetables.* Weekand. https://www.weekand.com/home-garden/article/plant-onions-next-other-vegetables-18057809.php

Hailey, L. (2022a, April 29). *31 Strawberry companion plants to grow with strawberries.* Epic Gardening. https://www.epicgardening.com/strawberry-companion-plants/

Hailey, L. (2022b, September 28). *15 Tips for vegetable gardening in small spaces.* Epic Gardening. https://www.epicgardening.com/gardening-limited-space/

Hassani, N. (2021, November 29). *The basics of companion planting garden crops.* The Spruce. https://www.thespruce.com/companion-planting-with-chart-5025124

Haynes, G. (2023, May 13). *How to grow and care for sunflowers.* Southern Living. https://www.southernliving.com/garden/flowers/how-to-grow-sunflowers#:

Healthy Living. (n.d.). *The power of parsley.* Healthy Living. https://healthyliving-herbs.co.za/the-power-of-parsley/#:

Hicks-Hamblin, K. (2021, September 29). *The benefits of companion planting.* Gardener's Path. https://gardenerspath.com/how-to/organic/benefits-compan ion-planting/

Hughes, R. A. (2023, April 2). *What noise does a plant make when it's under stress?* Euronews. https://www.euronews.com/green/2023/04/02/scientists-have-recorded-the-sound-plants-make-when-they-are-under-stress

Iannotti, M. (2022a, June 23). *Easy to grow comfrey wildflowers.* The Spruce. https:// www.thespruce.com/growing-comfrey-1402605

Iannotti, M. (2022b, July 29). *How to grow fragrant lavender*. The Spruce. https://www.thespruce.com/growing-lavender-1402779#:

Iannotti, M. (2022c, July 31). *How to grow rosemary indoors and out*. The Spruce. https://www.thespruce.com/grow-and-care-for-rosemary-plants-1403406

Iannotti, M. (2022d, August 20). *How to grow and care for chamomile*. The Spruce. https://www.thespruce.com/how-to-grow-chamomile-1402627

Iannotti, M. (2023, March 18). *How to grow blueberries at home*. The Spruce. https://www.thespruce.com/growing-blueberries-1401960

Insect Science. (2020a, July 7). *How to identify and get rid of aphids on garden plants naturally*. Home and Garden. https://shop.insectscience.co.za/garden-pests/aphids/

Insect Science. (2020b, July 8). *How to identify and get rid of thrips pests in your garden*. Home and Garden. https://shop.insectscience.co.za/garden-pests/thrips/

Insect Science. (2020c, July 8). *How to identify and get rid of whiteflies on houseplants*. Home and Garden. https://shop.insectscience.co.za/garden-pests/white-fly/

Insect Science. (2020d, July 10). *How to identify and control leaf miners naturally | insect science*. Home and Garden. https://shop.insectscience.co.za/garden-pests/leaf-miner/

Jill. (2019, October 29). *Crop rotation for home vegetable gardeners*. The Beginner's Garden. https://journeywithjill.net/gardening/2019/10/28/crop-rotation-for-home-vegetable-gardeners/

Johnson, Zach. *Garden Quotes We Love*. Maryland Plant Nursery & Garden Center in Bowie, MD | Patuxent Nursery. Last modified March 14, 2023. https://patuxentnursery.com/blog/garden-quotes-we-love/

Kanuckel, A. (2018, April 25). *Companion planting guide: Sow easy*. Old Farmers' Almanac. https://www.farmersalmanac.com/companion-planting-guide

Khait, I., Lewin-Epstein, O., Sharon, R., Saban, K., Goldstein, R., Anikster, Y., Zeron, Y., Agassy, C., Nizan, S., Sharabi, G., Perelman, R., Boonman, A., Sade, N., Yovel, Y., & Hadany, L. (2023). Sounds emitted by plants under stress are airborne and informative. *Cell, 186*(7), 1328-1336.e10. https://doi.org/10.1016/j.cell.2023.03.009

Kong, C.-H., Xuan, T. D., Khanh, T. D., Tran, H.-D., & Trung, N. T. (2019). Allelochemicals and Signaling Chemicals in Plants. *Molecules, 24*(15). https://doi.org/10.3390/molecules24152737

Landers, L. (2023, September 2). *What is a permaculture garden? Plus how to plant your own*. Better Homes & Gardens. https://www.bhg.com/what-is-a-permaculture-garden-7775333

Larum, D. (n.d.). *Companions for chamomile*. Gardening Know How.com. https://www.gardeningknowhow.com/edible/herbs/chamomile/chamomile-plant-companions.htm

Living Seeds. (n.d.). *Companion planting.* https://livingseeds.co.za/companion-planting.html

Love The Garden. (n.d.-a). *How to grow and care for sage.* https://www.lovethegarden.com/au-en/growing-guide/how-grow-care-sage

Love The Garden. (n.d.-b). *How to grow apple trees.* https://www.lovethegarden.com/au-en/growing-guide/how-grow-care-apple-trees#:

Magyar, C. (2021, February 10). *Bad neighbors - the ultimate guide to incompatible companion plants.* Rural Sprout. https://www.ruralsprout.com/incompatible-companion-plants/

Mane. (2021, April 30). *How to prune fruit trees in 8 steps.* Mehrabyan Nursery. https://www.mehrabyannursery.com/growing-guide/fruit-trees/how-to-prune-fruit-trees/

McCauley, T. (2023, July 6). *Companion planting: 43 Combinations for maximum yield.* https://www.tiffanymccauley.com/companion-planting/

Montoya, J. E., Arnold, M. A., Rangel, J., Stein, L. R., & Palma, M. A. (2020). Pollinator-attracting companion plantings increase crop yield of cucumbers and habanero peppers. *HortScience, 55*(2), 164–169. https://doi.org/10.21273/hortsci14468-19

Morini, R. (2023, February). *Biodiversity: Its meaning, importance and how home gardeners can help restore it.* Piedmont Master Gardeners. https://piedmontmastergardeners.org/article/biodiversity-its-meaning-importance-and-how-home-gardeners-can-help-restore-it/

Moulton, M. (2022, March 2). *12 Sunflower companion plants (& 3 plants to grow nowhere near).* Blooming Backyard. https://www.bloomingbackyard.com/sunflower-companion-plants/

New Mexico State University. (2015). *Propagation of grape vine cuttings: A practical guide | new mexico state university - BE BOLD. shape the future.* Pubs.nmsu.edu. https://pubs.nmsu.edu/_h/H322/index.html#:

Old Farmer's Almanac. (2019a, April 17). *Peaches.* https://www.almanac.com/plant/peaches

Old Farmer's Almanac. (2019b, April 22). *Chives.* https://www.almanac.com/plant/chives

Old Farmer's Almanac. (2019c, October 28). *The three sisters: Corn, beans, and squash.* https://www.almanac.com/content/three-sisters-corn-bean-and-squash

Oregon State University. (2010, June 4). *Rhododendrons and azaleas need a strong acidic soil.* Extension Communications. https://extension.oregonstate.edu/news/rhododendrons-azaleas-need-strong-acidic-soil

Pammy. (2014, January 29). *TSG: Companion planting: Petunias love beans.* TSG. https://thymesquaregarden.blogspot.com/2014/01/companion-planting-petunias-love-beans.html?m=1

Park Seed. (n.d.). *The-ultimate-guide-to-companion-planting-vegetables.* https://park seed.com/guide-to-companion-planting-vegetables/a/the-ultimate-guide-to-companion-planting-vegetables/

Peerless, V. (2021, November 8). *How to grow and care for nasturtiums.* BBC Gardeners World Magazine. https://www.gardenersworld.com/how-to/grow-plants/how-to-grow-nasturtiums/#harvesting

Plant Perfect. (2022, March 28). *How to design the perfect vegetable garden layout.* https://plantperfect.com/how-to-design-the-perfect-vegetable-garden-layout/

Pleasant, B. (2013). *Growing and harvesting garden dill.* GrowVeg. https://www.growveg.co.za/guides/growing-and-harvesting-garden-dill/

Rahbardar, M., & Hosseinzadeh, H. (2020). Therapeutic effects of rosemary (Rosmarinus officinalis L.) and its active constituents on nervous system disorders. *Therapeutic Effects of Rosemary (Rosmarinus Officinalis L.) and Its Active Constituents on Nervous System Disorders, 23*(9). https://doi.org/10.22038/ijbms.2020.45269.10541

Raman, R. (2018, February 22). *Cilantro vs coriander: What's the difference?* Healthline. https://www.healthline.com/nutrition/cilantro-vs-coriander#:

Restoration Seeds. (n.d.). *Germinating perennial seeds.* https://www.restorationseeds.com/blogs/news/7211932-germinating-perennial-seeds

Riesselman, L. (n.d.). *Companion planting: A method for sustainable pest control RFR-A9099.* https://dr.lib.iastate.edu/server/api/core/bitstreams/9f6c0efd-b8b1-4ecc-b8d1-2abbdfb16548/content#:

Saldanha, A. V., Gontijo, L. M., Carvalho, R. M. R., Vasconcelos, C. J., Corrêa, A. S., & Gandra, R. L. R. (2019). Companion planting enhances pest suppression despite reducing parasitoid emergence. *Basic and Applied Ecology, 41*, 45–55. https://doi.org/10.1016/j.baae.2019.10.002

Scavo, A., Abbate, C., & Mauromicale, G. (2019). Plant allelochemicals: Agronomic, nutritional and ecological relevance in the soil system. *Plant and Soil.* https://doi.org/10.1007/s11104-019-04190-y

Sciortino, D. G. (2023, September 3). *Cucumber is the secret weapon you need for a happy and healthy garden.* House Digest. https://www.housedigest.com/1381567/cucumber-natural-plant-fertilizer-thriving-garden/

Seeds Now. (n.d.). *33 Drought tolerant crops for dry or hot climates.* Www.seedsnow.com. https://www.seedsnow.com/blogs/news/120310727-33-drought-tolerant-crops-for-dry-or-hot-climates

Selemin, J. (2022, November 25). *Benefits of companion planting.* WebMD. https://www.webmd.com/a-to-z-guides/benefits-of-companion-planting

Seven in 10 Americans Say Gardening Allows Them to Gain Control over What They Eat. Digitalhub US. Last modified October 4, 2021. https://swnsdigital.com/us/

2021/08/seven-in-10-americans-say-gardening-has-allowed-them-to-gain-more-control-over-what-they-eat/

Sloan, J. (2023, May 31). *Understanding soil health and biota for farm and garden.* Extension Communications. https://extension.oregonstate.edu/catalog/pub/em-9409-understanding-soil-health-biota-farms-gardens

Strauss, M. (2023, April 12). *Can you grow tomatoes with basil?* Epic Gardening. https://www.epicgardening.com/tomatoes-and-basil/

Swainston, D. (2023, June 1). *12 Drought-tolerant vegetables that will grow well in dry conditions.* Homesandgardens.com. https://www.homesandgardens.com/gardens/best-drought-tolerant-vegetables

Sweetser, R. (2022a, October 25). *Crop rotation 101: Tips for vegetable gardens.* Almanac. https://www.almanac.com/crop-rotation-101-tips-vegetable-gardens

Sweetser, R. (2022b, November 11). *3 Simple DIY soil tests.* Old Farmer's Almanac. https://www.almanac.com/content/3-simple-diy-soil-tests

This Is My Garden. (2022, March 2). *Planting basil with tomato plants - how to grow incredible tomatoes!* https://thisismygarden.com/2022/03/planting-basil-with-tomato-plants/

University of Minnesota Extension. (n.d.). *Growing strawberries in the home garden.* Extension.umn.edu. https://extension.umn.edu/fruit/growing-strawberries-home-garden#harvesting-and-protecting-plants-in-winter--988762

USDA. (n.d.). *Medicinal botany.* https://www.fs.usda.gov/wildflowers/ethnobotany/medicinal/index.shtml#:

Van Elsas, J. D., Chiurazzi, M., Mallon, C. A., Elhottova, D., Kristufek, V., & Salles, J. F. (2012). Microbial diversity determines the invasion of soil by a bacterial pathogen. *Proceedings of the National Academy of Sciences, 109*(4), 1159–1164. https://doi.org/10.1073/pnas.1109326109

Vanderlinden, C. (2023, June 6). *Best (and worst) companion plants for cucumbers.* The Spruce. https://www.thespruce.com/companion-plants-for-cucumbers-2540044

Wikipedia. (2020, November 30). *Companion planting.* https://en.wikipedia.org/wiki/Companion_planting

Xiao, X., Cheng, Z., Meng, H., Liu, L., Li, H., & Dong, Y. (2013). Intercropping of green garlic (allium sativum L.) induces nutrient concentration changes in the soil and plants in continuously cropped cucumber (cucumis sativus L.) in a plastic tunnel. *PLoS ONE, 8*(4), e62173. https://doi.org/10.1371/journal.pone.0062173

Xu, W., Liŭ, D., Wu, F., & Liu, S. (2014). Root exudates of wheat are involved in suppression of Fusarium wilt in watermelon in watermelon-wheat companion cropping. *European Journal of Plant Pathology, 141*(1), 209–216. https://doi.org/10.1007/s10658-014-0528-0

Zhang, M.-M., Wang, N., Hu, Y.-B., & Sun, G.-Y. (2018). Changes in soil physico-chemical properties and soil bacterial community in mulberry (morus alba l.)/alfalfa (medicago sativa L.) intercropping system. *MicrobiologyOpen, 7*(2), e00555. https://doi.org/10.1002/mbo3.555

Ziton, A. T. (2023, March 27). *Permaculture 101 (definition, examples, pros, cons, & more)*. Couch to Homestead. https://couchtohomestead.com/permaculture-101/#is-permaculture-sustainable.